THE UNAUTHORIZED

X-FILES CHALLENGE

James Hatfield
and George "Doc" Burt

Authors of *THE ULTIMATE TREK TRIVIA CHALLENGE FOR THE NEXT GENERATION*

KENSINGTON BOOKS

KENSINGTON BOOKS are published by

Kensington Publishing Corp.
850 Third Avenue
New York, NY 10022

First Kensington Printing: October, 1996
10 9 8 7 6 5 4 3 2 1

ISBN 1-57566-096-2

Printed in the United States of America

This book is dedicated to:

Chris Carter, *The X-Files* creator, executive producer and "Mother Hen," for not only scaring the pants off of us, but for entertaining us in an intelligent way;

A true friend in sunshine and storms, and my partner in writing and publishing, George "Doc" Burt; and the love I waited 37 years for—Nancy Eileen Hatfield, my strength, support and partner in life.

—J.H.

Jim Hatfield, my comrade during the long wars, in which we shared the foxholes together; and all the X-Philes who know the truth is not always as black and white as some folks think.

—"Doc"

And Tracy Bernstein, our editor at Kensington, who had her own paranormal experience with the publication of this book. No one ever put more blood, sweat and tears into a manuscript than did this lovely lady.

ACKNOWLEDGMENTS

A project of this size and scope requires the assistance of many wonderful people and we owe them all a debt of enormous gratitude. They include Teddy Kuan, for that first introduction to *The X-Files;* Bryan Grayson, for putting out an APB for an X-Phile with a video library of all the episodes and for teaching a certain computer novice how to surf the Net; Michael Wolff & Company for providing the wormhole through cyberspace; Cliff Chen, Kymberlee Ricke, Lisa A. Salazar, Christopher Fusco, Simon Chin, Maria Atkinson, Doug R. Bailey, Sarah Stegall, Shanna Swendson, Paul Tang, Stephen R. Banks, Pat Gonzales, Charles Mcgrew, Paula J. Vitaris, and Pam Smith, for their indispensable episode guides, cast listings, productions credits, rantings and ravings, and links to other Internet *X-Files* research sources; Loren Coleman, veteran cryptozoologist and unabashed X-Phile, for exploring the show's Fortean underpinnings; *X-Files* author Brian Lowry for his invaluable reference book; Sue Harke, researcher extraordinaire, who graciously shared her time and unique connections to help us out once again when our backs were against the wall; Syndicated columnist Ian Spelling *(Inside Trek)* and online sci-fi editor Ruben Macias *(Warp 10* and *Subspace Chatter),* for being cognizant and responsive to the fan crossover between Trekkers and X-Philes; and those two good ol' Texas boys, Harold "Admiral" Skidmore and Billy Bob Walker. Finally, on a more personal note, thanks to the government guys, Eddie and Bill. They know why.

CONTENTS

INTRODUCTION:
Waiting to X-hale

The X-Files has made the rapid transition from a creepy cult favorite to a mainstream phenomenon. It's an hour of suspenseful television that draws viewers into a world of nightmares and realities—a place where you can truly trust no one. There's the weekly menace that must be faced, the government's clandestine operations to cover up strange occurrences and the sexual tension, but professional relationship, between Special Agents Mulder and Scully.

Since its premiere in 1993, *The X-Files* has continued to defy skeptics who refuse to believe that a show about two deadpan FBI agents investigating paranormal activities could succeed. But succeed it has. Capitalizing on antigovernment paranoia, the series postulates that Big Brother is covering up a wide array of paranormal, unusual and extraterrestrial activities. By skillfully blending old-fashioned conspiracy theories, sly humor, and stories drawn from today's headlines, *The X-Files* has won industry awards, topped network ratings (its third season premiere was watched by 30 million people), and is still attracting more viewers as word of mouth continues to spread.

While "interactive" is clearly an overused catchphrase in today's high-tech society, fan reaction to *The X-Files* has become as much a part of the series' story as the show itself. For an hour every Friday night, X-Philes sit glued to their TV sets; for much of the week in between installments of alien abductions, psychic forces, science experiments gone awry, voodoo, cults, clones, monsters, possession, and even life-after-death experiences, tens of thousands of X-Philes light up the Internet with forums, chat areas, newsgroups, mailing lists, Websites, and FTP archives with their thousands of digitized images and soundbites.

Far from being the quirky UFO-spotters the media suggested would form the show's cult following, X-Philes have gained a reputation for inquisitiveness, tasteful discrimination and native intelligence. Each week they critically review each episode, "netpick" the show's plot oversights and technical screw-ups, and chat online with *X-Files* creator Chris Carter or the show's stars Gillian Anderson and David Duchovny. But most of all, these devoted fans love to test their "X.Q." of *X-Files* trivia. Yet never has there been, in one volume, a collection of trivia questions and answers about this provocative, award-winning show.

Until now.

In the spirit of any worthwhile trivia challenge of this magnitude and scope, there are a variety of different quizzes in this book. The first three seasons' episodes are included in chronological order with each quiz containing questions relevant to the show on which it was based. Also included in the episode-by-episode sections is an X-travaganza of bloopers, scientific snafus, commentaries, factoids and background notes.

Strategically placed throughout the book, however, are trivia tests that address behind-the-scenes and on the set, character and actor profiles, "Mulderisms," "Scullyisms," and "X-Filisms," M.O.T.W. (Monsters of the Week), dialogue between the characters (X-pert Testimony), site locations of the episodes and a couple of helpings of Alphabet Soup ("What does the acronym NICAP stand for?"). Testing methods are just as varied with a combination of multiple choice, matching, short answer, true or false, and fill in the blank.

All trivia questions count as 1 point, except the specially designated **X-PERT X-TRA BONUS POINTS.** Because these questions are intended to challenge the die-hard X-Phile's X.Q., each correct answer counts as 5 points.

In the back section of this book you will find the answers, plus a specific line to calculate and enter your trivia X.Q. as you play along per category. On the very last page you will compute your total score, or X.Q., for this book's trivia challenge and compare it to the master score table.

You can start at the beginning and work your way through to the end, or flip around and pick out random questions that test your knowledge of particular episodes or categories, or pick a quiz and answer all the questions on that topic. However you want to do it, you are sure to know more about *The X-Files* when you've finished this book than you did when you started.

Read and enjoy, play and learn. May this unofficial and declassified *X-Files* trivia challenge be as interesting and entertaining to read as it was to write.

—James Hatfield and George "Doc" Burt

THE REALM OF X-TREME POSSIBILITY
The Beginning of The X-Files

"The X-Files stories take place in what I call the realm of extreme possibility. They have to be rooted in some sort of speculative scientific possibility or based on a progressive scientific idea. It must be believable that they could happen in the world we live in now. What if a man could hibernate and live much longer than the average life span? What if there was really such a thing as a shape-shifter? We take a little license with [the stories], but we still keep them rooted in scientific possibility."

—Chris Carter, Creator and Executive Producer

1. Which former TV series does Chris Carter acknowledge as his primary inspiration for the creation of *The X-Files*?
   A. *The Twilight Zone*
   B. *The Outer Limits*
   C. *Kolchak: The Night Stalker*

2. (True or False) Carter claims to be "a natural skeptic" who has personally never had a paranormal experience.

3. (Yes or No) Was the real-life Federal Bureau of Investigation asked to be involved in the series' development?

4. (Yes or No) The pilot episode was preceded by text saying, "The following is inspired by actual documented events." In Carter's opinion, do the X-Files *really* exist somewhere in the government?

5. (True or False) Ideas for the episodes come mostly from newspapers and magazines.

6. What actor did Carter consider to play Agent Mulder's father, but had to abandon the idea when schedules couldn't be worked out?

7. Identify the movie which helped spur the idea of using a pair of FBI agents—one a believer, the other a skeptic—who investigate cases involving the paranormal.

8. (True or False) The Ray Harryhausen fantasy movie, *Mysterious Island*, left a tremendous impression on Carter as a boy.

9. (Fill in the Blank) The origin of Agent Fox Mulder's name came from the maiden name of Carter's _____ and the first name of a kid he'd known growing up.

10. Carter named Dana Scully after which famous Los Angeles Dodgers broadcaster?

11. Identify "the most formative event" of Carter's youth, which inspired such nefarious and shadowy characters as Deep Throat and the Cigarette-Smoking Man.

12. (True or False) Carter pitched the concept of *The X-Files* to CBS first, but the network turned it down because they already had another "quirky and strange" show on their prime-time schedule—*Picket Fences*.

13. Which tongue-in-cheek horror movie were Fox executives afraid *The X-Files* would emulate if Carter and his production staff didn't write and film it seriously?
    A. *Ghostbusters*
    B. *American Werewolf in London*
    C. *Love at First Bite*

14. How many times did Carter have to pitch the series' premise to the Fox network before they bought it?
    A. 2
    B. 3
    C. 4

15. Carter created visual aids as a means of selling Fox executives on the show. What were the shape designs of Carter's charts?

16. Whose preferred choice was David Duchovny for the role of Agent Mulder? Carter's or Fox officials'?

17. (True or False) *The X-Files* turned out to be the only pilot script Duchovny's agent decided to send him during *The X-Files* formative year.

18. (True or False) A battle between Carter and Fox executives took place behind the scenes in the casting of the Dana Scully role as Carter pushed for Gillian Anderson and the network officials looked for the equivalent of *Baywatch*'s Pamela Anderson.

19. What is the significance of the name of Carter's production company, Ten Thirteen?

20. Name two of three reasons why the decision was ultimately made to film *The X-Files* in Vancouver rather than Los Angeles.

21. During which month in 1993 did filming begin on the series?

22. Where was the sequence actually filmed where Scully first met Mulder in the bowels of the FBI building that he called home to "the FBI's most unwanted"?
    A. An abandoned shopping mall
    B. A Canadian government office
    C. The Canadian Broadcasting Corporation

23. Before the season began, which Fox drama was the network's attention and hopes focused on instead of *The X-Files*?

24. (True or False) Scully's voice-over while typing up her field report notes at the end of each episode had been conceived in the series' planning stages to bring closure to a typically non-closed X-File case.

25. (True or False) The Cigarette-Smoking Man was a mysterious figure in the series' pilot and was supposed to remain that way.

26. Which fall entertainment magazine, listing synopses of the new series, wrote of *The X-Files*, "We know—this show's a goner"?
    A. *TV Guide*
    B. *Entertainment Weekly*
    C. *People*

27. Name the other two science-fiction series which premiered on the networks along with *The X-Files* in the fall of 1993.

X-PERT X-TRA BONUS POINTS #1

Whose voice says "I made this" at the end of the Ten Thirteen logo?

X-PERT X-TRA BONUS POINTS #2

Although a fan of *The Invaders, Project UFO* and *The Outer Limits,* name the classic science-fiction series of which Chris Carter admits he has never watched a single episode.

X-PERT X-TRA BONUS POINTS #3

According to the Nielsen ratings, how many million homes watched *The X-Files* pilot?

FILE NO. 1X01:

THE X-FILES: PILOT

Declassified Case Overview: FBI Special Agent and medical doctor Dana Scully was assigned by her Washington superiors to keep an eye on the activities of fellow agent Fox Mulder, a quiet and withdrawn loner who had a tendency to trawl through the X-Files—paranormal cases that were both inexplicable and unsolved. Although a skeptic at heart, Scully found herself drawn into Agent Mulder's latest X-File investigation: the murder of several high school classmates in the Pacific Northwest, whom he believed had been experimented on by aliens.

Nitpicking

The *X-Files'* research staff pays careful attention to detail. While each episode may have a certain level of implausibility, most remain within the outskirts of "extreme possibility," as Chris Carter terms it. But continuity problems, scientific inaccuracies, on-camera bloopers and plot holes do fall through the cracks occasionally and remain forever on film. For example, in the pilot episode, if Mulder lost nine minutes, and Scully lost nine minutes, and the car lost nine minutes, why didn't Mulder's watch lose nine minutes?

Trivia

1. How many tell-tale marks were found on the dead girl's back?

2. How many years had Dana Scully spent with the FBI prior to being assigned to the X-Files?

3. (Fill in the Blank) When Scully asked Mulder if he bothered to read her senior thesis, he assured her that he had but added, "It's just that in most of my work the laws of _____ rarely seem to apply."

4. What was lodged in the nasal cavity of one of the four dead classmates they exhumed?
   A. A metallic cylinder
   B. A worm-shaped parasite
   C. Hardened ammonia residue

5. (True or False) When Scully noticed marks on her back identical to the ones found on the dead girl, Mulder assured her that they were mosquito bites.

6. (Fill in the Blank) Mulder told Scully that his success as an investigator and "connections in _____" had allowed him a certain freedom to pursue his paranormal interests despite efforts to thwart his work.

X-PERT X-TRA BONUS POINTS

What was the name of the hypnotherapist who interviewed Billy at the end of the episode?

Investigative Field Report

The pilot episode opens like a more stylishly filmed, upscale version of NBC's *Unsolved Mysteries* or even Fox's own "reality-based" UFO *Sightings.* The highlight of the inaugural installment, however, is undoubtedly the exhumation of the corpse of a mysteriously slain student which had decomposed into some non-human, almost simian shrunken form that was obviously not of this world.

The hypnotherapist who interviews Billy is the same one who originally took Agent Mulder through regressive hypnosis to assist him in remembering his sister's abduction when they were children. Skeptics have claimed that many colorful "recollections" of alleged close encounters with extraterrestrials are mere products of the subject's imagination, rather than suppressed memories of actual events. When encouraged under hypnosis to reach back into memory and recall what the "saucer people" did to him or her, the subject may simply invent a "memory" of an event that never actually occurred.

FILE NO. 1X02:

DEEP THROAT

Declassified Case Overview: Ignoring the warnings of a mysterious and powerful high-ranking government official, Agents Mulder and Scully investigated the disappearance of one of the test pilots at a top secret Air Force base, which ultimately led to the implication of possible experimentation on UFOs by the military.

Nitpicking

When one of the MIBs (X-Phile slang for "Men in Black") removes the magazine from Scully's handgun, there is only one round of ammunition in it. Unless she just came from the target range, we doubt a highly trained and capable FBI field agent like Scully would have only one round of ammo in the magazine.

Trivia

1. How many pilots had turned up missing from Ellens Air Force Base since 1963?
    A. 4
    B. 6
    C. 8

2. (Fill in the Blank) Mulder told Scully the X-File case had a certain "paranormal _____."
    A. bouquet
    B. signature
    C. quality

3. What was the name of the restaurant where they went looking for "UFO nuts"?
    A. Spaced-Out Eats
    B. Flying Saucer Café
    C. Star Wars Cantina

4. (Fill in the correct number) Mulder explained to Scully that Ellens Air Force Base was rumored to be one of _____ sites where parts of the wreckage of the Roswell-UFO crash were taken.

5. What happened to Mulder after he was caught in a secret area witnessing one of the UFOs?

6. Who told Mulder that their lives were in danger and that "care and discretion are now imperative"?

X-PERT X-TRA BONUS POINTS

What did Colonel Budahas sprinkle on his food at a dinner party?

Investigative Field Report

The true-life threads of the so-called Roswell incident in 1947, one of the most celebrated cases in the history of UFO studies, are woven into the plot of this thoughtful and intense episode, which also introduces Jerry Hardin's Deep Throat character.

Because so many installments of *The X-Files* have to do with crashed UFOs and alien visitors, some X-Philes assumed for quite some time that Agent Scully was named after Frank Scully, the author in 1950 of ufology's first ever bestseller, *Behind the Flying Saucers*. Exposed as a hoax at the time, Frank Scully's book is currently being reappraised by modern-day investigators of the Roswell incident in case he might have been on to something after all.

The microfiched article on Ellens Air Force Base that Scully reads from in this episode was authored by a familiar name: Chris Carter.

FILE NO. 1X03:

SQUEEZE

Declassified Case Overview: A Baltimore murder investigation was hauntingly similar to a number of cannibalistic crimes that took place in 1903, 1933 and 1963. The search took Agents Mulder and Scully on the trail of a mutant serial killer who could gain access even to secure locked rooms and awoke from hibernation every 30 years to commit murder.

Nitpicking

One of the more memorable foes faced by our dynamic duo was the character known as Eugene Tooms, a cannibalistic mutation who could squeeze through the smallest gaps in pursuit of fresh human livers. The question of the hour asked by all nitpickers was: Why couldn't Tooms just squeeze himself out of the handcuffs?

Trivia

1. (True or False) In the opening scenes, a businessman was murdered in his office by a killer who slithered under a locked door.

2. After Mulder joined the investigation, what did he discover at the crime scene near a vent?

3. After staking out a previous crime scene, Agents Mulder and Scully caught a suspect, Eugene Tooms, slithering down an air conditioning conduit. Identify Tooms' employment, which he used as a convenient excuse for being in the vent at the time of his arrest.
   A. Building maintenance
   B. Animal control officer
   C. Air conditioning repairman

4. Why were the charges dropped and Tooms released from custody?

5. How did Mulder match Tooms' fingerprints with those found at the previous murder sites?
   A. A genetic bile coated each fingerprint
   B. The fingerprints were stretched by computer analysis
   C. Mulder exhumed the body of one of the 1963 victims

6. (Fill in the Blank) Going to the condemned building where Tooms lived in the '60s, Mulder and Scully found a nest of _____ and bile.

X-PERT X-TRA BONUS POINTS

According to Agent Mulder, why were Reticulans gray in color?

Investigative Field Report

Chris Carter in almost every interview has vocally acknowledged his debt of inspiration to the highly rated 1972 TV movie *The Night Stalker,* its equally popular follow-up *The Night Strangler,* and the short-lived 1974–75 series *Kolchak: The Night Stalker.* The premise and structure of

"Squeeze" owe much to *The Night Strangler* film, in which the wise-cracking, streetwise journalist, Carl Kolchak, stumbles upon evidence of an immortal serial killer very similar to Tooms.

While we always knew that Darren McGavin's newspaperman was going to kill or capture the mummies, vampires, werewolves and zombies, and that his vital evidence would end up lost, destroyed, or inconclusive, the prospects for Mulder and Scully are not always so certain.

"Squeeze" writers Glen Morgan and James Wong had a major falling out with Director Harry Longstreet over this episode, and re-shot much of the footage. They were considerably more satisfied with the sequel, "Tooms," directed by *X-Files* regular David Nutter.

FBI SERVICE RECORD
#118-366-047
Special Agent Fox Mulder

WARNING: This is an EYES ONLY personnel dossier and you must have a Level 2 Security Clearance to proceed. Unauthorized access to documents classified under the National Secrets Act can result in punishment of a $250,000 fine and/or five (5) years imprisonment. ENTER YOUR PASSWORD NOW!

1. What is Special Agent Mulder's middle name?

2. Which one of the following is his FBI badge number?
    A. JHH22530077
    B. JTT047101111
    C. GTBTDC486719

3. When was Mulder born?
    A. 13 October 1961
    B. 07 January 1961
    C. 20 September 1961

4.   (True or False) He was born in Bledsoe, Massachusetts.

5.   Identify the TV series Mulder enjoyed as a boy.
    A.   *Lost in Space*
    B.   *Star Trek*
    C.   *The Magician*

6.   Which position did he play in baseball when he was growing up?

7.   Which one of the following was the address of the Mulder family at the time of eight-year-old Samantha Mulder's alien abduction?
    A.   910 Northwest 10th Street
    B.   2790 Vine Street
    C.   24 Everleigh Drive

8.   What board game was young Fox Mulder playing at the time of her disappearance?
    A.   *Scrabble*
    B.   *Monopoly*
    C.   *Stratego*

9.   (True or False) Samantha Mulder's middle initial was "E."

10. Agent Mulder's wholehearted belief in the paranormal is driven by his sister's abduction by aliens. On which date was Samantha taken away?
    A.   27 November 1973
    B.   25 October 1972
    C.   27 December 1972

11. (True or False) Immediately after graduating from Oxford University in 1985 with a B.A. in psychology, Mulder entered the FBI's Quantico Academy.

12. As an FBI special agent assigned out of the Bureau's Washington, D.C. offices, Mulder lives in nearby Alexandria, Virginia. What is his apartment number?
    A.   44
    B.   42
    C.   24

13. (True or False) His telephone number at the apartment is (202)555-9355.

14. (True or False) Mulder has a photographic memory and the uncanny ability to process information and leap ahead to logical conclusions.

15. In 1988, he was assigned to the FBI's Violent Crimes Unit. Who was his supervisor?

16. On his first case, Mulder distinguished himself in the pursuit of a bank robber. What was this criminal's name?

17. In what year did Agent Mulder undergo regressive hypnosis with Dr. Heitz Werber, in an effort to recall memories of the day his sister was abducted?

X-PERT X-TRA BONUS POINTS #1

What is the population of Mulder's hometown?

---

18. Agent Mulder persuaded his superiors in 1991 to transfer him to the X-Files section. Who did he report to before Assistant Director Walter Skinner became his immediate supervisor?

19. (True or False) After trespassing on a crime scene under military jurisdiction and after charges of interfering with a military operation were lodged against him in 1993, Agent Mulder was called in for a hearing with Section Chief Edward Echols of the Office of Professional Responsibility.

20. Name the suspect who filed formal charges against Mulder, accusing him of engaging in harassment.

21. Mulder was armed with a Taurus 92 automatic, then later a Glock 19 and Sig Sauer 226 during his early years with the Bureau. Identify the standard FBI weapon he eventually began carrying.

22. In which branch of the federal government was Mulder's father, William, employed before retiring?
    A. Defense Department
    B. National Security Agency
    C. State Department

23. Name the government agent who assassinated Bill Mulder.

24. (Yes or No) Was Special Agent Mulder present at his father's house when he was shot to death?

25. Whose NICAP hat sometimes hung on Mulder's coat tree?
    A. Mike Bradshaw's
    B. Max Fenig's
    C. Doug Albert's

26. On which date did Special Agents Mulder and Scully first meet?
    A. April 28, 1992
    B. June 11, 1992
    C. March 6, 1992

27. Ever-helpful Danny Valodella is Mulder's (and later Scully's) mysterious and never-glimpsed Bureau insider. What does Mulder use to bribe Danny with to expedite license plate and adoption record searches?

28. What type of snack food is Mulder overly fond of eating?

29. What derogatory nickname was he given by his peers at the FBI early on in his career?

30. (True or False) Agent Mulder dislikes microfiche machines because they cause him to suffer from motion sickness.

31. What is his computer password (which Scully has easily cracked in the past)?

32. Mulder has a fondness for which type of music?
    A. Heavy metal
    B. Acid rock
    C. Classic rock

33. (True or False) Well known to have an interest in paranormal phenomena, Agent Mulder enjoys watching classic horror movies.

34. What is his preferred drink for stakeouts?
    A. Coffee with a teaspoon of Amaretto cream and two packets of artificial sweetner
    B. Iced tea
    C. Hot tea with nutmeg and a slice of lemon

35. (Fill in the Blank) Mulder has an intense fear of _____.
    A. fire
    B. snakes
    C. spiders

36. (Fill in the Blank) Mulder subscribes to *Celebrity Skin* and is known to read such porno publications as *Adult* _____ *News* in his free time.

37. Which NBA team is his favorite?
    A. Chicago Bulls
    B. Detroit Pistons
    C. New York Knicks

38. (True or False) Mark Mulder was the alias the special agent used when he investigated possible vampires at blood banks.

39. (True or False) Running Fox was a Native American name given to Agent Mulder during an X-File investigation.

X-PERT X-TRA BONUS POINTS #2

In 1993, Agent Mulder wrote an article on the Gulf Breeze UFO sightings for *Omni* magazine. Name the pseudonym he used for the publication.

---

40. Identify the alias Mulder favors during investigations when an assumed name is required.
    A. Mark Wardell
    B. George Hale
    C. Delbert Roberts

41. What breed is his dog?
     A. Border collie
     B. Norwegian elkhound
     C. Mixed

42. What is the rather unusual name of Mulder's dog?

43. (True or False) Agent Mulder keeps his notes for his field reports in a handwritten journal.

X-PERT X-TRA BONUS POINTS #3

What is Samantha Mulder's X-File number?

FILE NO. 1X04:

CONDUIT

Declassified Case Overview: When a young teenager disappeared from a trailer park in a flash of blazing light, Agent Mulder was forced to confront feelings about his own sister's abduction by aliens when they were children.

Nitpicking

The episode's Lake Okobogee, a "UFO hotspot" located near Sioux City, Iowa, has mountains on one side. The *X-Files* production staff have stated that Okobogee is a thinly disguised reference to the real-life Spirit Lake, which is in close proximity to Sioux City. Unfortunately, there are no mountains anywhere close to the body of water.

Trivia

1. What strange happening occurred in Darlene Morris' life in 1967?

2. (Fill in the Blank) Government agents grabbed Darlene and Kevin Morris, alleging that the boy's number-pictures held a code for a highly classified defense _____ transmission.

3. What did Mulder and Scully discover after examining the camp-site where Ruby Morris disappeared?
   A.   Incinerated grass
   B.   An unknown chemical composition
   C.   The body of the missing girl's boyfriend

4. What did Kevin use to construct a mural-sized picture of Ruby?

5. (Fill in the Blank) Returning to the woods, Mulder and Scully saw a blaze of lights that turned out to be _____.

6. Where did Mulder sit alone and cry for his missing sister, while Scully listened to his hypnotic regression therapy tapes?

7. Mulder recalled his sister's cries for help, a bright light that kept him paralyzed and a voice that assured him that Samantha would be returned. What was Mulder's reply when Scully asked him if he believed the voice?
   A.   "I want to believe."
   B.   "I have no other choice but to believe."
   C.   "Belief is the only thing that has kept me sane."

X-PERT X-TRA BONUS POINTS

What was unique about the two numbers that Kevin used to make his pictures?

Investigative Field Report

"Squeeze" gave the audience a week off from UFOs and saucer snatch-ers, but the series returned to its Fortean roots with this classic tale of alien abduction. Mulder's character background is substantially developed with the B-story concerning his sister's disappearance and how it tore the Mulder family apart.

The scene in which Mulder and Scully discover that Kevin has organized page after page of number doodlings on the floor, which from the aerial camera angle eerily reveals a huge mural of his missing sister, should have been nominated for an Emmy in the technical category.

Charles Cioffi, who returns as Scully's superbly obtuse and ambiguous FBI boss, is best remembered as the perverted killer from *Klute,* the other movie masterpiece from Alan Pakula, director of the paranoid conspiracy thriller *The Parallax View.*

Michael Cavanaugh, who portrays the sheriff in this episode, is also no stranger to extraterrestrial visitations. He was a regular on the syndicated series *Starman,* which was based on the theatrical movie about an alien that took the form of an earthling.

FILE NO. 1X05:

THE JERSEY DEVIL

Declassified Case Overview: The discovery of a vagrant's partially eaten corpse led Agents Mulder and Scully to a Sasquatch-type creature which lurked in the back alleys of Atlantic City. Was it myth or was it perhaps the missing link in human evolution?

Nitpicking

Although most X-Philes could not find any bloopers or inconsistencies with this episode, many fans thought the installment was "misinformed on the facts" concerning the "real" Jersey Devil. Several of them berated Chris Carter for describing the beast "as an East Coast Bigfoot." Internet chat groups complained that the real-life creature "has never been described that way" and lectured him publicly on electronic bulletin boards with such postings as "a little research by Carter and Company would have gone a long way to prevent this." *The X-Files* creator replied with, "The idea was not to make this a monster per se, but almost a missing link."

Trivia

1. In what year did this episode begin?
   A. 1949
   B. 1948
   C. 1947

2. (Fill in the blank with the correct body part) In the opening scene, a man was pulled away from his car and later found with his _____ eaten off.

3. Cut to the present, and a homeless man was found with parts of him eaten. What physical evidence was discovered on the body to suggest a cannibalistic human was the suspect?

4. (True or False) After Mulder staked out the spot where the creature was known to lurk, he was arrested by the local police and thrown in the drunk tank.

5. Who told Mulder he found the body of a male creature in the woods and turned it over to the authorities?

6. The female creature fled into the woods, where the police killed her. After an examination was conducted, what was found in her digestive system?

X-PERT X-TRA BONUS POINTS

What was Mulder's room number at the Galaxy Gateway motel in Atlantic City?

Investigative Field Report

Once again, the influence of *Kolchak* was manifested in "The Jersey Devil." The idea of authorities covering up horror stories to avoid damaging the tourist trade was a constant theme in *The Night Stalker* series.

The Jersey Devil, sometimes called the Leeds Devil, has in reality been the state's "official demon" since the 1930s. The earliest mention of a half-human monster dates back to 1735, when a Mrs. Leeds, as a consequence of her thirteenth pregnancy, is said to have given birth to a "devil child" which escaped up her chimney.

The Jersey Devil has been variously described by witnesses as: ram-headed and winged in the late 1700s tales; a phantom livestock-killer in 1840; the "Devil" in 1873–74; unidentifiable footprints in 1894–95; again a ram-headed winged creature in 1909; a "flying lion" in 1926; "a large, speedy, feathered animal running on all four legs" in 1927; a "horrible monster" in 1928; a half-man, half-beast in 1932; an upright "devil" in 1932; a "green male monster" in 1949; "something" killing chickens in 1952; and a "seven feet tall . . . faceless" hairy creature in 1966.

FILE NO. 1X06:

SHADOWS

Declassified Case Overview: The discovery of two terrorists' corpses led Mulder and Scully to a frightened young secretary whose boss had recently committed suicide. Further investigation involved the two FBI agents in a tangle of Middle Eastern religious extremism, a possible poltergeist and an ambiguous relationship between the forlorn secretary and her dead employer.

Nitpicking

In several instances during this episode, the vehicles that appear on-screen obviously have no license plates, or at least the numbers have been blacked out. Pay close attention to the scene in which Mulder and Scully's car crashes in the FBI vehicle compound and in the car park just before Lauren Kyte complains about the reassignment of Graves' parking space.

Trivia

1. How many men tried to attack Lauren before they were killed by an unseen force?

2. (True or False) Mulder and Scully were called in to examine the bodies because the corpses exhibited signs of residual electro-magnetic charge.

3. What was unusual about the victims' throats?
    A. They were internally crushed
    B. They had been cut from ear to ear
    C. The Adam's apple had been surgically removed

4. (True or False) Lauren was awakened by Graves' voice as blood streamed down the bathroom sink drain, letting her know his death was a result of murder, not suicide.

5. Identify Graves' nefarious former partner.
    A. Carlton
    B. Dorland
    C. Morland

6. CIA agents told Mulder and Scully that they believed Graves' company had been illegally doing business with a Mideast extremist group. What was being sold?
    A. Ammunition/weapons
    B. Computer technology
    C. The names of CIA undercover agents working in the Mideast

7. Lauren moved on to a new job in a new city. What happened to a co-worker who became surly with Lauren?
    A. Her letter opener flew into the wall
    B. Her correction fluid exploded all over her desk
    C. Her coffee cup began to rattle

X-PERT X-TRA BONUS POINTS

Whose words of wisdom were prominently displayed in Graves' office?

Investigative Field Report

With the series' first traditional ghost story, writers Glen Morgan and James Wong repeatedly subvert the audience's expectations throughout the episode, which has now become a classic trait that separates *The X-Files* from other pale imitations such as CBS' *American Gothic* and Fox's own *Kindred: The Embraced*.

The script for "Shadows" is tight and crisp and the Mulderisms and Scullyisms come in rapid fire succession. The veteran *X-Files* screenwriters also effectively capture the insular and isolated world of office politics, despite the fact that they tried in vain to have a different setting for this episode. At Fox's insistence, Morgan and Wong, who wanted to pen a *Poltergeist*-like installment set in a haunted suburban house, were forced to change the episode's principle milieu.

S & M: SEASON ONE

Much of The X-Files' appeal, and edge, comes from the onscreen chemistry between Agents Scully and Mulder. X-Philes have coined the droll comments from poker-faced Mulder as "Mulderisms" and the witty comebacks from his cool-headed partner as "Scullyisms." Identify the episodes in which the following S & M interplay occurred.

1. MULDER: "I think I saw some of these people at Woodstock."
    SCULLY: "Mulder, you weren't at Woodstock."
    MULDER: "I saw the movie."

    Episode _____

2. SCULLY: "The answers are there. You just have to know where to look for them."
    MULDER: "That's why they put the 'I' in FBI."

    Episode _____

3. SCULLY: "So, why did you two go your separate ways?"
   MULDER: "I'm a pain in the ass to work with."
   SCULLY: "No, seriously."
   MULDER: "You mean I'm *not* a pain in the ass to work with?"

   Episode _____

4. SCULLY: "I know by now to trust your instincts."
   MULDER: "Why? Nobody else does."

   Episode _____

5. MULDER: "You've got a brother, don't you, Scully?"
   SCULLY: "Yeah, I have an older one and a younger one."
   MULDER: "Have you ever thought about calling one of them all day and then the phone rings and it's one of them?"
   SCULLY: "Does this pitch somehow end in a way for me to lower my long distance charges?"

   Episode _____

6. SCULLY (at the door): "Who is it?"
   MULDER: "Steven Spielberg."

   Episode _____

7. (Inside Mulder's trashed hotel room)
   SCULLY: "What's going on?"
   MULDER: "Looks like housekeeping hasn't been here yet."

   Episode _____

8. MULDER: "I was merely extending her a professional courtesy."
   SCULLY: "Oh, is *that* what you were extending?"

   Episode _____

9. SCULLY: "There's something up there, Mulder."
   MULDER: "Well, I've been saying that for years."

   Episode _____

10. MULDER: "Now, this . . . that's . . . west."
    SCULLY: "What does the map say?"

MULDER (crumpling up and dropping the map): "That we should be there already."

Episode _____

11. SCULLY: "Mulder, I know what you did wasn't by the book."
     MULDER: "Tells you something about the book, doesn't it?"

     Episode _____

12. SCULLY (looking at a desiccated corpse): "It's male."
     MULDER: "Barely."

     Episode _____

13. SCULLY: "Those lights the driver saw may have been swamp gas."
     MULDER: "Swamp gas?"
     SCULLY: "It's a natural phenomenon in which phosphane and methane rising from decaying organic matter ignite, creating globes of blue flame."
     MULDER: "Happens to me when I eat Dodger Dogs."

     Episode _____

14. SCULLY: "Mulder, did you see their eyes. If I were that stoned ..."
     MULDER: "Ohhhh, if you were that stoned *what?*"

     Episode _____

15. SCULLY: "Genetics might explain the patterns. It also might explain the sociopathic attitudes and behaviors. It begins with one family member who raises an offspring, who raises the next child ..."
     MULDER: "So what's this, the anti-Waltons?"

     Episode _____

16. MULDER: "You should have seen her, Scully. She was beautiful."
     SCULLY: "Yeah? Well, she just about ripped your lungs out."

     Episode _____

17. SCULLY: "I just don't think it's a good idea to antagonize the local law enforcement."

MULDER: "Who, me? I'm Mr. Congeniality."
SCULLY: "You never know, we might need his help one of these days."
MULDER: "I'll send him a bundt cake."

Episode _____

18. MULDER: "You think he does it because he gets off on it?"
SCULLY: "No, I think he does it because *you* do."

Episode _____

19. SCULLY: "What do you think?"
MULDER: "I think I'm gonna suggest we sleep with the lights on."

Episode _____

20. SCULLY: "We can't rule out the possibility that the person we're talking about is a transvestite."
MULDER: "I think Don Juan in there knows the difference between the male and female of the species."

Episode _____

21. MULDER: "You have to admit that was exciting, Mission Control and all."
SCULLY: "Yeah. Ranks right up there with getting a pony and learning to braid my own hair."

Episode _____

22. SCULLY: "You're saying that time disappeared! Time can't just disappear. It's a universal constant!"
(Dead car starts itself)
MULDER: "Not in this zip code."

Episode _____

23. SCULLY: "That's why Blevins has you hidden away down here."
MULDER: "You're down here, too."

Episode _____

24. SCULLY (on the phone): "What's that sound in the background?"
MULDER: "That's someone getting sick."
SCULLY: "Mulder, where are you? The drunk tank?"

Episode _____

25. SCULLY: "Did Boggs confess?"
MULDER: "No, no, it was five hours of Boggs' channeling. After
three hours I asked him to summon up the soul of Jimi Hendrix
and requested *All Along the Watchtower*. You know, the guy's
been dead twenty years, but he still hasn't lost his edge."

Episode _____

26. SCULLY: "These are the most paranoid people I have ever met.
I don't know how you could think that what they say is even remotely plausible."
MULDER: "I think it's remotely plausible that someone might
think you're hot."

Episode _____

27. MULDER: "How are you feeling?"
SCULLY: "First time I've ever played the target."
MULDER: "Let's make sure it's not the last."

Episode _____

28. SCULLY: "You've got that look on your face, Mulder."
MULDER: "What look is that?"
SCULLY: "The one where you've forgotten your keys and you're
trying to get back in the house."

Episode _____

X-PERT X-TRA BONUS POINTS

(Fill in the blank dialogue from the episode "The Jersey Devil")
SCULLY: "Working hard, Mulder?"
MULDER (indicating centerfold of porno magazine): "This
woman claims to have been taken aboard a spaceship and held
in an _____ chamber without food and water for three
days."

GHOST IN THE MACHINE

Declassified Case Overview: Agents Mulder and Scully were asked to assist a perplexed fellow agent when all the evidence pointed to the murder of a company's CEO by his own computer, which appeared to have developed a life of its own.

Nitpicking

In this episode, Scully spools through a digital audio tape while sitting at a desk. Unfortunately, DAT machines do not make that type of spooling noise. The recording/dubbing editor has confessed that the sound was made by an analogue audio tape machine instead to enhance the audible effects.

When the Eurisko computer calls Scully's computer the phone rings on her bedside nightstand. She picks it up and hears the modem screeching on the line. Scully then goes to her computer and notices that someone (or something) is accessing her computer files. Why doesn't she lose her online connection when she picks up the bedroom extension?

When Mulder's former partner is killed, he appears to be pushed to the floor of the elevator by G-forces. But if the elevator is falling down, shouldn't he be plastered to the ceiling?

Trivia

1. What was the name of Eurisko's slain CEO?
    A. Benjamin Drake
    B. Lawrence Burk
    C. Mark Wohl

2. Identify Mulder's former partner who asked him to assist with this X-File.

3. (True or False) The CEO's office audio taping system proved that Brad Wilczek was the last person to speak to him before he was killed.

4. While Wilczek watched helplessly on a monitor, an elevator plummeted to the bottom. How many stories did it fall?
   A. 20
   B. 25
   C. 30

5. Who told Mulder that the Defense Department was interested in Wilczek because he had successfully created artificial intelligence?

6. A building security worker tried to stop Mulder from implanting a virus in the computer system. Who did the guard *really* work for?
   A. CIA
   B. Defense Department
   C. NSA

X-PERT X-TRA BONUS POINTS

What two word question did COS ask as it was being neutralized with Mulder's computer virus?

Investigative Field Report

The supercomputer with a mind of its own has been rehashed more times than we care to remember on TV and in movie theaters (*2001: A Space Odyseey* and *Demon Seed*, to name a couple). Still, the well-worn premise is handled effectively and the episode does have its share of striking visual sequences, especially the scene involving Scully and the vacuum-sucking fan.

A true life case of technology possibly becoming sentient involved a computer installed in an architect's office in Stockport, England. Video recordings of the antics of the rogue Amstrad PC 1512 were a major attraction at a computer exhibition in London in 1988. Although it was nowhere near a power source, it would switch itself on, begin the start-up procedures, attempt to write onscreen, and then cut out half a minute later with a sound like a groan. One expert believed that the Amstrad was trying to communicate something important.

FILE NO. 1X08:

ICE

Declassified Case Overview: Mulder and Scully's latest X-File led them to an isolated Arctic research station where they discovered extraterrestrial parasitic worms had been unearthed in the deep underground drilling at the base and were burrowing their way into host bodies.

Nitpicking

When Mulder points his Glock 19 handgun at the dog the audience hears the cocking of the pistol's hammer. Unfortunately, that particular weapon has an internal hammer and makes no such noise.

The dog purges the alien worms out of its body via a bowel movement. If the parasitic creatures had attached themselves to glands in the brain, how did they turn up in the dog's digestive tract?

At the end of the episode, we see Hodge informing Mulder and Scully that the research station has been incinerated by government forces. How come these characters are standing outside in the freezing Arctic weather, but we don't see their breath (although Hodge is blowing into his hands to keep them warm and Mulder is seen crossing his arms as he shivers)?

Trivia

1.   (True or False) Mulder and Scully watched a satellite link-up recording in horror as two surviving scientists slit their throats in a suicide pact rather than kill each other.

2.   (Fill in the Blank) Scully found _____ in the victims' blood as well as a small, single-celled creature that she believed was the larval stage of a larger animal.

3.   Who decked Mulder when he suggested that they employ a quarantine because of their exposure to the unknown organism?
     A.   Da Silva
     B.   Murphy
     C.   Bear

4. (Days or Weeks?) Mulder tried to radio for help but was told they would be trapped for _____ by the storm.

5. (Fill in the Blank) The worm penetrated the _____ gland in the brain, causing aggressive behavior in its host.

6. (True or False) Da Silva questioned whether they should kill it, saying the worm probably came to Earth from another planet, one that sustained ammonia-based life.

7. After she examined a blood sample, Scully found that when larva from two different worms invaded the same host they killed each other. How did she prove her theory?

8. Who became infected and required an implant of another worm, Hodge or Da Silva?

X-PERT X-TRA BONUS POINTS #1

Who torched the research station after they were rescued?

X-PERT X-TRA BONUS POINTS #2

According to Mulder, what was the approximate age of the worm-shaped extraterrestrials?

Investigative Field Report

Although chilling (pardon the pun), unnerving and visually impressive, "Ice" was devised as a one-set budget-cruncher to eliminate the need for location shooting, and the episode is a flagrant and shameless knockoff of other, very prominent creative sources—*The Thing* by way of *Alien*, with creatures reminiscent of "The Invisibles" from *The Outer Limits* and "The Conspiracy" aliens who attempted to take over Starfleet Command in *Star Trek: The Next Generation*.

Antarctica, the ice-covered southernmost continent, occupies a peculiar place in UFO lore. Albert Bender, a prominent figure in the early history of the UFO phenomenon in America, thought the remote and seemingly lifeless area was the site of a vast installation under the ice, where aliens extracted some mysterious but valuable substance from sea water. A wave of UFO sightings near the region, at Deception Island in the South Shetland Islands, was reported in 1965. Argentine, British and Chilean personnel stationed there reported seeing UFOs, including a noiseless, luminous, round or oval object that moved from east to west and exhibited oscillations in its trajectory.

X-Files coordinator Ken Kirzinger plays Richter, one of the men in the standoff scene at the beginning of the episode.

FILE NO. 1X09:

SPACE

Declassified Case Overview: When NASA's latest space shuttle launch was beset by numerous minor acts of sabotage, mechanical failures and irregularities, the finger of suspicion pointed to Lt. Col. Marcus Belt, supervisor of the shuttle program and a former astronaut idolized by Agent Mulder.

Nitpicking

Michelle Generoo is involved in a serious automobile accident, which leaves a deep cut on her eyebrow and quite a lot of blood on her head. Later on in the episode she has no visible cuts.

Isn't Scully a physician? Why then did Mulder call for a doctor when his medically trained partner was present?

Lt. Colonel Belt is shown on a shuttle mission in 1977, but the first space shuttle wasn't launched until 1981.

Don't most states have laws requiring hospitals to have windows that people *can't* jump out of?

Trivia

1. (True or False) Lt. Colonel Belt was the former commander of *Gemini 6* and had flashbacks of a spacewalk where he saw a sculpted face in the landscape of Mars looking down at him.

2. (True or False) Generoo told Mulder and Scully that a recent shuttle launch had been aborted only seconds before liftoff and that she feared a piece of equipment had been sabotaged.

3. (Fill in the blank dialogue) The shuttle felt a "dull thump" and experienced an oxygen leak while the astronauts told Mission Control, "There's some kind of _____ outside the ship!"

4. (True or False) Mulder and Scully examined records that proved that Belt knew about the equipment flaws and possibly the O-ring failure on the *Challenger*.

5. After collapsing, Belt confessed that an astral force had lived in him and controlled his actions. At his urging, the shuttle's trajectory was altered, preventing the craft from burning up on re-entry. Name the city and state where the shuttle made its emergency landing.

6. After Belt leapt to his death, who said, "Something had possessed him. Something he had seen out there in space"?

X-PERT X-TRA BONUS POINTS

What position did Michelle Generoo hold at NASA?

Investigative Field Report

Although the dialogue references to documented paranormal phenomena, popular faction, and real events added authenticity to this truly science-fiction episode, the allusion to the far-too-recent *Challenger* disaster was in rather questionable taste.

The ever increasing camaraderie between Mulder and Scully is perfectly orchestrated through her affectionate amusement at, and tolerance of, Mulder's boyish enthusiasm for Lt. Col. Belt, his childhood hero of the space race era.

The so-called "Face on Mars" has become a symbol of the belief in extraterrestrial intelligence. The geological formation, revealed by photos returned to Earth from an American Mariner probe in 1976, resembles a stylized human face turned skyward, and is located near a set of symmetrical, pyramidal structures that have been compared to a "city." Through an exercise in imagination, the alleged face and city have been interpreted both in the U.S. and in the former Soviet Union as possible works of engineering produced by extraterrestrials.

ALPHABET SOUP

Like the federal government itself, The X-Files is chockfull of acronyms—words formed from the first (or first few) letters of several words. Decipher the following acronyms into their full compound terms. Each correct answer will count as a 5-point X-PERT X-TRA BONUS. This section may take you a little longer, but please try to complete it and move on to the next part of the trivia test PDQ (Pretty Damn Quick).

1. **Acronym:** COS
    Compound Term: _____

2. **Acronym:** AICP
    Compound Term: _____

3. **Acronym:** APU
    Compound Term: _____

4. **Acronym:** NICAP
    Compound Term: _____

5. **Acronym:** DNA
    Compound Term: _____

6. **Acronym:** IEBED
    Compound Term: _____

7. **Acronym:** FFS
    Compound Term: _____

8. **Acronym:** SETI
    Compound Term: _____

9. **Acronym:** ASL
    Compound Term: _____

10. **Acronym:** ACIC
    Compound Term: _____

11. **Acronym:** AFOSI
    Compound Term: _____

12. **Acronym:** SAC
    Compound Term: _____

13. **Acronym:** VCU
    Compound Term: _____

14. **Acronym:** OPR
    Compound Term: _____

15. **Acronym:** DOJ
    Compound Term: _____

16. **Acronym:** NIS
    Compound Term: _____

17. **Acronym:** ASAC
    Compound Term: _____

18. **Acronym:** INS
    Compound Term: _____

19. **Acronym:** INTERPOL
    Compound Term: _____

20. **Acronym:** NCIC
    Compound Term: _____

21. **Acronym:** CDC
    Compound Term: _____

22.   **Acronym:** BATF
       Compound Term: _____

23.   **Acronym:** DEA
       Compound Term: _____

24.   **Acronym:** WAO
       Compound Term: _____

25.   **Acronym:** EBE
       Compound Term: _____

FILE NO. 1X10:

FALLEN ANGEL

Declassified Case Overview: The mysterious informant, Deep Throat, directed Agent Mulder to a government cover-up involving a crashed UFO. Mulder risked his career to prove the existence of a top secret UFO clean-up team and intercept a fugitive alien on the run from the military.

Nitpicking

When UFO enthusiast Max Fenig has a seizure and Mulder assists him in lying down, the FBI agent notices a V-shaped scar behind Fenig's right ear. Back at the hotel, Mulder informs Scully that the scar is behind his left ear.

After discovering Fenig's Melleril medication, Scully immediately concludes that he suffers from schizophrenia. However, the *Physician's Desk Reference* clearly states that the pheonthiazine derivative is prescribed for anxiety, tension, agitation, psychosomatic disorders, sleep disturbances, difficulties of concentration, intractable pain and alcohol withdrawal—not exclusively for schizophrenia, as Scully claimed.

At the hospital, the doctor reports that the deputy and the others were admitted with 5th and 6th degree burns over 90 percent of their bodies. Isn't a body burned to the bone in 4th degree? Red Cross first aid courses teach that a person burned more severely would be incinerated to ash.

Trivia

1. (Fill in the Blank) A military commander told his radar observer to report the sighting of a crashed UFO as a _____.

2. Deep Throat told Mulder that a top secret government UFO retrieval team had been dispatched. How many hours did Mulder have to locate evidence before the area was "sanitized"?
    A. 12
    B. 24
    C. 48

3. (Fill in the Blank) Mulder infiltrated the field operation, code-named OPERATION _____, but was caught photographing the wreckage as troops sought the escaped UFO pilot.

4. (Fill in the blank dialogue) Held prisoner, Mulder met Max Fenig, a member of NICAP, a national organization dedicated to the scientific exploration of the UFO phenomenon. Fenig told Mulder that the clandestine government involvement at the crash site was "like the _____ cover-up all over again."

5. (True or False) Deep Throat came to Mulder's aid, informing him that he was in deep trouble in Washington and that the X-Files section was on the verge of being shut down.

6. What happened to the soldiers who encountered the translucent body-possessing alien fugitive?
    A. Their bodies exploded
    B. They were burned horribly
    C. Their bodies imploded

7. Army radar tracked another UFO, which was larger than the first. A radar operator noted that it was hovering over a small town in what state?
   A. Iowa
   B. Nebraska
   C. Wisconsin

8. (Fill in the blank dialogue) Back in Washington, a committee grilled Mulder, but he asked defiantly, "How can I disprove _____ that are stamped with an official seal?"

X-PERT X-TRA BONUS

(Fill in the blank dialogue) Mulder told the committee, "No one, no government agency, has _____ over the truth."

Investigative Field Report

The core of this riveting episode is the UFO clean-up team, which is a popular and logical paranoia of the flying saucer brigade. Among the most famous alleged UFO "sanitation" efforts by the U.S. military was the Aztec incident, which reportedly occurred in 1948 near Aztec, New Mexico. The bodies of 14 to 16 aliens were said to have been recovered from their crashed but undamaged saucer.

Rumor has it that the craft was inspected by a team of distinguished scientists including Dr. Robert Oppenheimer, director of the U.S. A-bomb project at Los Alamos, New Mexico, during World War II; and Dr. John von Neumann, the Hungarian-born U.S. mathematician who helped develop the first electronic computers. According to one report, the "fallen angel" was disassembled and taken to Los Alamos, then moved to another location several months later.

FILE NO. 1X11:

EVE

Declassified Case Overview: On two different coasts, two men were killed simultaneously in the same bizarre manner by their respective daughters, who were identical to each other. The evidence pointed to a deadly eugenics experiment funded by the government.

Nitpicking

If Teena Simmons had the Eve-strength to get her father into the swing without leaving tell-tale signs of a struggle, then how did Mulder manage to restrain her with one arm *and* Cindy Reardon with the other?

Sally Kendrick, the adult Eve, said she had *extra* chromosomes. According to scientists specializing in genetics, multiple extra chromosomes would result in spontaneous abortion of the fetus long before birth.

When the girls and Eve are in the motel room they drink from throwaway paper cups. However, when Mulder and Scully later retrieve one of the cups, it has miraculously turned to glass.

Trivia

1. How old were the murdered men's twin daughters?
      A.   6
      B.   7
      C.   8

2. (True or False) Each of the two men died from the result of having a massive amount of blood drained from their bodies.

3. (Fill in the blank dialogue) The first girl, Teena, speaking in a peculiarly adult manner, told Mulder and Scully that "men from the clouds" came for her father and "wanted to _____ him."

4. From what type of facility was Teena kidnapped?
   A. Juvenile detention
   B. Social services
   C. Children's ward of a hospital

5. (True or False) Teena and Cindy killed their aunt by injecting her with her own excrement over a prolonged period.

6. (Yes or No) Did Teena and Cindy know of each other's existence?

X-PERT X-TRA BONUS POINTS

(Fill in the blank with the correct number)
Eve 6 alleged that her extra chromosomes gave her heightened intelligence and that her I.Q. could "top _____."

Investigative Field Report

"Eve" is classic *X-Files* with its marvelously convoluted and complex plot, which keeps the audience guessing from beginning to end as the story we think we're being told is continuously re-routed. What's particularly notable is that Mulder and Scully are both consistently wrong in every single assumption they make during the course of their investigation.

Our apprehension and discomfort over cloning, of screwing around with both science and nature simultaneously, is accompanied by the fun-horror of the two pint-sized monsters (eerily played by Vancouver twins Erika and Sabrina Krievins) and the more close-to-home horror of the two loving fathers being killed by their previously innocent and devoted daughters when the genetic "sleeper" switch is engaged.

X-PERT TESTIMONY: PART I

With the assistance of some well-placed government informants, we have been allowed unprecedented access and review of all the X-Pert testimony contained in the highly classified X-Files. It is now your assignment to determine the identity, means, motives or opportunities of the eyewitnesses who made the following statements.

1. Who boasted, "Let's just say I'm in a position to know quite a lot of things"?
    A.   Cigarette-Smoking Man
    B.   Mr. X
    C.   Deep Throat

2. In the episode "Anasazi," who said, "Gentlemen, that was the phone call I never wanted to get"?
    A.   Krycek
    B.   Cigarette-Smoking Man
    C.   Skinner

3. (True or False) Chaco said in "Our Town," "Living a long life is a mixed blessing."

4. Who told Agent Scully in "Ghost in the Machine," "We enjoy walking down unpredictable avenues of thought, turning new corners, but, as a general rule, scruffy minds don't commit murder"?
    A.   Nancy Spiller
    B.   Mulder
    C.   Brad Wilczek

5. (Fill in the blank dialogue) Scully philosophized in "Soft Light," "Darkness can hide a multitude of _____."

6. In which episode did Mulder say (while undergoing a full body examination), "Before anyone passes judgment, may I remind you, we are in the Arctic"?

7. Who issued the warning "It knows you now" in "The Calusari"?
    A. Calusar
    B. Scully
    C. Kosseff

8. (True or False) Chief Koretz said in "Fallen Angel," "Well, sir, the meteor seems to be hovering over a small town in eastern Indiana."

9. In "Humbug" who said of Mulder, "Can you imagine looking like *him* for the rest of your life"?
    A. The Curator
    B. Dr. Blockhead
    C. The Conundrum

10. Which character said in "Shapes," "I coulda sworn I saw . . . red eyes . . . and fangs"?
    A. Jim Parker
    B. Running Horse
    C. Sheriff Spencer

11. Name the "Miracle Man" who proclaimed, "I've laid my hands on the ill, given them health. I've healed the sick. I've even touched the dying and given them life."
    A. Preacher
    B. The Reverend Kearns
    C. Samuel Hartley

12. In "E.B.E." who told Mulder, "That's why I like you . . . Your ideas are even weirder than ours"?
    A. The Lone Gunmen
    B. Deep Throat
    C. Two Air Force PROJECT FALCON intelligence officers

13. Who said in "Dod Kalm," "Everything stopped. Everything. Even the sea. Even the wind"?
    A. Ionesco
    B. Halverson
    C. Captain Barclay

14. (True or False) Deep Throat admitted in "Shadows," "I would never lie. I willfully participate in a campaign of misinformation."

15. (True or False) In the episode "Colony," Samantha Mulder said, "The certainty . . . becomes a comfort that allows you to move on. We bury our memories so deep after that has been destroyed."

16. Who said that " 'Fresh Bones,' they pay good, but I go there for the frogs. You find the best frogs at the cemetery"?
    A. Groundskeeper
    B. Chester Bonaparte
    C. Pierre Bauvais

17. In "Ascension" which government informant issued the warning, "No one can help you now. Your channels of appeal and recourse are closed"?

18. Another Ambiguous Government Warning: Who said, "Duane Barry is not what Mulder thinks he is"?
    A. Krycek
    B. Scully
    C. Kazdin

19. (True or False) The Cigarette-Smoking Man said in "F. Emasculata," "Don't believe—for a second—this is an isolated incident!"

20. Identify the episode in which Sophie the Ape "said" in American Sign Language, "Bright light. Man save man."

21. Who screamed "WHERE IS SHE?!" in "End Game"?
    A. Bill Mulder
    B. Samantha Mulder
    C. Fox Mulder

22. In the episode "Die Hand Die Verletzt," what was Mulder referring to when he said, "It'd make a great coffee table"?
    A. A woodland altar
    B. A small pine coffin
    C. A mummified corpse

23. (Fill in the blank with the correct name) Scully said in "Irresistible," "It is somehow easier to believe, as Agent _____ does, in aliens and UFOs, than in the kind of inhuman, cold-blooded monster who could prey on the living to scavenge from the dead."

24. Who asked Scully in "The X-Files: Pilot," "So, who did you tick off to get stuck with this detail?"

25. Which character in "Space" spouted the technobabble, "The valve is made of ferrocarbon titanium. To score that material would take extreme temperatures, *launchpad* temperatures"?
    A. Lt. Col. Belt
    B. Scully
    C. Michelle Generoo

26. (Fill in the blank dialogue) Scully said about the Bigfoot-like monster in "The Jersey Devil," "This thing chewed somebody's _____ off! That's not exactly a *DEFENSIVE* posture!"

27. Who admitted in "Conduit," "I knew that if I screamed loud and long enough that someone would listen. But I never expected the FBI."?
    A. Ruby Morris
    B. Tessa
    C. Darlene Morris

28. (True or False) Mulder asked in "Squeeze," "Is there any way I can get it off my fingers quickly—without betraying my cool exterior?"

29. (Fill in the blank with the correct number) Mulder said in the "Fire" episode, "This is classic Phoebe Green, Mind Game Player Extraordinaire. _____ years it's taken me to forget about this woman and she shows up in my life with a case like this!"

30. Which diabolical character was Mulder referring to when he said at the age of six he "slaughtered every animal in his housing project. When he was thirty, he strangled five family members over Thanksgiving dinner and then sat down to watch the fourth quarter of the Detroit-Green Bay game"?

31. In which episode did Mulder accuse Scully of almost doing "the wild thing with some stranger"?
    A. "Irresistible"
    B. "GenderBender"
    C. "Fire"

32. Who cried out, "You *are* Jack Willis!" when it was painfully obvious that the former FBI agent had somehow risen from the dead like "Lazarus"?
    A. Scully
    B. Warren Dupree
    C. Mulder

33. Who was Mulder referring to in the episode "Young at Heart," when he said that the character had "found the perfect disguise—youth!"?
    A. Jerry Lamana
    B. Reggie Purdue
    C. John Barnett

34. (Fill in the blank dialogue) In "Darkness Falls," Mulder said, "It'll be a nice trip to the _____" in Washington State where people were disappearing.

35. (True or False) Scully said in "Born Again" that "Jumpers tend to open the window before they jump."

36. Which character said that " 'Roland' isn't exactly a rocket scientist"?
    A. Scully
    B. Mulder
    C. Dr. Keats

37. In which episode did Mulder comment, "The man we met yesterday kept this place looking like he was waiting for the people from *Good Housekeeping* to show up. I would never have pegged him as one to do all this—or do a Greg Louganis out the window"?
    A. "Born Again"
    B. "The Erlenmeyer Flask"
    C. "Tooms"

38. Who confessed in "Little Green Men," "I wanted to believe . . . But the tools have been taken away"?
    A. Senator Matheson
    B. Walter Skinner
    C. Agent Mulder

39. (Fill in the blank dialogue) Alex Krycek stated in "Sleepless" that "The autopsy revealed forty-three separate internal hemorrhages and skeletal fragments which just don't happen _____, not without some corresponding external trauma."

40. How old was the real estate agent Mulder referred to in the episode "Blood," who murdered "four people with his bare hands"?
    A. 42
    B. 56
    C. 68

41. (Fill in the blank dialogue) Scully concluded in "The Host," "Nature didn't make that thing, Mulder, _____ did."

42. Identify the character who said in "Excelsius Dei," "I put it back in that drawer—with all those other videos that aren't yours."
    A. Dorothy
    B. Scully
    C. Mulder

43. In which episode did Mulder say, "You know, for a holy man, you've got quite a knack for pissing people off"?

44. Who acknowledged in "Firewalker" that "We're not exactly 'proper channels' "?
    A. Peter Tanaka
    B. Dr. Adam Pierce
    C. Agent Mulder

X-PERT X-TRA BONUS POINTS

Identify the character who made the following statement in a second season episode: "I don't have to be psychic to see that you are in a very dark place. Much darker than where my sister is. Willingly walking deeper into the darkness cannot help her at all."

FILE NO. 1X12:

FIRE

Declassified Case Overview: The investigation into a sadistic, pyrokinetic killer got very hot indeed when Agent Mulder had to help an ex-lover, a Scotland Yard inspector, protect a visiting member of British Parliament.

Nitpicking

In an obvious cost-cutting attempt, the production crew utilized stock footage from previous episodes. When Scully is seen working at a computer, it is *exactly* the same shot as seen in "Squeeze."

Trivia

1. (Fill in the Blank) Anticipating Sir Malcolm Marsden's arrival in the U.S., Cecil L'ively killed the estate's _____ and took his place.

2. What type of local establishment did L'ively patronize and then torch after he ignited his arm?

3. What were the names of Sir Malcolm's two children?
   - A. Michael and Jimmy
   - B. Nancy and Susan
   - C. Bryan and Carla

4. (Fill in the blank dialogue) Scully profiled L'ively, ascertaining that he was probably "prone to excessive fantasies about _____."

5. Who rescued the Marsden children after the Cape Cod estate erupted in flames?
   - A. Mulder
   - B. Scully
   - C. Phoebe Green

6. Who doused L'ively with a fire accelerant?

7. (True or False) Via narration, Scully said L'ively sustained fourth- and fifth-degree burns over his entire body but was rapidly healing and would fully recover within a month.

X-PERT X-TRA BONUS POINTS

What was the name of the caretaker of Marsden's estate?

Investigative Field Report

So what if Mulder has a phobia of fire? Who wouldn't be afraid of the grand scale infernos displayed in this episode. Amazingly, when "Fire" was shown in England, the BBC was so concerned about the subject of spontaneous combustion they seriously considered not televising the episode or at least censoring portions of it.

Once again, Carter (who wrote this episode) essentially reworked one of his creative influences. Does anyone remember Stephen King's bestseller *Firestarter* or the movie version of the same name, starring a young Drew Barrymore?

Charles Dickens was fascinated by Spontaneous Combustion—the sudden, virtual destruction of a human body by fire. He studied known cases at great length, and eventually used his knowledge in his novel *Bleak House.*

In chapter 32, Dickens describes the death of Krook, a depraved drunk. His charred remains are discovered in his seedy room by Weevle and Guppy: ". . . there is a smouldering suffocating vapour in the room, and a dark greasy coating on the walls and ceiling . . . Here is a small burnt patch of flooring; here is the tinder from a little bundle of burnt paper . . . seeming to be steeped in something; and here is— is it the cinder of a small charred and broken log of wood sprinkled with white ashes . . . ? Call the death by any name . . . attribute it to whom you will . . . it is the same death eternally—inborn, inbred, engendered in the corrupted humours of the vicious body itself . . .— Spontaneous Combustion, and none other of the deaths that can be died."

FILE NO. 1X13:

BEYOND THE SEA

Declassified Case Overview: After Scully's father died, the agent's usually routine skepticism was put to the test by a death row convict who claimed that by using his recently acquired psychic abilities he could assist in the apprehension of a serial killer.

Nitpicking

When Scully is sitting in her car at the intersection, her hair is parted on the left as she notices the Hotel Niagara, which is the psychic sign of "water falling" that Boggs told her about. But after Scully turns to look at the statue of the angels on the other side of the street, her hair is suddenly parted on the right.

Trivia: The Numbers Game

(NOTE: Because of the difficulty of the following questions, all correct answers will count as a 5-point X-PERT X-TRA BONUS.)

1. Scully wakes up on the couch in her living room to see her father sitting in a chair. What was the time digitally displayed on the VCR atop her television?

2. How much did a month's supply of the men's hair spray paint for baldness cost (as advertised during an early morning commercial on Scully's TV)?

3. Mulder showed Scully a police mug shot of Luther Lee Boggs. Identify his prisoner's number shown in the photo.

4. What was the time of Captain Scully's funeral?

5. In her Washington, D.C. office, Scully glanced at the cover of a red X-File folder titled "Visionary Encounters w/ the Dead." What was the file's number?

6.   Including Dana Scully, how many mourners were in attendance at her father's seaside funeral service?

7.   (Fill in the blank number) Mulder told Scully that it was important that they plotted their moves in the investigation because Boggs was already _____ steps ahead of them.

8.   Mulder tried to trick Boggs with a fake newspaper article with headlines that read: "KIDNAPPED COLLEGE STUDENTS FOUND SAFE. POLICE SEEK SUSPECT." How many people knew that the story was bogus?

9.   Identify the prisoner's number shown in Lucas Jackson Henry's mug shot.

10.   (Fill in the blank number) Investigators believed that Boggs' last _____ murders had been committed with a partner.

11.   How old was Scully when she snuck outside to smoke one of her mother's cigarettes?

12.   Boggs killed five of his family members on Thanksgiving Day. How many brothers and sisters did he murder?

Investigative Field Report

The all-important "hook" to "Beyond the Sea" is, of course, the idea of Mulder and Scully's roles of believer and skeptic being reversed. Although there is more than a passing resemblance to *Silence of the Lambs* in several of the sequences involving Scully and death-row inmate Luther Lee Boggs, the episode is notably redeemed by some visceral punch-in-the-gut scenes such as the scary teaser involving Scully's recently deceased father and the long corridor of victims haunting Boggs on his way to his execution.

Several of Duchovny's fellow *Twin Peaks* alumni appear in various *X-Files* episodes; Don Davis (who portrays Captain Scully) was the major in the quirky, short-lived series who had an extraterrestrial encounter in the woods.

"Beyond the Sea" remains a personal favorite of writers Glen Morgan and James Wong, creator Chris Carter and, of course, Gillian Anderson, because of the depth of emotion her character was allowed to display in this episode. For all the right reasons, it is also one of the X-Philes all-time favorites.

When Mulder presents Boggs with a supposed piece of torn material from one of the missing teenagers during the channeling session, the agent is utilizing a psychic technique known as "Psychometry." Through objects such as a ring or watch or clothing which have been worn by the subject in question, practitioners are able to ascertain the emotional state of the owners and to reveal details of their characters by "reading" the vibrations given off by the object. Traumatic events in a subject's life also seem to register particularly strongly.

One psychic was given a very ordinary piece of stone to read, and instantly began to sob, later revealing that she had an upsettingly vivid picture of a monk being hauled up a hill to his death. It appeared that the stone actually came from the ancient site of Glastonbury Tor, in Somerset, England, where Abbot Whyting and two other monks had been hung over 400 years previously.

FILE NO. 1X14:

GENDERBENDER

Declassified Case Overview: The search for a gender-changing killer took Mulder and Scully's investigation into an Amish-style community where a black-clad group of religious recluses named the Kindred held bizarre midnight rituals in their underground catacombs.

Trivia

1. (True or False) At the beginning of the episode, a man died after being seduced by a woman in a health club.

2. Who called the killer "a walking aphrodisiac" and "the ultimate sex machine"?
     A. Mulder
     B. Scully
     C. Detective Kosterman

3. Three women and two men died in the throes of passion. What was the cause of death?
     A. Brain hemorrhage
     B. Coronary failure
     C. Chemical imbalance

4. (Fill in the Blank) Each victim's body contained large amounts of pheromones, the essence of _____ attraction.

5. (True or False) Andrew told Scully of Brother James, one of the Kindred who "left to become one of you."

6. Identify the Kindred member who tried to seduce Scully.
     A. Michael
     B. Andrew
     C. Martin

7. (Fill in the blank dialogue) Humans, Brother Andrew said, "enjoy _____ we can't."

8. (Fill in the blank dialogue) After discovering that the Kindred had disappeared from their compound, Mulder said, "They're gone and by no _____ means of transportation."

X-PERT X-TRA BONUS POINTS

What was the killer's name?

Investigative Field Report

Although the episode is basically flawless in the nitpicking area of plot oversights, production problems and scientific snafus, this is the first outright turkey in the series. Unlike most episodes before it, "GenderBender" develops predictably almost from start to finish. The idiotic final frame showing crop circles seems almost like an attempt by writers Larry and Paul Barber to throw in something so off-the-wall as to make at least one element of the episode a surprise.

Crop circles have been linked tentatively with UFO activity with little or no firm evidence to support an association, although peculiar lights have reportedly been observed in the skies before the crop circles appeared. There is evidence of intelligent design and execution behind the crop glyphs, but to attribute them to extraterrestrial visitors is premature.

X MARKS THE SPOT: SEASON ONE

Federal law enforcement agents are not restrained by state boundaries or limitations and Special Agents Mulder and Scully and the Bureau's X-Files section are no exceptions. Their federal jurisdiction covers all fifty states and their authority supersedes all local and state law enforcement agencies. Match Mulder's and Scully's nationwide on-site investigations with the corresponding X-Files episodes. NOTE: Locations were selected by site of main conflict; many episodes covered more than one location.

1. _____ Baltimore, MD   A. "Miracle Man"

2. _____ Colson, WA   B. "Fallen Angel"

3. _____ Raleigh, NC   C. "Conduit"

4. _____ Sioux City, IA   D. "Squeeze"

5. _____ Marin County, CA   E. "Shapes"

6. _____ Townsend, WI   F. "GenderBender"

7. _____ Georgetown, MD   G. "Roland"

8. _____ Browning, MT   H. "Erlenmeyer Flask"

9. _____ Steveston, MA   I. "Ghost in the Machine"

10. _____ Kenwood, TN   J. "Beyond the Sea"

11. _____ Bellefleur, OR   K. "The X-Files: Pilot"

12. _____ Crystal City, VA   L. "Eve"

X-PERT X-TRA BONUS POINTS #1

In "Deep Throat," Ellens Air Force Base was located in the southwest corridor of what state?

X-PERT X-TRA BONUS POINTS #2

Identify the national forest in the Pacific Northwest in which the prehistoric green parasites dwelt in "Darkness Falls."

X-PERT X-TRA BONUS POINTS #3

Arthur Graves' company in "Shadows" was officed in the northeast United States. Name the city and state.

X-PERT X-TRA BONUS POINTS #4

What was the name of the remote cape in Alaska where Mulder and Scully encountered ancient alien worms in the episode "Ice"?

X-PERT X-TRA BONUS POINTS #5

Eugene Tooms was discharged from a mental hospital and took up residence in what city and state in his namesake episode?

FILE NO. 1X15:

LAZARUS

Declassified Case Overview: Scully's former lover, Agent Jack Willis, was either suffering from trauma or was possessed by the spirit of a dead bank robber after a fatal shoot-out that supposedly killed them both.

Nitpicking

If Jack Willis was diabetic, then why did it take so long for him to go into a coma without insulin?

When Willis is revived and has Dupre's consciousness within his body, he goes to the morgue and severs Dupre's finger to retrieve his wedding band. Why did it fit perfectly on his "new" body?

The kidnappers use Scully's cell-phone, but Mulder says they can't trace it. If that's true, then how did the Cigarette-Smoking Man locate Mulder later on in the "Anasazi" episode?

Trivia

1. During a foiled bank robbery, Scully shot Warren Dupre, a notorious bank robber, while fellow agent and former lover, Jack Willis, was seriously wounded. After flatlining for a long time, where was Willis revived?
    A.   Onboard a Care Flight helicopter
    B.   In the back of an ambulance
    C.   In a hospital emergency room

2. Willis had spent a year pursuing Dupre, who along with his accomplice/wife, Lula, robbed a multitude of banks. How many people had they killed during their robbery spree?
    A.   7
    B.   10
    C.   12

3. Who called the FBI, demanding $1 million ransom for Scully?

4. Scully gave Willis a watch for his birthday. What were the words engraved on the back?

5. (True or False) After Willis/Dupre died, Scully discovered that Willis' watch had stopped at the exact time he had gone into cardiac arrest.

6. What was Lula's last name?

X-PERT X-TRA BONUS POINTS

What disappeared from Willis/Dupre's body after he died?

Investigative Field Report

"Lazarus" sadly blows most of its opportunities to rise above the mediocre, the low point being the unnecessary manifestation of the bank robber's tattoo on Willis' arm, a rather silly tell-tale visual gimmick that is painfully at odds with the series' usual subtleties. Nevertheless, the early scene in the emergency room with shocks being administered to one corpse while another jolts unnoticed in the background is the kind of classic that we've come to know and expect from this series.

We can't help but think that "Lazarus" would have been a much better episode, though, if Mulder had been the character to experience "soul switching," as originally scripted before the Fox network vetoed the idea.

FILE NO. 1X16:

YOUNG AT HEART

Declassified Case Overview: A murderous robber whom Agent Mulder helped convict years earlier and thought had died in prison, suddenly began stalking him and committing a new string of crimes.

Nitpicking

Toward the climax of the episode, Barnett takes a hostage at the cello recital. In the almost full body camera shot, Mulder is wearing a black communications ear piece. But in the close-up camera frame of his head and gun, the device is missing.

Trivia

1. Mulder was called by his former partner, Reggie Purdue, to a jewelry store robbery scene, where the "calling card" of John Barnett had been left. What did the note say?
    A.   "Fox can't guard the chicken coop"
    B.   "A hunted Fox eventually dies"
    C.   "The Fox has been outfoxxed"

2. What was Barnett's middle name?

3. (Fill in the blank number) Records proved Barnett had died in prison four years earlier, but analysis showed a _____ percent probability that the handwriting on the note to Mulder was a match.

4. (True or False) Mulder found another note on his car that read, "A hunted Fox eventually gets trapped."

5. How was Reggie Purdue killed?

6. (Fill in the Blank) Dr. Ridley, who had pronounced Barnett dead, had his license revoked for _____ malpractice.

7. (Fill in the Blank) Dr. Ridley had sawed off Barnett's hand and grew him a new one using _____ cells.

8. How did Barnett know that Scully was going to a cello recital?
    A. He listened to the messages on her answering machine
    B. He tapped her phone
    C. He overheard her telling Mulder

X-PERT X-TRA BONUS POINTS

On the banks of what river were Barnett's cremated ashes scattered?

Investigative Field Report

With its gradual discarding of Mulder's former colleagues associated with the Barnett case, Scully as the woman partner-in-jeopardy, and the overworked cliché of Mulder's troubled past, this is basically the retread plot of many a TV cop show.

In the previous episode, Scully was abducted (the first of what turned out to be several times) and in "Young at Heart" she is in peril. Isn't Scully a highly trained and skilled FBI field agent?

FILE NO. 1X17:

E.B.E.

Declassified Case Overview: When an Iraqi jet shot down a UFO, it signaled the beginning of an elaborate and sophisticated cover-up to conceal the spacecraft's survivor and Agent Mulder realized there were limits to what even Deep Throat would tell him.

Nitpicking

In the scene where the Lone Gunmen assist Mulder and Scully in breaching the government facility, they encounter an MP guarding a door. If you look closely, you will notice that the soldier is wearing the rank of Sergeant-Major on his uniform. Our military advisers have informed us that SGMs occupy staff level positions only and are never allowed to do the "dirty work of low-ranking peons," such as guarding doors.

When Mulder and Scully are about to enter the truck transporting the "rescued" extraterrestrial, Scully has her flashlight, but in the next camera shot it's gone.

Trivia

1. (True or False) The UFO crashed near a U.S. installation along the Iraq/Iran border.

2. Name the town in Tennessee where a truck driver lost power, stating he saw a saucer and lights.

3. Which one of the Lone Gunmen bragged that he had breakfast with "the guy who shot John F. Kennedy"?
   A. Frohike
   B. Byers
   C. Langly

4. In what denomination of currency was the metallic strip that the Lone Gunmen claimed was used to track U.S. citizens?

5. Deep Throat told Mulder he was "on a dangerous path" and gave him a packet directing him to an installation in what state?
   A. Alabama
   B. South Carolina
   C. Georgia

6. (Fill in the blank with the correct state) Tracking the vehicle, Mulder and Scully journeyed to _____, where they were stopped suddenly by a blinding light, and found the truck abandoned.

7.   Which notorious UFO incident laid the groundwork for an international pact governing the disposal of E.B.E.s?

X-PERT X-TRA BONUS POINTS

(Fill in the blank with the correct number)
Deep Throat confessed that he was one of ＿＿＿＿＿＿＿ men to have carried out the act of exterminating an E.B.E., an unfortunate event that haunted him and galvanized him to use Mulder as his means for personal redemption.

Investigative Field Report

After a string of misses and near-misses, this engaging episode has to be credited with getting the series back on track with its successful mix of UFOs, captured ETs, Deep Throat, secret sinister networks within the government, Roswellian undertones, bluffs and double-bluffs and consistent surprises all along the way.

The E.B.E. concept is difficult to reconcile with many reported elements of UFO encounters, including the high velocities and radical maneuvers executed by UFOs in flight. Such conditions, it is believed, would be impossible for biological entities, or at least humanoids like ourselves, to survive. In any event, there appears to be no unequivocal evidence, in the form of tissue samples or anything else, of the actual existence of E.B.E.s on Earth.

FBI SERVICE RECORD
#121-627-161
Special Agent Dana Scully, M.D.

WARNING: As with Special Agent Fox Mulder's personnel dossier (which you illegally accessed), you must have a Level 2 Security Clearance to proceed. Further access of this and other classified Department of Justice documents could result in the most severe judicial punishment allowable by law. CEASE AND DESIST NOW!

1.   What is Special Agent Scully's FBI I.D. number?
     A.   22530-077
     B.   2317-616
     C.   7271-2714

2.   (True or False) Her birthdate is February 24, 1964.

3.   (True or False) Agent Scully's place of birth was Baltimore, Maryland.

4.   What is Scully's middle name?
     A.   Katherine
     B.   Christine
     C.   Katheryn

5.   (Yes or No) Was Scully a tomboy when she was growing up?

6.   What was her father's name?
     A.   James
     B.   Robert
     C.   William

7.   What was his rank in the United States Navy?

8.   Although Agent Scully's father was formal and reserved, he

called her "Starbuck" after the able lieutenant in the classic *Moby Dick*. What nickname did she call him?

9. (True or False) Agent Scully's father died of a heart attack in 1993.

10. What is the name of Scully's mother?
    A. Madeleine
    B. Margaret
    C. Marcia

11. (True or False) Agent Scully's mother, a devout Catholic, gave her a tiny cross when she was twelve, which she has continued to wear into adulthood.

12. (Yes or No) Does Scully's mother have psychic ability and premonitory dreams?

13. (True or False) Agent Scully has two brothers (one older, one younger) and an older sister, Melissa, who was known to entertain certain New Age philosophies.

14. Melissa was killed in a botched attempt on Agent Scully's life. Identify her assassin.
    A. Crew-Cut Man
    B. Cigarette-Smoking Man
    C. Agent Alex Krycek

15. Who is the executor of Agent Scully's living will?
    A. William Scully
    B. Charles Scully
    C. Maggie Scully

16. (True or False) Agent Scully spent the first year of her undergraduate studies at the University of California, Berkley, near the Alameda Naval Air Station, where her father was posted.

17. From which university did she earn a B.S. in physics before completing a medical degree?
    A. University of California
    B. University of Maryland
    C. University of Southern California

X-PERT X-TRA BONUS POINTS #1

What was the title of Scully's senior thesis?

---

18. In what area of specialized medicine did Agent Scully complete her residency?

19. She joined the FBI directly from medical school. How many years did she teach at Quantico Academy?
    - A.   2
    - B.   2-1/2
    - C.   3

20. Name the FBI instructor with whom Agent Scully maintained an open relationship during training.

21. (True or False) Assistant Director Skinner assigned Scully to the X-Files section.

22. Name the psychotic fugitive who kidnapped Agent Scully in October 1994.

23. Identify the hospital where she was discovered in a deep coma with no witnesses or records of her admission.
    - A.   North Georgetown University Hospital
    - B.   Baltimore General
    - C.   St. Mary's Regional

24. (True or False) Upon her recovery, Agent Scully returned to duty, claiming to have had no memory of the events of her disappearance.

25. Who was wanted for questioning as an accomplice in Scully's abduction?

X-PERT X-TRA BONUS POINTS #2

What is Agent Scully's cellular phone number?

---

26. How does Scully drink her coffee?
    A. 1 cream, no sugar
    B. 1 cream, 1 sugar
    C. 2 creams, no sugar

27. Which is her preferred type of underwear?
    A. Flannel
    B. Cotton
    C. Silk

28. What is Scully's home phone number?
    A. 202-555-6432
    B. 202-555-6431
    C. 202-555-4631

29. To what position was Scully assigned after the X-Files section was temporarily closed?

30. What is her own X-File case number?
    A. X73317
    B. X43215
    C. X27778

31. What is the name of Scully's best friend?
    A. Jacqueline
    B. Ellen
    C. Helen

32. (True or False) Scully's godson is named Brent.

33. In the field, what type of Macintosh computer has Scully been known to use?

X-PERT X-TRA BONUS POINTS #3

What is Agent Scully's E-mail address?

FILE NO. 1X18:

MIRACLE MAN

Declassified Case Overview: If a young evangelist's gift of healing was truly a gift from God, then who was responsible when his touch began killing the faithful flock?

Trivia

1. What was the name of the evangelical traveling tent ministry Mulder and Scully were called in to investigate?
    A. Mission Ministry
    B. Miracle Ministry
    C. Jehovah's Followers

2. (True or False) Although young Samuel had the power to heal, he had also laid hands upon three people who died shortly thereafter.

3. Whom does Mulder have visions of throughout this episode?

4. (True or False) After being freed from jail, Samuel touched a woman in a wheelchair who went into a seizure and died.

5. Who said, "God never lets the Devil steal the show"?
    A. Mulder
    B. Samuel
    C. Scully

6. What was used to poison each of the victims?
    A. Arsenic
    B. Cyanide
    C. Battery acid

7. Who committed suicide after seeing a vision of Samuel?

X-PERT X-TRA BONUS POINTS #1

Like the biblical Moses, Samuel was found as an infant on the banks of a river. Name it.

X-PERT X-TRA BONUS POINTS #2

(Fill in the blank number) The episode began _____ years earlier, with a mere boy bringing a horribly burned man back to the living.

Investigative Field Report

"Miracle Man," although seemingly free of bloopers and technical screw-ups, is usually ranked toward the bottom of the barrel when first season episodes are rated and reviewed by X-Philes.

But if the episode's not a saint, it's not a sinner, either. The installment's biblical Christ parallels are adroitly handled, and the motives of the true villain—or Judas—give pause for thought. In true *X-Files* fashion, the obvious chicanery and exploitation is laced with a touch of genuine supernatural ability.

Healing, achieved by the laying on of hands without recourse to conventional medicine, has been practiced for centuries. Until the reign of George I, the British monarchy was traditionally supposed to have the power to heal a hideous skin disease called *scrofula,* or the King's Evil. Charles I evidently cured a hundred sufferers at Holyrood on St. John's Day in 1633.

FILE NO. 1X19:

SHAPES

*Declassified Case Overview: Jim Parker was interested only in the boundaries be-
tween his ranch and a neighboring Indian reservation until he shot a wild animal and ended up with a naked Native American corpse—with fangs. Mulder
and Scully's investigation led them all the way back to the very first X-File on
record.*

Nitpicking

When Lyle is in the bathroom transforming into the fanged beast, we
see him shred the shower curtain with his fingernails. But when his
hand splits open a moment later, it's obvious that his nails are short
and dull.

When Mulder and the sheriff are talking to the old Indian man, the
sheriff turns into the light and his makeup line is very evident to the
TV audience.

Why can Lyle hear Scully say right outside the bathroom door, "I
want to take you to the hospital," but she can't hear him when he's
howling incredibly loudly? There's even a keyhole in the door.

Why couldn't Mulder call Scully on his cell-phone while in his car?
In future episodes he calls her from inside a boxcar buried in a canyon
and in "F. Emasculata" Mulder receives a phone call from within his
car. Obviously, the vehicle's blockage of the cell-phone's reception is
only a plot device.

While investigating Joe Goodensnake's death, Mulder discovers
tracks in the mud, human steps immediately followed by animal
steps. Based upon the description Ish gives Mulder, and more importantly, the painful transformation from man to beast we see Lyle
go through in the bathroom, it is obvious that the metamorphosis is
not as quick as Clark Kent changing into Superman in a telephone
booth. It doesn't seem possible that Joe Goodensnake is able to go
through the agonizing transmutation and still continue to walk a normal path.

Trivia

1. At the beginning of the episode, who was wounded by the creature before it was killed?
    A. Jake Parker
    B. Jim Parker
    C. Lyle Parker

2. (True or False) Jim Parker's barn had been burned and his horses slaughtered.

3. FBI Director J. Edgar Hoover himself initiated the very first X-File. Identify the year that it was opened.
    A. 1946
    B. 1952
    C. 1958

4. (True or False) Although the animal-like suspect in the first X-File was subsequently killed, the murders resumed in 1955, '60, '65, '79 and '94.

5. Which famous explorers wrote of "Indian men who could change into a wolf"?

6. Who took an unconscious Lyle Parker to the hospital?

7. What was the Algonquin name for an evil spirit capable of changing a man into a beast?

8. (Fill in the blank with the correct number) The tribal leader warned Mulder, "FBI, see you in about _____ years."

X-PERT X-TRA BONUS POINTS

What was Sheriff Tskany's first name?

Investigative Field Report

Once we get past the ludicrous premise of lycanthropy, this conventional monster show is a welcome relief after a seemingly endless parade of serial killers and saucer-spottings.

Usually the series' location shooting in British Columbia (which is cheaper than in Los Angeles) distracts from the story because it is painfully obvious that the episode is not actually taking place in Idaho ("Deep Throat") or Sioux City, Iowa ("Conduit"). But in "Shapes," the fog, the dreary overcast, the dark forest and the remoteness of the rural highways adds an eerie sense of loneliness and detachment to this tale of American Indian mysticism.

Donnelly Rhodes, who portrays rancher Jim Parker, is usually seen clean-shaven in loud sitcom roles (he was Dutch on *Soap*). *Twin Peaks* alumnus Michael Horse plays the stoic and proud Sheriff Tskany.

FILE NO. 1X20:

DARKNESS FALLS

Declassified Case Overview: While investigating the disappearance of loggers in a Pacific Northwest forest, Agents Mulder and Scully found themselves terrorized by a swarm of deadly prehistoric insects when an ancient tree was cut down.

Nitpicking

How was it possible for Spinney to have been killed by the bugs while standing in the headlights of the car? If the insects swarmed on his shadowy, unlit side, why then did they not swarm on the unlit sides of Mulder, Scully and the ranger while they spent the night in the cabin?

When the agents are riding downhill in a Jeep, the reflection off the camera lens makes it appear as if there's another vehicle following them.

When the ancient, felled tree is discovered, Mulder scrambles up on to the stump to investigate. The growth rings have a distinctive crack at the center and are irregular in shape. However, the close-up camera shot of the stump has neither.

Trivia

1. How many loggers had disappeared?
    A. 30
    B. 40
    C. 50

2. (Fill in the blank with the correct number) Mulder stated that a similar incident happened in the same area _____ years earlier.

3. What was the forest ranger's name?
    A. James Elliot
    B. George Collier
    C. Larry Moore

4. (Fill in the Blank) After they found their car tires had been flattened by spikes, the group (including Mulder and Scully) hiked to the camp, where they found one of the missing loggers drained of fluid inside a huge white _____.

5. (Fill in the blank dialogue) One of the eco-terrorists, Doug Spinney, stated that there was a force that came out at night and devoured people alive. "Darkness is our _____," he warned them.

6. Who concluded that the ancient insect eggs had been affected by radiation from local volcanic activity?
    A. Spinney
    B. Mulder
    C. Scully

X-PERT X-TRA BONUS POINTS

What was the name of the security chief for the logging company?

Investigative Field Report

Although not specifically written to preach a sermon about environmental conservation, this episode takes a sensible ecological stance as it remains honestly objective about the livelihood arguments of the logging industry while subtly condemning the childish extremism of eco-terrorists.

Essentially spectators in "Darkness Falls," it is refreshing to see Mulder and Scully genuinely frightened in a dire predicament, especially in the shocking conclusion, which nearly kills the dynamic duo.

As always, Mark Snow's music contributes to the brooding, apprehensive feel of this episode.

ON CLOSER X-AMINATION: PART I

Agents Mulder and Scully have encountered highly trained specialists in a variety of occupations while investigating the X-Files. Some of them have been dedicated to making the world a better place, yet many others have had secret agendas. Correctly match the X-Pert below with his or her specialty.

1. ___ Dr. Sheila Braun   A. Transgenics/aging specialist

2. ___ Dr. Joe Ridley   B. Genetics specialist

3. ___ Dr. Adam Pierce   C. Psychologist/hypnotic regression

4. ___ Dr. Ronald Surnow   D. Aeronautics/propulsion specialist

5. ___ Dr. Terrence Berube   E. Sleep specialist

6. ___ Michelle Generoo   F. Toxicologist

7. ___ Dr. Spitz   G. Computer scientist/developer

8. ___ Dr. Denny Murphy   H. Pediatric psychologist

9. ___ Dr. Saul Grissom   I. Detective/retired

10. ___ Dr. Nancy Da Silva   J. Geologist/specializing in ice flow

11. ___ Frank Briggs   K. NASA communications specialist

12. ___ Brad Wilczek   L. Volcanologist

ON CLOSER X-AMINATION
PART II

1. ___ Dr. Sally Kendrick   A. Sleep specialist

2. ___ Dr. Jay Newman   B. Professor/Anthropology

3. ___ Dr. Francis Gerrardi   C. Medical doctor

4. ___ Dr. Hodge   D. Psychiatrist

5. ___ Dr. Anne Carpenter   E. Inspector/Scotland Yard

6. ___ Dr. Diamond   F. Aeronautics/propulsion

7. ___ Dr. Del Hakkie   G. Eugenics specialist

8. ___ Phoebe Green   H. Volcanologist

9. ___ Dr. Keats   I. Coroner/general practitioner

10. ___ Dr. Daniel Trepkos   J. Specialty unknown

11. ___ Dr. William Secare   K. Pathologist

X-PERT X-TRA BONUS POINTS #1

Mulder consulted quite often with the four publishers of the magazine *The Lone Gunman*. What were the known names of this quartet of conspiracy buffs (yes, all four)?

X-PERT X-TRA BONUS POINTS #2

Name the rare disease that Dr. Ridley was treating at the National Institutes of Health in the episode "Young at Heart."

FILE NO. 1X21:

TOOMS [A.K.A. SQUEEZE 2]

Declassified Case Overview: With Eugene Tooms released from a sanitarium, Agents Mulder and Scully had to prevent him from killing again while finding tangible proof of his mutant abilities.

Nitpicking

Writers Morgan and Wong repeatedly remind the viewing audience that Tooms has lived at 66 Exeter for sixty years, while coming out of dormancy every thirty years to eat five livers and then hibernate again. We know that he didn't own the residence because it was sold and turned into a shopping mall while he was on one of his extended vacations. So how did he pay the rent for all those years?

Trivia

1. (True or False) Eugene Tooms was institutionalized in the Druid Park Sanitarium.

2. (True or False) Tooms had come up for parole, contingent on protests and the results of "impact statements" from the families of his previous victims.

3. (Fill in the blank with the correct number) Mulder alarmed the psychiatric board by contending that Tooms was a genetic mutant, more than _____ years old, who survived on a diet of human livers.

4. (Yes or No) Scully was criticized by Assistant Director Skinner for not debunking enough of Mulder's investigations. Did the Cigarette-Smoking Man say anything during the meeting?

5. Pursuing the case, Scully returned to Frank Briggs, the detective who originally investigated Tooms. What was the name of the retirement home where the former cop lived?
    A. Twin Cedars
    B. Lynne Acres
    C. Oak Ridge

6. With Mulder in pursuit, how did Tooms escape after attempting to kill a new victim?
    A. He slithered through an air conditioning conduit
    B. He wriggled through a barred window
    C. He slid under a locked door

7. Which original sci-fi classic was playing on Mulder's TV when Tooms entered the agent's apartment?
    A. *The Fly*
    B. *The Thing*
    C. *The Blob*

8. (Fill in the blank number) The psychiatrist who fought for Tooms' release from the asylum stopped by to visit him and became his _____ victim.

X-PERT X-TRA BONUS POINTS

At the episode's conclusion, what was Mulder looking at when he told Scully, "Change is coming"?

Investigative Field Report

Although a competent and ultimately satisfying sequel to "Squeeze" (the only return engagement by an *X-Files* villain), the open-ended tag of the original episode suggested that Tooms escaped through the small window of his jail cell door rather than remaining incarcerated.

The highlight of the episode (besides Skinner's inaugural appearance and the first line of dialogue from the Cigarette-Smoking Man) is finally seeing a psychiatrist personally reap the consequences of releasing from prison an obvious danger to society.

Claims of shape-shifting have been around for centuries with reports of humans who could actually take on another form altogether. The most notorious account of someone who could change in bodily shape centered on the infamous 19th-century medium, Daniel Dunglas Home, who grew in height by a full fifteen centimeters while in a state of trance, something he was seemingly able to perform at will.

FILE NO. 1X22:

BORN AGAIN

Declassified Case Overview: When two Buffalo cops were murdered, the evidence pointed to an eight-year-old girl, who was perhaps the reincarnation of a murdered man.

Nitpicking

How could an Oxford-educated psychologist like Mulder confuse Multiple Personality Syndrome with schizophrenia?

Seemingly within an hour or two of Detective Barbala's suicide (and while local police investigators are still examining the crime scene), Mulder and Scully arrive in Buffalo. An FBI agent informed us that after a crime is committed (over which the Bureau has federal jurisdiction), it takes several hours for special agents to be assigned to the case not to mention travel time. Even if specific FBI agents are requested by local cops in the field, the wheels of the bureaucracy grind slowly.

When Michelle is asked to describe the hair color of the man who was in the room before Barbala plummeted to his death, the little girl says it was light like hers rather than dark like Mulder's. The computer operator composing the digital mug shot then colors the man's hair dark and no one corrects him.

Trivia

1. According to Michelle's mother, how many nannies had the little girl run off?
   - A. 2
   - B. 3
   - C. 4

2. How many years had police officer Charlie Morris been dead?
   - A. 7
   - B. 9
   - C. 12

3. What type of powers did Michelle possess?

4. Who said of Michelle, "Sometimes she frightens me . . . She sees things I can't see"?

5. Michelle appeared at the scene of another "accident" that resulted in the death of another former cop, Barbala's partner. How was he killed?

6. (Fill in the blank dialogue) Reincarnation, Mulder noted, was a tenet of many major religions, adding that they're "one short step away from proving the _____ of the human soul."

7. (True or False) After Fiore's admission of complicity in Morris' murder, Michelle was taken away by a government research agency against her mother's and Mulder's objections.

X-PERT X-TRA BONUS POINTS

What was Michelle Bishop's mother's first name?

Investigative Field Report

"Born Again" is usually rated by X-Philes in the bottom three or four episodes from the first season. With its premise similar to "Lazarus" and other recently aired soul transference or possession-themed installments, most fans strongly felt that with this episode the series was beginning to plagiarize itself.

Although the episode did deal with reincarnation, the producers originally wanted to do a show based upon the alleged Tujunga Canyon alien abduction/reincarnation case in California, in which a young woman claimed to have been marked on her back with a glyph resembling the astrological symbol for the planet Jupiter. The mark, she indicated, was the extraterrestrials' way of identifying her in successive incarnations. (It's difficult to understand how, since the body decays soon after death. Wouldn't the reincarnated soul have to be tracked down and marked again in its new body?)

Trivia alert: Actress Maggie Wheeler, who plays Detective Lazard in this episode, previously appeared with David Duchovny in the theatrical release, *New Year's Day*. Reportedly the two dated during filming of the movie.

FILE NO. 1X23:

ROLAND

Declassified Case Overview: When two research scientists were killed at a jet propulsion laboratory, the finger of suspicion pointed to a mentally retarded janitor, not to mention a dead scientist's cryogenically frozen brain.

Nitpicking

Everyone who has ever watched this episode always asks the same question: Why didn't these supposedly brilliant propulsion research scientists simply stand in the corner to one side of the fan instead of directly in the line of the maximum flow of wind?

Can a human being *really* hold on to a metal grill by the fingertips for as long as a few seconds in a thousand-mile-an-hour wind?

Trivia: The Numbers Game

(Note: Because of the difficulty of the following questions, all correct answers will count as a 5-point X-PERT X-TRA BONUS.)

1. At the beginning of the episode, Roland tried twice to successfully enter his numerical I.D. into the electronic keypad. What was his three-digit code?

2. (Fill in the blank number) Against Dr. Nollette's wishes, Surnow refused to jeopardize _____ years worth of work on the Icarus Project.

3. (Fill in the blank number) Dr. Surnow was the second scientist to die on the propulsion program in the past _____ months.

4. According to Mulder, what time was Dr. Keats' computer files turned off the night of his murder?

5. Mulder correctly ascertained Arthur Grable's computer password based upon a series of numbers doodled by Roland on a piece of paper. Identify the five-digit numerical access code.

6. On what day in July of 1952 were twins Arthur Grable and Rolland Fuller born?

7. How old was Roland when he was placed in the Heritage Halfway House program?

8. What was Roland's I.Q.?

9. Identify the number of the storage unit which housed Arthur Grable's preserved head in liquid nitrogen.

10. What was the normal stabilized temperature for the storage units?

11. Identify the much sought-after mach speed that the propul-

sion program was trying to reach with experimental jet engines.

12. What was the final set-point of Grable's cryogenic storage capsule at the conclusion of the episode?

Investigative Field Report

"Roland" is another rip-off installment with creative echoes from hundreds of other cryogenic films and television episodes—from *The Twilight Zone* to Mel Gibson's *Forever Young* to the Sylvester Stallone-Wesley Snipes action vehicle, *Demolition Man*. Sometimes it appears that the *The X-Files* writers spend most of their time wandering through the rows and rows of videos at Blockbuster in an effort to jump-start their creative engines.

The idea of Roland's twin brother controlling his actions has a basis, though, in real science. Researchers believe that twins' similar medical histories and personalities can be explained by genetics. They have discovered that most twins, even if they have not spent all their lives together, teethe at the same time and go bald together. Girl twins often begin to menstruate on the same day.

FILE NO. 1X24:

THE ERLENMEYER FLASK

Declassified Case Overview: Agents Mulder and Scully discovered evidence of a supersecret government experiment involving extraterrestrial DNA. When Mulder disappeared his partner had no choice but to turn to his mysterious informant, Deep Throat.

Nitpicking

If Scully is a medical doctor by training, then why didn't she take a tissue sample for further investigation before handing over the alien fetus?

This episode purportedly takes place in Washington, D.C., but a sign glimpsed briefly during the opening car chase clearly reads: "VANCOUVER DRYDOCK COMPANY LTD." Also seen during the beginning teaser: a CN (Canadian National) engine pulling the train.

Scully tells Mulder that chloroplasts are plant cells instead of saying that chloroplasts are part of some plant cells.

Trivia

1. At the outset of the episode, what color was the fleeing man's blood trail?

2. To which *Star Wars* character did Mulder compare Deep Throat?
    A. Yoda
    B. Obi-Wan Kenobi
    C. Darth Vader

3. Who killed Dr. Berube?

4. (True or False) Scully took samples of Dr. Berube's research to Dr. Bernstein, a Georgetown research microbiologist.

5. What two words were written on the bottom of the Erlenmeyer flask?

6. (Fill in the Blank) Dr. Berube's cloned bacteria DNA possessed a fifth and sixth _____ that existed "nowhere in nature" and was, by definition, extraterrestrial.

7. According to Mulder, who issued the order to shut down the X-Files section?
    A. The FBI Director
    B. The top of the executive branch
    C. The chiefs of the intelligence branches

X-PERT X-TRA BONUS POINTS #1

Provide the name and address of the warehouse where Mulder found the experimental subjects.

X-PERT X-TRA BONUS POINTS #2

How many experimental subjects did Mulder find in the warehouse?

Investigative Field Report

"The Erlenmeyer Flask" is a classic *X-Files* paranoid conspiracy yarn which X-Philes consistently rate as one of their overall favorite episodes of the first season. Intelligent, well-written, and thoughtful, this effective mixture of *Blade Runner* and *The Fugitive* takes the shocking step of killing off the mysterious Deep Throat *and* closing down the X-Files unit.

Chris Carter was quoted as saying, "You can't go too far, but you've got to go further than *just far enough*," referring to the need for a series like *The X-Files* to keep its viewers on their toes. By assassinating Deep Throat, who had propped up Mulder's investigations in seven of the initial twenty-four episodes, Carter certainly concluded the series' freshman year in a way that would keep us all guessing as to what twists and turns would occur in *The X-Files* second season.

MONSTER MASH: SEASON ONE

Though the pilot and the first episode of The X-Files dealt with UFOs, ETs and saucer snatchers, the series quickly began engaging Agents Mulder and Scully with M.O.T.W. (X-Phile slang for "Monsters of the Week")—genetic mutant serial killers, pyrokinetic assassins, shape-shifters, prehistoric parasites, Bigfoots and a host of other creatures great and small. Test your X.Q. with the following questions about M.O.T.W.s.

1. (Fill in the Blank) In the sequel to "Squeeze," the examination of the 1933 skeleton exhibited Tooms' _____ marks on the victim.

2. When referring to the two dead men, Agent Jack Willis and robber Warren Dupre, who asked "One came back, but which one?"
    A. Agent Bruskin
    B. Agent Mulder
    C. Lula Philips

3. According to Mulder (who had authored the murderer's psychological profile), why did Luther Lee Boggs kill?

4. Identify the chemical L'ively used to enhance the burn capacity of his victims in "Fire."
    A. Apalaxoline S-7
    B. Phenoropoline
    C. Argotypoline

5. (Fill in the Blank) Deep Throat informed Mulder of the _____ Project, a supersecret 1950s eugenics program that created identical little girls named Eve and boys named Adam.

6. At the conclusion of "The Jersey Devil," what was seen hiding in the brush as a father and son hiked through the woods?

7. Who surmised in "Ghost in the Machine" that COS killed Benjamin Drake as an act of self-preservation?

8. At the conclusion of the episode "Ice," who wanted to return to the Arctic research base to study the one remaining parasitic alien worm?

9. (Fill in the Blank) After Mulder, Scully and the park ranger were rescued from the ancient tree bugs' cocoon in "Darkness Falls," a quarantine unit stated that they would utilize controlled burns and pesticides as _____ procedures for the forest.

10. (True or False) In "Shapes," Gwen Goodensnake presented Scully with an elongated fang which once belonged to her brother.

11. Identify the type of insects that swarmed into the courtroom during Samuel's bail hearing in "Miracle Man."

12. (True or False) In the Frankenstein-like "Young at Heart," Dr. Ridley told Scully that John Barnett was the last surviving test subject from his experiments with age process reversal.

13. (True or False) In one of many flashbacks in "Space," former astronaut Lt. Col. Marcus Belt screamed as the astral presence escaped his body, transferring its energy-form into Michelle Generoo.

14. (Fill in the blank number) At the beginning of "Shadows," Howard Graves' former employee, Lauren Kyte, was attacked by _____ men, who were then killed by an unseen force.

X-PERT X-TRA BONUS POINTS

How did Tooms gain entry into Mulder's apartment in his namesake episode?

BEHIND THE SCENES: PART 1

1. What did Doug Hutchinson, who played mutant killer Eugene Tooms in the episodes "Squeeze" and "Tooms," send to Chris Carter to thank him for the acting role?

2. Chris Carter has appeared in one episode of *The X-Files*. Which one was it?
    A. "The Erlenmeyer Flask"
    B. "Tooms"
    C. "Anasazi"

3. Which episode did Carter consider to be a landmark in that it strayed from the alien milieu and demonstrated "the sky's the limit" in terms of paranormal material to be found in *The X-Files*?

4. Identify the magazine that glowingly described the series as having "the makings of a classic" and "as scary as *The Twilight Zone*, and much sexier."
    A. *Entertainment Weekly*
    B. *US*
    C. *The New Yorker*

5. (True or False) During its second season, *The X-Files* won the Golden Globe Award as outstanding drama and then received Fox Broadcasting's first-ever Emmy nomination for an outstanding drama series.

6. (True or False) The series' producers and writers considered having Scully give birth to an alien baby when Gillian Anderson became pregnant in real-life.

7. (True or False) Anderson herself feared she might be dropped from the show, first confiding in Carter about her condition, then Duchovny, though her pregnancy was kept secret from the crew and press for several months.

8. Which grisly scene in "The Host" did Fox threaten to censor, but was successfully argued for by Carter?

9. In terms of personal favorites, which two episodes does Carter always mention?
    A. "Beyond the Sea" and "Ice"
    B. "Deep Throat" and "The Erlenmeyer Flask"
    C. "Anasazi" and "The Blessing Way"

10. During its first season, which category did the series win its lone Emmy award?

11. Which episodes have featured altered "tag lines"?

12. (True or False) The show was budgeted at $1.2 million per

episode the first season, $1.5 the second year and a bit more than that in season three, owing in part to salary increases.

13. (True or False) The show's research department only began amassing its own library of collected articles and paranormal material in early 1995.

14. On Chris Carter's desk sits a jar containing what looks like an alien fetus covered by a paper bag. What is written on the bag?
    A. "My God, Mulder . . . It's trying to Communicate"
    B. "You've never been closer"
    C. "The truth is out there"

15. *The X-Files* writers seem to love the "name game"—hiding names or references in the script, such as the many clocks that read "11:21." What is the significance of those numbers?

16. (True or False) Carter, who wrote three of the first five episodes at the beginning of the third season, wrote 18 of the first 54 episodes of the series, or exactly one third of the total.

17. How many days did it take the makeup special effects department to create the Flukeman costume?
    A. 7
    B. 10
    C. 12

18. Name the episode in which Mulder first fired his gun.

19. In which episode did Scully fire her gun for the first time?

20. (True or False) David Duchovny's favorite episodes are "Duane Barry" and "One Breath."

21. Identify Gillian Anderson's two favorite episodes.
    A. "The Erlenmeyer Flask" and "Beyond the Sea"
    B. "Irresistible" and "Ice"
    C. "Beyond the Sea" and "Irresistible"

22.   What was the name of Dana Scully's one and only date?

23.   Whom did Mitch Pileggi state was the inspiration for his character, Assistant Director Walter Skinner?
   A.   His father
   B.   His brother
   C.   His college football coach

24.   (True or False) Steven Williams, a.k.a. Mr. X, landed the role at the last minute because it had originally been conceived as a woman.

25.   (Yes or No) Is Doug Hutchinson, who played the liver-eating mutant Eugene Tooms, a vegetarian in real-life?

26.   Although there were some parallels between the episode "Squeeze" and the '70s TV movie *The Night Strangler* (the second *Night Stalker* movie), the writers said they drew their inspiration from a notorious real-life serial killer. Who was he?

27.   Name the only episode to be filmed without Gillian Anderson.

28.   Nicholas Lea portrayed the perfidious Agent Alex Krycek in "Sleepless" and other episodes. What role did he play in "GenderBender"?

29.   In which episode did the mysterious Mr. X make his first appearance, although the audience only saw the back of his head as he spoke on the phone?

30.   Gabrielle Rose played the part of Dr. Zenzola in "The Host." What character did she portray in the "Deep Throat" episode?

31.   (True or False) In an interview David Duchovny once said that he would consider Mulder Jewish until told otherwise.

32.   Name the first episode in which Mulder killed someone.

33.   In the episode "Fire," who was the British lord, Malcolm Marsden, named after?
   A.   Chris Carter's father-in-law
   B.   The show's chief hairdresser
   C.   One of the show's cameramen

X-PERT X-TRA BONUS POINTS #1

Name the only episode in which the Lone Gunmen have appeared without Dean Haglund's "Langly" character.

X-PERT X-TRA BONUS POINTS #2

Name the three women we have seen Mulder kiss and the episodes in which they appeared.

---

34. What was the inspiration for the title of the third season episode "Piper Maru"?

35. (True or False) The severed heads in the trophy case belonging to Walter Chaco in "Our Town" were portraits of various real people.

36. In real life, who or what were the aliens that ran past Scully within the mountain storage facility in the third season "Paper Clip" episode?
    A. Midgets
    B. Children
    C. Monkeys

37. To what famous movie serial did Duchovny compare the narrative course of the three-part episodes "Anasazi," "The Blessing Way" and "Paper Clip"?
    A. The Indiana Jones films
    B. The three *Alien* movies
    C. The *Star Wars* trilogy

38. "Paper Clip" also carried a memoriam to a major fan of the show who had organized online sessions on the Internet. What was his name?

39. On-screen, Alex Krycek shot Agent Dana Scully's sister, Melissa. What is the real-life connection between Nicholas Lea, who plays Krycek, and Melinda McGraw, who played Melissa?

40. A tag line at the end of "The Blessing Way" read, "In Memoriam. Larry Wells. 1946–1995." Who was he?
    A. A costume designer on the series
    B. A makeup special effects technician
    C. A stunt double for Mitch Pileggi

41. Name the second episode in which Mulder killed someone.

42. What did Gillian Anderson actually put in her mouth (but not swallow) during the filming of "Humbug"?

43. How many languages other than English have appeared in *The X-Files*?
    A. 12
    B. 13
    C. 15

44. In "Die Hand Die Verletzt," who were the characters Paul Vitalis and Deborah Brown named after?
    A. Prominent online X-Philes
    B. Research assistants on the show
    C. TV critics who gave the series glowing reviews during the first season

45. Dwight McFee made his third *X-Files* appearance in "Irresistible." Identify the other two episodes in which he appeared.
    A. "Beyond the Sea" and "Ice"
    B. "Fire" and "Lazarus"
    C. "Shapes" and "Little Green Men"

46. (True or False) The bones and skulls used in "Aubrey" and "Our Town" were real, although their origin was animal rather than human.

47. Sheila Moore appeared in "Deep Throat" as Verla McLennen. In which later episode did she portray a convalescent home director?

48. Who did "One Breath" writer Glen Morgan say he named Nurse Owens after?
    A. His sister-in-law
    B. His grandmother
    C. His great-aunt

49. In which episode did Mitch Kosterman reprise his role of Detective Horton from "GenderBender"?

50. Name the *X-Files* novel author whose name appeared on the passenger manifest Scully scrutinized in "Little Green Men."

51. In "Little Green Men," a senator called Richard Matheson was a nod to the great Hollywood scriptwriter and author of many classic science-fiction and horror stories, including several episodes of Chris Carter's favorite series, *Kolchak: The Night Stalker.* What was the title of Matheson's early novel about vampire-like mutants, which was the basis for the 1970s Charleton Heston science-fiction movie *The Omega Man*?

52. In which episode did Mulder tell the story for the first time instead of the usual Scully voice-over?

53. In which episode did the Cigarette-Smoking Man speak for the first time?

54. (True or False) In the interest of artistic integrity, Doug Hutchinson played the final scene as Eugene Tooms under the escalator nude and covered with Karo syrup and food coloring to look like bile.

55. Which episode was honored at the Environmental Media Awards?

56. Duchovny suffered a burn severe enough to leave a scar on his hand during the filming of an *X-Files* scene. Name the episode.

57. (Yes or No) Did the "Eve" episode utilize real-life twins?

58. Deep Throat's warning to Mulder in "Fallen Angel" to "Keep your friends close, but keep your enemies closer" is a quote from which gangster movie?
    A. *The Valachi Papers*
    B. *The Godfather*
    C. *Goodfellas*

59. Which episode was designed to be an inexpensive hour (after

the series had exceeded its budget on some earlier episodes), but ended up being the most expensive episode of the first season?

60. David Duchovny, unlike his character, has no love of sunflower seeds. Who, on the other hand, is addicted to them?
     A.   Chris Carter
     B.   Gillian Anderson
     C.   Mitch Pileggi

61. Andrew Johnson portrayed the mind-altered Colonel Budahas in "Deep Throat." What was his character's name in "Colony"?

62. (True or False) An earlier script of "Ghost in the Machine" had several scenes that never made it past the final cut, among them a bar scene in which Lamana reminisces over the bachelor party Mulder once arranged for him, which included a table dance by two Asian girls named Chu Me Soon and Chu Me Too.

63. In which episode did the real-life father of Duchovny's dog, Blue, make an appearance?

X-PERT X-TRA BONUS POINTS #3

What was the "biblical" reference written on a wall by the vampires in "3"?

X-PERT X-TRA BONUS POINTS #4

What is the English translation for *die hand die verletzt?*

X-PERT X-TRA BONUS POINTS #5

The high school in "Die Hand Die Verletzt" was called Crowley High School, which was an appreciative nod to Alistair Crowley. Who was he?

X-PHILE EPISODE RANKING: SEASON ONE

The following ranking of The X-Files' first season episodes (with 10.0 being the highest) have been posted by fans in various manifestations at official conventions and on the Internet.

Ranking	Episode Title	Ranking	Episode Title
1. 9.07	"Ice"	13. 7.84	"Fallen Angel"
2. 9.02	"The Erlenmeyer Flask"	14. 7.81	"Miracle Man"
3. 8.88	"Squeeze"	15. 7.60	"Fire"
4. 8.80	"Beyond the Sea"	16. 6.76	"The Jersey Devil"
5. 8.77	"Tooms"	17. 6.50	"Roland"
6. 8.63	"The X-Files: Pilot"	18. 6.44	"Young at Heart"
7. 8.60	"Deep Throat"	19. 6.38	"Lazarus"
8. 8.57	"E.B.E."	20. 6.35	"Born Again"
9. 8.45	"Darkness Falls"	21. 6.24	"Ghost in the Machine"
10. 8.44	"Eve"	22. 6.09	"Shadows"
11. 7.93	"Conduit"	23. 6.03	"Shapes"
12. 7.88	"GenderBender"	24. 5.33	"Space"

FILE NO. 2X01:

LITTLE GREEN MEN

Declassified Case Overview: With the Bureau's X-Files section closed, Agent Mulder covertly searched for evidence of alien contact at an abandoned SETI site in Puerto Rico while Scully was reassigned to a teaching post at Quantico.

Nitpicking

In "The X-Files: Pilot" Mulder tells Scully that he and his sister, Samantha, were in bed at the time of her abduction by extraterrestrials. But in "Little Green Men" the flashback scene clearly shows them wide awake and in the living room where they were arguing over a board game.

Mulder's password (TRUSTNO1) is only eight characters, but when Scully enters it into his computer, it is obvious that she types nine keystrokes and a RETURN.

Camera shots of Mulder's printer show that it is an ink jet, but the sound effects are those of a laser type.

A radio transmission with a wide bandwidth does not mean that the source is close by, but rather that the transmission is covering a great many frequencies. A radio transmission with a narrow bandwidth does not mean that the source is far away, but actually covering a small range of frequencies.

Location filming problems continue to plague the series: The Miami International Airport is obviously just a soundstage in Vancouver (especially with a phone prop that only charges 20 cents a call), a Miami newspaper being read at the same airport is unmistakably the *Toronto Globe* on the back page, and if you have ever visited Puerto Rico you never saw so many pine trees and evergreens.

Trivia

1. Name the NASA unmanned probe which was sent to contact other intelligent life in the universe.

2. Senator Matheson, who had supported Mulder's work, told him to go to a site in Puerto Rico and that he had 24 hours to contact alien visitors there before government agents would be dispatched. Identify the federal soldiers who would be sent to respond.
    A.   Special Operations React Team (SORT)
    B.   Blue Beret UFO Retrieval Team
    C.   Extraterrestrial React & Retrieval Squad (ERRS)

3. What one word did the senator use as his reply when Mulder asked, "What am I looking for?"

4. Informed that Mulder was missing, who assured Skinner that Scully would find him?

5. At the SETI site Mulder met a frightened man who spoke only Spanish. What did he draw on the wall?

6. (Fill in the blank dialogue) Back in Washington, Skinner chewed Mulder out for abandoning his more mundane assignment and the Cigarette-Smoking Man told the agent, "Your _____ is over."

X-PERT X-TRA BONUS POINTS

Name the composer and title of the classical music Senator Matheson played for Mulder in his Capitol Hill office.

Investigative Field Report

Director David Nutter admits that he became somewhat apprehensive during filming of this episode because the series had received so much media attention during the summer hiatus between seasons one and two. He was fully aware that "Little Green Men" had to appeal not only to established viewers of the show, but to new ones as well, all the while incorporating a storyline arc that would carry the series through the year. "I wanted to avoid the pitfalls of these shows that become really hot and then fade away really quickly," the director acknowledged. "So in that regard, I thought 'Little Green Men' was a tough show to do. The introduction of the episode was wonderful, and I loved the paranoia we were able to generate, especially during that first, tentative meeting between Mulder and Scully. I also very much liked the bookending of the show, opening with Mulder on a mundane surveillance assignment and closing the same way."

The expression, little green men, which is widely used to refer to alleged extraterrestrials, is believed to have originated in a series of science fiction magazine *Amazing Stories* in the late 1940s. The installments, "The Green Man" and "The Green Man Returns," were by Harold Sherman and involved an extraterrestrial with psychic ability. Also, accounts of small humanoid aliens having green-colored skin or wearing green clothing may be found in numerous eyewitness accounts reported over the years.

THE HOST

Declassified Case Overview: Angry at being given meaningless assignments by his Bureau superiors, Agent Mulder considered leaving the FBI until his "routine murder case" opened up a brand-new can of worms and led to the discovery of a genetically mutated creature living in Newark's sewers.

Nitpicking

Scully quotes from research material that states that flukes or flatworms have a scolex with hooks and suckers. Unfortunately, those characteristics belong to tapeworms; flatworms have no scolex and definitely no hooks.

The impellers in tanker trucks that clean out portable toilets slice and dice their retrieval contents into small pieces, which should have been the demise of the escaping Flukeman.

Trivia: The Numbers Game

(NOTE: Because of the difficulty of the following questions, all correct answers will count as a 5-point X-PERT X-TRA BONUS.)

1. During the pre-credits teaser, how many miles off the coast of New Jersey was the Russian cargo freighter?

2. What was the wiretap number Mulder was working on during his "meaningless assignment"?

3. Identify the case number of Scully's John Doe autopsy.

4. According to Scully, how much did John Doe's body weigh?

5. How many million people did Scully estimate were infected with flukes or flatworms, which attached themselves to the bile duct that connects to the liver?

6.   (Fill in the blank dialogue with the correct number) The sewage treatment plant foreman told Mulder that "_____ people call my office every day on the porcelain telephone."

7.   What was the telephone number on the side of A & A Anderson tanker truck which cleaned out the Lake Betty Park portable toilets?

8.   What time of the morning did the tanker truck arrive at the campsite?

9.   According to Scully, how many hooking spikes did flatworms have on their bodies?

10.   (Fill in the blank dialogue with the correct number) Mulder told Scully that "_____ species disappear off the planet every day."

Investigative Field Report

" 'The Host' has become a real popular episode," recalled Chris Carter. "That's one of our traditional monster shows—although we obviously don't do *traditional* monsters. I was in a funk when I wrote that episode. We were coming back from hiatus and I was trying to find something more interesting than just the 'flukeman.' I was irritated at the time, and I brought my irritation to Mulder's attitude. Basically, he had become fed up with the FBI. They had given him what he felt was a lowly assignment, which was sending him into the city after a dead body. But lo and behold, he finds that this is a case that for all intents and purposes is an X-File."

Producer J.P. Finn remembered: "Chris' scripts tend to deal with alien subject matter. Although we had done some creature parts the first year, this time we got to see more than we had before . . . At one point we actually went into a real sewage plant to shoot, which was a very hard day for those exterior shots. That was the real McCoy. It was also a hot, summer day—about 90 degrees—and it was a pretty difficult and smelly day for the cast and crew."

"The Host," which has elements of *The Creature from the Black Lagoon*, also takes the audience into the familiar monster-strewn terrain of the sewers *(It, C.H.U.D.* and *Alligator)* before making a sharp turn into the *Ghoulies*-in-the-commode territory and finally emerging into the series' well-known and frequently used *Alien, Thing* parasite arena.

Trivia alert: Scully refers to the autopsy of John Doe in this episode as case number DP112148—the initials and birthdate of Chris Carter's wife, Dori Pierson.

X-MAN: DAVID DUCHOVNY

David Duchovny, the actor who portrays FBI Agent Fox Mulder, is reluctant to give interviews ("I hate these things," he once said) and for quite some time he even resisted cyber-chatting with X-Philes online the Internet. He readily admits that the attention of fans has made his life "a bit more enclosed, a bit more insular." The X-Files weekly episodic tag line is "the truth is out there," yet getting the truth from a nefarious government agent can turn out to be a great deal easier than getting detailed information on Duchovny. Meet the trivia challenge and see if you can score successfully on this background check on The X-Files' mystery man.

1. (True or False) Duchovny was born on August 16, 1960.

2. How old was he when his parents divorced?
    A. 10
    B. 11
    C. 12

3. Duchovny's father is in public relations and authored an off-Broadway play, which ran for about a week in 1967. What was the name of this disastrous theatre production?
    A. *The JFK-Marilyn Monroe Affair*
    B. *The Trial of Lee Harvey Oswald*
    C. *The Ruby-Oswald Conspiracy*

4. When he was 13, Duchovny, always a good athlete and student,

won a scholarship to New York's elite Collegiate School. Identify the other well-known celebrity who has attended the school.
   A.   Tommy Lee Jones
   B.   John F. Kennedy, Jr.
   C.   Tom Brokaw

5.   (True or False) Duchovny went to Yale, where he majored in English literature and then pursued grad lit studies at Princeton.

6.   (True or False) Duchovny, who wasn't too fond of his preppy classmates, referred to them as vampires.

7.   What is Duchovny's middle name?

8.   (Fill in the Blank) The Russian translation for Duchovny (pronounced doo-KUV-nee) is _____.

9.   At the urging of an actor friend in college, Duchovny tried out and was hired for a TV commercial. Which product did he pitch in his first paying gig as an actor?
   A.   Beer
   B.   Laundry detergent
   C.   Men's underwear

10. Name the artsy 1989 Henry Jaglom improv film that Duchovny performed a small part in and which ultimately forced him to head to California for better roles.
   A.   *Labor Day*
   B.   *New Year's Day*
   C.   *Memorial Day*

11. Identify the 1991 low-budget erotic drama in which Duchovny had a minor role as a dial-a-perv.
   A.   *Julia Has Two Lovers*
   B.   *Sunset Striptease*
   C.   *The Misadventures of Lotta Head*

12. Which small, off-beat role did Duchovny play in 1991's *The Rapture*?
   A.   TV evangelist
   B.   Born-again insurance salesman
   C.   Religious fanatic homicide investigator

13. (True or False) Duchovny portrayed a temperamental film director in 1992's *Chaplin*.

14. Name the Kennedy assassination movie in which he had a bit role.

15. (True or False) Duchovny's filmography includes minor roles in *Working Girl* and *Bad Influence*.

16. Identify the movie in which he played a writer authoring a book on serial killers.

17. In which film did Duchovny appear with another Fox TV series star?

18. Identify the movie in which he did NOT make an appearance.
     A. *Denial*
     B. *Venice/Venice*
     C. *JFK*

19. One of Duchovny's co-stars in 1993's *Kalifornia* was a former cast member of *Star Trek: The Next Generation*. Who was the actress?
     A. Marina Sirtis
     B. Denise Crosby
     C. Michelle Forbes

20. What was the name of the successful 1992 movie in which Duchovny portrayed a yuppie villain?

21. Name the racy cable show in which he plays what he calls "the conduit through which America views the soft underbelly of women's erotic desires."

22. Which acting role did Duchovny once consider as the "beginning and end" of his career?

23. (True or False) Duchovny has done TV commercials for AT & T and MCI.

24. What was the name of the transvestite detective he played on David Lynch's short-lived cult TV series *Twin Peaks*?

    A. Carl/Carla
    B. Dennis/Denise
    C. James/Jane

25. *X-Files* creator Chris Carter told Duchovny to wear a tie to his audition for the part of FBI agent Fox Mulder. What was unique about the tie he wore?
    A. It was a bow tie
    B. It had been given to him by a real-life FBI agent
    C. It had pink pigs on it

26. How many actors did he compete against in his audition for *The X-Files*?
    A. 3
    B. 2
    C. 1

27. (True or False) Duchovny's character, Agent Mulder, always wears suits with tastefully bold ties, but in real-life the actor has a reputation for being a "horrible dresser."

28. Duchovny's alter ego tangles with ETs, vampires, mutants, and serial killers on TV every week. What is the actor truly frightened of the most?
    A. Spiders
    B. Snakes
    C. Playing one role for 7 years

29. Which two writers for *The X-Files* does Duchovny believe wrote some of the best scripts for the series?
    A. Darin Morgan and Howard Gordon
    B. Paul Brown and Chris Ruppenthal
    C. Glen Morgan and James Wong

30. Which two directors for *The X-Files* does Duchovny respect the most?
    A. Robert Mandel and Daniel Sackheim
    B. David Nutter and Rob Bowman
    C. Fred Gerber and Jerrold Freedman

31. (True or False) Duchovny didn't want to be on a weekly TV series, so he accepted the part of the UFO-busting G-man Fox Mulder because he didn't expect the show to last a season.

32. For which person associated with *The X-Files* does he have the most admiration?

33. Who described Duchovny as "a morose S.O.B." in a December 1995 interview with *Starlog* magazine?

34. Duchovny is one of the most intelligent and educated actors on TV. How long does his *X-Files* co-star, Gillian Anderson, say it takes her to decipher one paragraph of what he says in a print interview?
    A. Fifteen minutes
    B. A half hour
    C. An hour

35. Identify the role he played on HBO's talk-show send-up *The Larry Sanders Show*.
    A. David Duchovny on a star trip
    B. The cross-dressing detective from *Twin Peaks*
    C. An Olympic gold medalist swimmer (in a Speedo suit)

36. How many months a year does Duchovny spend in Vancouver filming *The X-Files*?
    A. 10
    B. 11
    C. 12

37. Duchovny has become the hottest sci-fi sex symbol since Patrick Stewart of *Star Trek: The Next Generation* fame. What did he wear on a second season episode that almost caused a global systems overload on the Internet computer lines?

38. At the end of *The X-Files* second season, he re-negotiated a new contract from $35,000 to $100,000 per episode. How many more years did he agree to star on the series?

39. (Fill in the Blank) Duchovny, with degrees in literature, writes _____ in his trailer between filming scenes on *The X-Files*.

40. (True or False) Duchovny is a vegetarian who religiously practices yoga.

41. (Fill in the Blank) His former girlfriend, Perrey Reeves, whom he met while shopping for a new suit, played a _____ on a second season episode of *The X-Files.*

42. (True or False) Duchovny at one time dated actress Maggie Wheeler, who played Janice, Chandler's sometime girlfriend on the hit NBC series *Friends.*

43. Which comedian plays basketball with Duchovny on a semi-regular basis?
     A.   Billy Crystal
     B.   Gary Shandling
     C.   Dennis Miller

44. (Fill in the Blank) Duchovny is interested in directing future *X-Files* installments, but beginning with "Colony," he has shown more enthusiasm for _____ episodes.

45. Identify the acting teacher from the famous Actors' Studio in New York who taught Duchovny to "show whatever you're feeling at the moment, even if it seems to be wrong"?
     A.   Judith Echols
     B.   Tracy Bernstein
     C.   Marsha Haufrecht

46. Which career does Duchovny's sister, Laurie, and their mother, Margaret, both share?
     A.   Teaching
     B.   Banking
     C.   Publishing

47. What is the name of Duchovny's faithful, mixed-breed dog?

48. What does Duchovny do for an hour almost every morning at a public park in Vancouver?
     A.   Run
     B.   Bicycle
     C.   Swim

49. (Yes or No) Has Duchovny ever been married?

50. (Yes or No) Does he personally believe in the existence of UFOs?

51. Which weekly magazine profiled the quirky Duchovny with a headline that read: A GENUINE X-CENTRIC?
     A. *TV Guide*
     B. *Entertainment Weekly*
     C. *People*

52. Name the movie in which he played a disgraced doctor forced into a shadowy underground involving the Mafia's wounded.

X-PERT X-TRA BONUS POINTS #1

What was the title of Duchovny's senior thesis at Princeton?

X-PERT X-TRA BONUS POINTS #2

What was the date of the *Entertainment Weekly* cover story on Duchovy that boldly proclaimed: EXPOSING THE X-FILES' HOTTEST UFO (UNLIKELY FANTASY OBJECT)?

FILE NO. 2X03:

BLOOD

Declassified Case Overview: When several residents of a small town went on killing sprees without explanation, Agent Mulder began to suspect the influence of an outside force when the only physical evidence consisted of damaged electronic devices and a mysterious organic substance.

Nitpicking

After Mrs. McRoberts kills the auto repairman, Mulder and the other investigative officers inspect the crime scene. When Mulder takes a clipboard off the wall to examine it, he is seen wearing white rubber gloves, but when he runs his finger down the page his hand is bare. When he goes to shake hands in the very next scene, he inadvertently draws more attention to the blooper when he says, "Pardon my rubber."

Trivia

1. A 42-year-old real estate salesman went on a massacre in the claustrophobic confines of an elevator after seeing the words "KILL 'EM ALL" on a digital display. How many people did he murder with his bare hands?
    A. 2
    B. 4
    C. 6

2. (Fill in the blank with the correct number) The local sheriff told Agent Mulder that the elevator murders was the seventh such killing spree, accounting for _____ deaths in the area.
    A. 12
    B. 18
    C. 22

3. (True or False) A local woman killed an auto repairman in response to a similar display, which read "HE'LL RAPE YOU. HE'LL ENJOY KILLING YOU. KILL HIM BEFORE HE KILLS YOU."

4. Who shot Mrs. McRoberts when she tried to stab Mulder?

5. (True or False) An examination of her body revealed adrenaline levels 200 times normal, adrenal glands showing signs of wear, and an unknown compound.

6. What was the truck scooping into the gutter?

7. (Fill in the Blank) Mulder sought the assistance of the Lone Gun-

men, who told him about _____, a trial insecticide that acted as a natural pheromone, heightening a fear response among insects.

    A. LDSM
    B. LMDS
    C. LSDM

X-PERT X-TRA BONUS POINTS

What was the specific name and model number of the micro video camera that the Lone Gunmen told Mulder could be back-packed on a fly?

Investigative Field Report

"We wanted to do a show about postal workers and one about paranoia about pesticides, so we decided to merge the two ideas," said episode co-writer Glen Morgan. "We took some heat for the ending when William Sanderson climbs a tower and starts shooting people. Everyone would say, 'Couldn't they come up with something more original?' "

Chris Carter recalled that the episode's origin came "from films Darin Morgan had seen of the medfly pesticides being sprayed on unknowing populations by a government that actually said this was good for you. I think the show works because it feels like something that can happen in your own backyard."

Sorry to disagree, Chris, but the convoluted, conspiracy-laden storyline doesn't work. The phenomenon of previously peaceful and undemonstrative townfolk suddenly cracking up and going on killing sprees is certainly frightening enough without embellishment. Rather than the two ideas writer Morgan described, there are at least six *X-Files*-worthy story concepts struggling to emerge from what turned out to be an improbable and unresolved disappointment.

William Sanderson, who portrays Ed Funsch, the gun-blazing laid-off postal worker, is best-known for his quirky role as Larry on the TV sitcom, *Newhart*, and as the childlike android inventor Sebastion in the sci-fi classic *Blade Runner*.

FILE NO. 2X04:

SLEEPLESS

Declassified Case Overview: While investigating a series of bizarre deaths, Agent Mulder and his new partner, Alex Krycek, discovered evidence of a government-controlled experiment to create the perfect soldier—one that no longer needed to sleep.

Nitpicking

When Agents Mulder and Krycek are stuck in traffic, Mulder's new partner is shown not wearing a tie. A few seconds later, without explanation, Krycek is magically dressed like a *GQ* cover model.

Trivia

1. When Dr. Saul Grissom saw flames shooting into his apartment, he called 911 for help. What was the mysterious circumstance surrounding his death?
    A. There was no sign of fire in the room
    B. His body showed signs of being dead for at least 48 hours
    C. The room had been incinerated but his body was left unscarred

2. What type of clinic did Dr. Grissom operate?

3. (True or False) Scully's autopsy showed damage to Grissom's internal organs "as if his body believed it were burning."

4. (Fill in the blank with the correct number) Another man was murdered, a Marine special forces officer, stationed at the same spot where Grissom had worked _____ years earlier.
    A. 22
    B. 24
    C. 26

5. The last survivor of the military unit was Augustus Cole, but when the agents went to the V.A. hospital to question him, he was missing. What was Cole's nickname?
   A. Preacher Man
   B. Preacher
   C. Reverend

6. Who told Mulder of a secret project to create the perfect soldier by eradicating the need for sleep?

7. (True or False) Cole had gone without sleep for 26 years.

8. (True or False) Guessing that Cole would seek revenge on the other doctor involved in the project, the agents went to the airport to apprehend him.

X-PERT X-TRA BONUS POINTS

What was Dr. Grissom's apartment number?

Investigative Field Report

Director Rob Bowman addressed the ambiguity of "Sleepless": "You couldn't tell who the good guy was and who the bad guy was," he explained. "The apparent antagonist, played by Tony Todd [best remembered as Worf's brother, Kurn, on *Star Trek: The Next Generation* and *Deep Space Nine*], was on a mercy mission. You could absolutely support this guy's point of view. He's out killing people, but the reason he's killing people is well documented. His victims want to die."

"I really love that show," Chris Carter has stated in interviews. "It's a great idea, well executed. I guess the hardest part was that it required a lot of night shooting, and, of course, we were shooting in the middle of the summer in Vancouver, where it's the land of the midnight sun. That was a challenge for the cast and crew. Production-wise, I think there's a lot of suggestion of violence there rather than what you see. You're shown what's going to happen, but you don't actually see it."

DUANE BARRY [PART 1 OF 2]

Declassified Case Overview: Former FBI agent Duane Barry, who claimed to have been experimented upon by aliens, escaped from the mental hospital where he was a patient and took several people hostage—including Special Agent Dana Scully.

Nitpicking

When an agitated Duane Barry walks away from Mulder he says, "I'm tired of this BS!" but you can actually read his lips as they form the word "bullshit."

After Barry's alleged alien abduction, he was sent to a mental hospital in Marion, Virginia. While at the institution he kidnaps a doctor and drives into downtown Richmond, where he holds several people hostage at a travel agency. It's at least a five-hour road trip from Marion to Richmond. Why couldn't the Virginia State Police or the FBI have been able to set up roadblocks somewhere in between during this long time period?

Trivia

1. At the beginning of the episode, Duane Barry was shown being abducted by aliens. What year was it?
    A.   1979
    B.   1985
    C.   1988

2. What was the name of the mental health hospital where Barry was institutionalized?
    A.   Davis Correctional Treatment Center
    B.   Amsterdam Treatment Center for Mental Diseases
    C.   Virginia State Hospital for the Criminally Insane

3. (True or False) When the power abruptly went off in the travel agency, Barry fired into the darkness, wounding two hostages.

4. Barry, a former FBI agent, had at one time been shot in the line of duty. What effect did the wound have on his brain?

5. Who believed they found the key to Barry's bizarre behavior in the century-and-half-old medical case of Phineas Gage?

6. Where was Scully when the piece of metal removed from Barry's stomach went berserk?
    A. In the X-Files basement office
    B. In the supermarket
    C. In her car, driving down the Beltway

X-PERT X-TRA BONUS POINTS

What was Agent Kazdin's first name?

Investigative Field Report

"Duane Barry" was Chris Carter's first outing as a director of *The X-Files.* "It was a chance for me to show people what I thought the series could be and should be, and I think I was very successful."

Although the episode seems disjointed at times, it is only fair to mention that it was hastily thrown together to cover for Gillian Anderson's surprise pregnancy. Carter and Company should also be commended for coping with her unavailability without insulting our intelligence with improbable writing and storylines.

At one point in the episode, Barry tells Mulder that the government knows all about UFOs and alien abductions. The theory that Washington has been hiding the truth about extraterrestrials has been circulating since the first highly publicized UFO sighting in 1947. Although the U.S. government has officially denied such stories, the most telling evidence in support of the view that there is indeed a high-level cover-up occurred in 1978. Arizona-based UFO research organization Ground Saucer Watch (GSW) obtained through the Freedom of Information Act more than 1,000 pages of CIA papers relating to UFO incidents from 1947 to the mid-1970s.

S & M: SEASON TWO

The amusing banter and deftly orchestrated verbal counter punches between Agents Scully and Mulder continued with their "Scullyisms" and "Mulderisms" in the second season. Identify the episodes from which the following S & M interplay occurred.

1. SCULLY: "According to the briefing, prisoners escaped by hiding in a laundry cart."
    MULDER: "I don't think the guards are watching enough prison movies."

    Episode _____

2. SCULLY: "Hey, how you feeling?"
    MULDER: "Like I got a bad case of freezer burn."

    Episode _____

3. MULDER: "Well, I don't want to jump to any rash conclusions, but I'd say he's definitely our prime suspect, huh?"
    SCULLY: "Mulder, the man we're talking about is 77 years old."
    MULDER: "Well, George Foreman won the heavyweight crown at 45. Some people are just late bloomers."

    Episode _____

4. MULDER: "I think this area is being subjected to a controlled experiment."
    SCULLY: "Controlled by who? By the government, by a corporation, by Reticulans?"

    Episode _____

5. MULDER: "Scully, are you familiar with subliminal messages?"
    SCULLY: "You mean like sex in ice cubes in liquor ads? That's paranoia."

    Episode _____

6. SCULLY: "Mind if I sit here?"
    MULDER: "I have to warn you, I'm having violent impulses."
    SCULLY: "I'm armed. I'll take my chances."

    Episode _____

7. MULDER: "Are you familiar with the Ten Commandments,
    Scully?"
    SCULLY: "You want me to recite them?"
    MULDER: "Just number four, the one about obeying the sabbath,
    the part where God made heaven and earth but didn't bother to
    tell anybody about his side projects."

    Episode _____

8. SCULLY: "All of them share one strange detail, Mulder."
    MULDER: "Well, they seem to have lost their heads."

    Episode _____

9. SCULLY: "I was just down the street. Somebody fired more shots
    at the White House again last night."
    MULDER: "Got to wonder about a country where even the pres-
    ident has to worry about drive-by shootings."

    Episode _____

10. MULDER: "I'd be willing to admit the possibility of a tornado,
    but it's not really tornado season. I'd even be willing to entertain
    the notion of a black hole passing over the area or some cosmic
    anomaly, but it's not really black hole season, either. If I were a
    betting man, I'd say it was—
    SCULLY: "—an invisible elephant?"
    MULDER: "I saw David Copperfield make the Statue of Liberty
    disappear once."

    Episode _____

11. MULDER: "I brought you something . . . *Superstars of the Super
    Bowl.*"
    SCULLY: "I knew there was a reason to live."

    Episode _____

12.   SCULLY (looking at broken doorbell): "This is odd."
      MULDER: "Frustrated Jehovah Witnesses?"

      Episode _____

13.   MULDER: "How big can these things get?"
      SCULLY: "Sorry, for a second there it felt like old times."

      Episode _____

14.   SCULLY: "Must be nice not having someone questioning your
      every move, poking holes in all your theories."
      MULDER: "Oh, yeah . . . yeah, it's great. I'm surprised I put up
      with you for so long."

      Episode _____

15.   MULDER: "This isn't where you tell me some terrible story about
      sushi, is it?"
      SCULLY: "Maybe you'd rather hear what you can catch from a
      nice rare steak?"
      MULDER: "So . . . what? The murder weapon was a nice top sir-
      loin?"

      Episode _____

16.   SCULLY: "I mean, there's nothing weird about—"(toads start
      falling from the sky, then stop)
      MULDER: "So, lunch?"
      SCULLY: "Mulder, toads just fell from the sky!"
      MULDER: "Guess their parachutes didn't open. What did you
      say about this place not feeling odd?"

      Episode _____

17.   SCULLY: "I've got a bad feeling about this case, Mulder."
      MULDER: "What do you mean?"
      SCULLY: "Well, nothing about it makes sense. We've got
      three deaths of identical victims, no bodies, a virtual non-
      suspect."
      MULDER: "Sounds just like an X-File."

      Episode _____

18. MULDER (looking very sick): "You're lucky you inherited your father's legs."
SCULLY: "What?"
MULDER: "Sea legs."

    Episode _____

19. (Discussing the possibility that a man was eaten by a snake)
SCULLY: "That's impossible. It would take a large python hours to consume and weeks to digest a human body."
MULDER: "You really do watch the Learning Channel."

    Episode _____

20. MULDER: "You see this a helium balloon here and the only thing I learned in kindergarten is when you let them go they float up, up and away. But you see, this is moving away from him. Horizontally."
SCULLY: "Did you learn about wind in kindergarten?"

    Episode _____

21. SCULLY: "He's non-verbal, non-responsive to voice, touch or pain. The neurologists suspect he suffered a severe concussion in the crash, resulting in amnesia."
MULDER: "That's a plausible diagnosis, though I'm more interested in how he came back to life."

    Episode _____

22. (After Mulder gets hit by a car)
SCULLY: "How are you feeling?"
MULDER: "Like I should have used the crosswalk."

    Episode _____

23. MULDER: "I think from the . . . 'information' . . . here, this is clearly some kind of poltergeist act."
SCULLY: "Mulder, this information is the same reason why I'll see a newspaper photo with Jesus' face appearing in the . . . the foliage of an elm tree."

    Episode _____

X-PERT X-TRA BONUS POINTS #1

(Fill in the blank dialogue from the episode "Humbug")
MULDER: "We're being highly discriminatory here. Just because
a man was once afflicted with excessive _____, we've no
reason to suspect him of aberrant behavior."
SCULLY: "It's like assuming guilt based solely on skin color,
isn't it?"

X-PERT X-TRA BONUS POINTS #2

Name the individuals Mulder was referring to in "Fearful Symmetry" when Scully asked, "Where are you going?" and her partner replied, "To talk to the animals."

FILE NO. 2X06:

ASCENSION [PART 2 OF 2]

Declassified Case Overview: Agent Mulder desperately sought to rescue the kid-
napped Scully before Duane Barry turned her over to the aliens who had previ-
ously abducted him.

Nitpicking

Duane Barry takes Scully to Skyland Mountain in Virginia via a long,
high altitude aerial tram. Although it's supposed to be late autumn,
where's the snow at this obvious ski resort?

Why is it so dark in the hallway scene with Mr. X when the time is
given as 11:45 A.M.?

In the following scene in Assistant Director Skinner's office, everyone is dressed the same as in the previous scene, although the time is reported as 8:11 A.M. and no date change is noted.

Trivia

1. How did Mulder know Scully had been kidnapped by Barry?

2. Who said she had a dream about Scully being taken away?

3. Barry shot a patrolman who pulled him over on the interstate, an incident caught on tape. How did Mulder ascertain that Scully was in the trunk of Barry's car after analyzing the film?

4. Who alerted the Cigarette-Smoking Man to Mulder and Krycek's Skyland Mountain destination?

5. Why did Mulder have to squirm out of the aerial mountain tram and take off on foot after Barry?

6. Who was present with Barry when he died of cardiac arrest?

7. (Fill in the blank dialogue) When Krycek asked the Cigarette-Smoking Man why they didn't simply kill Mulder, his superior replied that doing so "risks turning one man's religion into a _____."

8. Who intercepted Mulder at the capitol, stating that Senator Matheson couldn't help him "without committing political suicide"?
    A.   Mr. X
    B.   ADA Skinner
    C.   Cigarette-Smoking Man

X-PERT X-TRA BONUS POINTS

Identify the interstate that Barry was traveling which led to the Blue Ridge Parkway.

Investigative Field Report

"Jim Wong made the cable tram scene work," said *X-Files* producer and frequent screenwriter Glen Morgan of his partner, "because he's a really good editor. It was missing a lot of stuff. If you go back and look at it again, you'll see all kinds of little inserts. Jim said, 'You've got to show the dial, you've got to see the other car'—and that kind of thing. And that ending is the kind of thing I wish I had done. Mulder is just standing at a point where he feels he's completely lost. Let's face it, Mulder loves Scully. It's the same thing he felt for his sister and now he's lost her, too."

In episodes prior to "Ascension" we only had Mulder's assertion—his own apparent belief—that his sister's disappearance was attributable to a UFO abduction. We previously had been left to wonder whether Mulder imagined the whole thing, whether it was a hoax, a delusion or a lie. When the audience actually sees Samantha floating out the window in the visually explicit flashback, there's not much left to speculate about. If the series has a developing flaw, it is a tendency to show far too much onscreen.

FILE NO. 2X07:

3

Declassified Case Overview: With the X-Files officially reopened, Mulder kept his sanity after Scully's disappearance by investigating a series of homicides that followed the pattern of the so-called Trinity Murderers, a trio of blood-sucking killers.

Nitpicking

When Mulder suspects that John's vampire beliefs are delusional, the agent leaves him in a holding cell in hopes that the fear of the "rising sun" will scare him enough to tell the truth about the murders. It is obvious, however, that the sun is setting rather than rising.

Trivia

1. At the beginning of the episode, a businessman was murdered by a woman and her accomplice. Which of his body parts were they biting and drawing blood from?
    A. The shoulder
    B. An arm
    C. The chest

2. After having obviously been away for months, Mulder returned to his Washington-based office. What did he extract from Scully's X-File?

3. (Fill in the blank with correct number) Afterwards, Mulder arrived at the scene of the businessman's murder, explaining that there had been _____ similar killings in Memphis and Portland where the victims' blood was drained.

4. (Fill in the blank dialogue) When John asked Mulder if he wanted to live forever, he replied, "Not if _____ pants come back into style."

5. What did Mulder refuse to do which caused Kristen to leave the club with another man?

6. How many bodies were found in the charred remains of the house?

X-PERT X-TRA BONUS POINTS

Name book, chapter and verse of the "Bible" passage written on the wall.

Investigative Field Report

Episode co-writer Glen Morgan acknowledged that it was indeed a mistake to have an X-File concerning vampires. "This is a show that should be able to do anything, but it seems clear from feedback from fans that they don't want to see vampires. My feeling is, why not? But we did the manitou last year, which was essentially a werewolf, and they hated that too . . . We're a horror show and, like a rock band should be able to play 'Johnny B. Goode' as well as originals, we should be able to do the classics."

Morgan's writing partner, James Wong, has admitted that "3" was a disappointment in that "the script was much better than the show. The problem is two-fold: the network's standards people really had lots of problems with that show. We had the blood fetish stuff going on. When you took away all that stuff, it really didn't make much sense anymore. The kinkiness really helped the vampire aspect of it work, as well as making the show a lot more interesting. We had to take that away, which really lessened the impact."

The main problem with this garbled and confused mess of an episode was addressed by Wong: "Perrey Reeves [who played Kristen] is David [Duchovny'] girlfriend. I think that because the two of them have a sexual relationship off screen, there was the kind of tension missing that you have with two people who haven't messed around. That's why I think it wasn't successful."

FILE NO. 2X08:

ONE BREATH

Declassified Case Overview: Agent Scully was discovered comatose in a Washington, D.C. hospital while Mulder confronted the Cigarette-Smoking Man, whom the agent suspected of being the head of the cabal responsible for her condition.

Nitpicking

You'll have to tape this episode and freeze-frame two different scenes to catch this one, but Mulder's signature on the hospital paperwork is not the same handwriting as on his photo ID shown in the credits sequence at the beginning.

How come the doctors didn't notice the large hole in Scully's abdomen or the branched DNA?

The brand name of Hewlett Packard has been taped over on Mulder's laser printer. Only LaserJet 4 can be seen.

Trivia

1. What did Mulder steal from the hospital?

2. (Fill in the Blank) The Lone Gunmen informed Mulder that someone had experimented with Scully's _____.

3. (Fill in the blank dialogue) After Mulder confronted the Cigarette-Smoking Man at gunpoint, he said, "I have more respect for you, Mulder. You're becoming a _____."

4. Who told Mulder his resignation was "unacceptable"?

5. Who arranged an ambush so Mulder could seek vengeance against Scully's abductors?

6. What happened to Mulder's apartment while he was sitting at Scully's hospital bedside?

7. (Fill in the blank dialogue) When Scully awoke to find Mulder at her side, she told him, "I had the strength of your _____."

X-PERT X-TRA BONUS POINTS

What was the Cigarette-Smoking Man's street address?

Investigative Field Report

"One of our most popular episodes," remembered Chris Carter. "I guess that's really the third episode of the 'Duane Barry' trilogy. It's the return of Gillian [after giving birth in real-life] and it has very little paranormal stuff in it. I think there were some people at Fox who didn't like it for that reason, but our fans called it one of our best."

The episode also marked a significant development of the Mr. X character, as he assassinates two men—in front of Mulder. "At first, Steve [Williams] wasn't going over that well," confessed co-screenwriter Glen Morgan. "I said, 'Jerry Hardin brought so much to Deep Throat, and we're kind of giving Mr. X Jerry's lines.' That's why we didn't use X for a while . . . Deep Throat was a guy willing to lose his life for letting out the secret, whereas X is a guy who's still scared. He's somewhere between Mulder and Deep Throat."

A real highlight of "One Breath" is when Mulder confronts Cigarette-Smoking Man. Ironically, Chris Carter initially told Morgan and Wong not to give Bill Davis, the actor who portrays the nefarious character, much to do except smoke cigarettes incessantly because Carter thought he might be an actor of limited potential (even though Davis is an acting teacher and worked for the British National Theatre).

Melinda McGraw, discovered by Morgan and Wong when they wrote for *The Commish*, was a major find as Scully's New Age sister.

ANOTHER HELPING OF ALPHABET SOUP

Fill in the blank with the correct answer that corresponds to the letter of the alphabet. Example: S is for . . . Pet name given to Scully by her father. Answer: Starbuck.

A is for . . .

1. Readout on Mulder's cell-phone at the conclusion of "Blood" (which is used by many X-Philes when signing off online): _____.

2. Pornographic magazine Mulder reads occasionally: _____.

3. Song Mulder requested Jimi Hendrix to sing via Luther Lee Boggs: _____.

B is for . . .

4. Bobby Darin song played at Captain Scully's seaside funeral: _____.

5. He originally investigated the 1933 murders committed by shape-shifter Eugene Tooms: _____.

6. Name of the pilot who flew Mulder, Scully and three doctors and scientists up to Alaska in "Ice": _____.

C is for . . .

7. Deep Throat's assassin: _____.

8. Classmate of Scully's who initially investigated the Tooms case in "Squeeze": _____.

9. Hollywood club where Mulder first encountered the mysterious Kristen: _____.

D is for . . .

10. Remote town in Alaska where Mulder searched for his sister: _____ .

E is for . . .

11. Name of slain CEO Benjamin Drake's high-tech firm: _____.

F is for . . .

12. In "Fresh Bones" this was the name of the Haitian refugee camp: _____.

13. Roland's last name: _____.

G is for . . .

14. The writer who penned the scripts for "Born Again" and "Fire-walker": _____.

15. The actor who portrayed the Rev. Cal Hartley in "Miracle Man": _____ (Hint: Both his first and last names begin with "G")

H is for . . .

16. One of the scientists sent to Icy Cape, Alaska with Mulder and Scully: _____.

17. Name of the actress who played Sally Kendricks, Eve 8: _____.

I is for . . .

18. One of the few episodes with no paranormal angle to it: _____.

J is for . . .

19. Young Kevin's heavenly-sent protector against evil in "Revelations": _____.

K is for . . .

20. She was born the same year as Howard Graves' deceased daughter: _____.

21. After seeing these words on a digital elevator, a real-estate salesman murdered four people: _____.

X-PERT X-TRA BONUS POINTS

E is for . . .

The former marine drill sergeant turned character actor who portrayed the con artist evangelist, Reverend Finley, during the pre-credit sequence of the episode, "Revelations."

FILE NO. 2X09:

FIREWALKER

Declassified Case Overview: Reunited at last, Agents Mulder and Scully were flown to an erupting volcano to investigate a scientific research team whose discovery of a parasitic life-form was causing a series of mysterious deaths.

Nitpicking

For a subterranean organism that lives in the intense heat of a volcano, wouldn't you believe that the human body would seem a rather cold host at only 98.6 degrees?

The snakelike spike spores eventually burst through the neck of their hosts. This particular area of the human anatomy is crowded with the spine, windpipe, and esophagus, not to mention major arteries and veins. It's doubtful that there was sufficient space for the parasite to reach its reproductive maturity without causing physical discomfort to the host during the process.

When O'Neil dies, a puff of spores come flying out of the crack in the door. If it only takes one spore to infect a body, then why wasn't at least one of them inhaled by Scully, who was handcuffed to O'Neil?

Trivia

1. What was the name of the volcano?

2. Who was the research expedition's leader?

3. (True or False) Mulder found the words "NEW LIFE-FORM" written in Tanka's notes.

4. What tetravalent nonmetallic element was the basis of the subterranean organism?

5. Who was the descent team's robotics engineer?

6. (True or False) Mulder told rescuers there were only two survivors.

X-PERT X-TRA BONUS POINTS

Who used a geologist's pick to attack Mulder?

Investigative Field Report

After weeks of soapy theatrics necessitated by the Scully abduction storyline, it was a relief to see this episode move back to a straightforward, self-contained mystery. In other words, "Firewalker" was specifically an X-File case, although most fans complained that essentially the episode was a brazen re-working of first season's "Ice," complete with skin-bursting parasitic life-forms.

While troubled by the similarities to "Ice," Glen Morgan nonetheless enjoyed creating another parasite that jumps from victim to victim. "I went to the museum where I learned about an ant in Africa that sometimes ingests this peculiar virus, which causes it to climb up a tree and hang from it—and then this spike juts out of its head. Howard Gordon [the script writer] and I talked about that, and he put it out through the neck, which is gorier."

Unfortunately, the similarities to "Ice" in this episode are unnerving. *The X-Files* has always had a nasty habit of borrowing creative ideas from other series and movies, but if the show begins to cannibalize itself, then its run on television will indeed be short-lived.

FILE NO. 2X10:

RED MUSEUM

Declassified Case Overview: When several missing teenagers were found wandering through the woods in their underwear with the words "HE IS ONE" scrawled on their backs, Wisconsin cattle ranchers believed the series of abductions to be the work of a bizarre local religious cult.

Nitpicking

When Mulder and Scully are eating at the café, he removes his napkin before going outside to see what the kids are yelling and screaming about. As he is walking along, he removes the napkin again.

New technology is being developed every day, but we have yet to find a camcorder that can film through a peephole. Maybe we should check with the Lone Gunmen.

Trivia

1. (Fill in the blank with the correct number) A teenage boy disappeared, then was discovered _____ hours later with the words "HE IS ONE" written on his bare back.

2. The local sheriff thought possession was involved and suspected a local religious order whose acolytes believed in soul transference and abstained from eating meat. What was the name of the cult?

3. After a missing teenage girl was found, what did medical tests detect in her blood?
   A. Trace levels of ammonia
   B. A strange opiate
   C. Large quantities of a muscle relaxant

4. What was Richard Odin's former profession?

5. (Fill in the Blank) One of the townsfolk led Mulder and Scully to a farm, where they witnessed men injecting cattle with genetically engineered _____ hormones.

6. How many teenage girls had been raped in the previous year by high school boys?
   A. 7
   B. 10
   C. 12

7. Who killed the Crew-Cut Man?

Investigative Field Report

A sequel of sorts to "The Erlenmeyer Flask," this episode deals with several diversified elements which all congeal together to create a distinctly unique episode. The biggest complaint from the fans, however, was bringing back Deep Throat's assassin and then having him killed off-screen. Most X-Philes stated online that they would have preferred to have seen an entire episode based upon the Crew-Cut Man's reappearance and Mulder's vengeance for Deep Throat's murder.

Originally planned as a crossover episode with the CBS series *Picket Fences*, Mulder was to have gone to Rome, Wisconsin to investigate the paranormal phenomena of cows giving birth to human children, believing it would provide information on the "Red Museum" X-File. Ultimately, the investigation would have proven fruitless when the bizarre cow mystery turned out to involve a doctor using cows as surrogate wombs for couples with fertility problems. Both episodes were ultimately produced, but with Mulder absent from the *Picket Fences* show.

FILE NO. 2X11:

EXCELSIUS DEI

Declassified Case Overview: Mulder and Scully's investigation proceeded to a convalescent home where a young nurse claimed she was raped by an invisible force, but before long the two agents were deeply involved in psychic desires, experimental medication, magic mushrooms, and the spirits of former residents.

Nitpicking

This *X-Files* installment is repeatedly spelled two different ways in publications and online. The Friday night of its premiere, Fox referred to it in television guide listings as "Excelsius Dei," but during the episode the name on the metal gate of the convalescent home plainly reads: Excelsis Dei. Which is correct?

The doctor informs Mulder and Scully that he has been using an experimental drug called Deprenyl on the Alzheimer's patients to increase their acetylcholine levels. Acetylcholine is a chemical that acts as a neurotransmitter and carries messages between nerve cells, as is dopamine. Deprenyl, which is in reality an experimental Alzheimer's treatment drug, primarily affects dopamine levels in the nervous system, not acetylcholine.

Trivia

1. Michelle Charters, a nurse in the Excelsius Dei convalescent home, was pinned down and raped by an invisible assailant. Name the seventy-four-year-old patient she accuses.

2. The crime of rape isn't normally a federal offense. Identify the mitigating circumstance that established the FBI's jurisdiction in the investigation.
    A. The convalescent home received federal funds for operations
    B. Nurse Charters sued the U.S. government, making it a party to the case
    C. Nurse Charters' salary was reimbursed through Medicare payments

3. Who killed one of the orderlies by knocking him out of a window?

4. Identify the orderly whose body Mulder found in the mushroom beds in the basement.

5. (Fill in the blank dialogue) Gung told Mulder that "the souls who died here continue to _____" and had been awakened.

6. Who was locked in the flooding bathroom with Mulder?

X-PERT X-TRA BONUS POINTS

What was Gung's last name?

Investigative Field Report

James Wong recalled that "Excelsius Dei" was "one of the hardest shows we've put on because the script came in in really bad shape and Chris [Carter] was rewriting it until the last minute, even while we were shooting it. The show had some neat stuff in it, but I don't think it came together at the end."

Most X-Philes rate this episode somewhere in the middle overall for the season. We appear to be as lonely as the Lone Gunmen in our opinion that this chilling and effective *X-Files* installment (inspired by actual claims of ghost-rape) is a near-classic. It was also a daring stroke of genius by the writers to make the rape victim so utterly unsympathetic.

Eric Christmas, who portrays nursing home resident Stan Phillips, also played a hapless government scientist with a proclivity for opening time warps in *The Philadelphia Experiment.*

X-PERT TESTIMONY: PART II

1. In which episode did Mulder tell his partner, "That's one of the luxuries of hunting down aliens and genetic mutants. You rarely get to press charges"?

2. In "Shadows," which of the following was Scully's response when Mulder asked her if she believed in the afterlife?
    A. "I've had enough in this one. I don't want a second helping."
    B. "I'd settle for a life in this one."
    C. "Not if I have to spend it with you."

3. (True or False) In the episode "Squeeze," Mulder said, "Oh God . . . it smells like . . . I think it's bile."

4. In "The X-Files: Pilot," which character stated simply, "Agent Mulder believes we are not alone"?
    A. Cigarette-Smoking Man
    B. Chief Blevins
    C. Agent Scully

5. Who urged Mulder to get out "while you still have a job" in "Deep Throat"?

6. Also in the "Deep Throat" episode, who told Mulder, "*They* have been here for a very, very long time"?

7. In the third season episode, "The Blessing Way," who related the ancient Native American proverb, "Something lives only as long as the last person who remembers"?
    A. Albert Hosteen
    B. Eric Hosteen
    C. Camouflage Man

8. Which character once told Assistant Director Skinner "I think you overestimate your position in the chain of command"?
    A. Mulder
    B. Scully
    C. Cigarette-Smoking Man

9. Who asked Scully, "Would you say your hair is normal, or dry?" in "Irresistible"?

10. Who left a note for Mulder at the scene of a jewelry store robbery that read, "Fox can't guard the chicken coop"?

11. Who warned Mulder to "forget what you saw—or what you think you saw" in "Fallen Angel"?
    A. Deep Throat
    B. Commander Henderson
    C. Lt. Fraser

12. In "One Breath," who bragged to Mulder, "I've watched presidents die"?
    A. Overcoat Man
    B. Cigarette-Smoking Man
    C. Skinner

13. (True or False) In the episode "3," Kristen Kilar told Mulder after they had sex, "Everybody else just dies, but we come back."

14. (Fill in the blank dialogue) When the mysterious Mr. X first called Mulder anonymously, he told him, "You have a _____ in the FBI."

15. In "Little Green Men," who responded with "Contact," when Mulder asked, "What am I looking for?"
    A. Scully
    B. Cigarette-Smoking Man
    C. Senator Matheson

16. Who told a nurse in "Fire," "I'm just dying for a cigarette"?

17. Which government informant warned Mulder that there "still exist some secrets that should remain secret"?

18. In the episode "The Host," who told Mulder, "We all take our orders from someone"?
    A. Skinner
    B. Scully
    C. Bristentine

19. Who told the Cigarette-Smoking Man in "Sleepless" that Scully was "a much larger problem than you described"?

20. In which episode did old Harry Cokely tell Mulder and Scully, "I sit here in front of the TV twenty-four hours a day"?

21. In "End Game," who pointed a gun at Skinner's head and said, "I've killed men for far less"?

22. (Fill in the blank dialogue) In "End Game," Scully concluded, "Ultimately, it was _____ that saved Agent Mulder's life."

23. (Fill in the blank dialogue) In the third season episode "Paper Clip," Mulder told Skinner, "Your cigarette-smoking friend killed my father for that _____."

24. Who said in "Anasazi," "Nothing vanishes without a trace"?
     A. Cigarette-Smoking Man
     B. Mr. X
     C. Bill Mulder

25. What did Mulder find at the crime scene in "Squeeze" to cause him to say the killer "ought to stick out with ten-inch fingers"?

26. (Fill in the blank with the correct year) With one murder left in Tooms' cycle, Mulder said in "Squeeze," "If we don't get him now, we won't have another chance til _____."
     A. 2010
     B. 2018
     C. 2023

27. Who told Mulder in "Space," "You make the front page today only if you screw up"?

28. In the episode "Ice," which two characters both said the line, "It all ends right here, right now," but at different times and in wholly different contexts?
     A. Scully and Richter
     B. Mulder and Richter
     C. Campbell and Dr. Da Silva

29. When Mulder was searching for Scully in "Ascension," who told him, "They'll tell you where she is. The military's in on it. Just ask 'em"?

30. In which episode did Mulder ask, "Did you really think you could summon the Devil, then ask him to behave?"

31. Who said "The Statue of Liberty's on vacation" in "Fresh Bones"?

A. Col. Wharton
B. Agent Mulder
C. Mr. X

32. (Fill in the Blank) In "The Calusari," who yelled, "You marry a devil! You have a devil child!"

33. (True or False) Mulder said in "Soft Light," "Dead men can't keep promises. Next time the blood and regret could be yours."

34. Who told Mulder in "Soft Light," "You're choosing a dangerous time to go it alone"? Scully or Mr. X?

35. In "The Blessing Way" episode, who screamed at Albert Hosteen, "I want Mulder and I want those files!"?
A. Cigarette-Smoking Man
B. Skinner
C. Mr. X

36. Who told Mulder in "The Jersey Devil," "Unlike you . . . I would like to have a life"?
A. Detective Thompson
B. Dr. Diamond
C. Scully

37. (True or False) At the conclusion of "E.B.E.," Mulder told Deep Throat, "I'm wondering which lie to believe."

38. (True or False) After catching sight of an image of his sister, Mulder said in "Miracle Man," "I think people are looking hard for miracles, so hard that they make themselves see what they want to see."

39. (Fill in the blank dialogue) In the "Miracle Man," Mulder said to Scully (when she suggested they venture backstage), "Hang on. This is the part where they bring out _____."

40. Who said in "Shapes" that the Lewis and Clark expedition "wrote of Indian men who could change into a wolf"?
A. Dr. Josephs
B. Mulder
C. Lyle Parker

41. Who warned the agents in "Shadows," "My advice to you is don't get rough with her," when they sought to question Lauren Kyte?
    A. Robert Dorland
    B. Ellen Bledsoe
    C. Agent Mulder

42. (True or False) In the "Darkness Falls" episode, Mulder said, "Maybe they woke up hungry," after he concluded that the ancient insect eggs were affected by radiation.

43. (True or False) Mulder warned the psychiatric panel in "Tooms," "If you release Eugene Tooms, he will kill again. It's in his genetic makeup."

44. What were Deep Throat's dying words to Scully?
    A. "The truth is out there."
    B. "Deny everything."
    C. "Trust no one."

45. Who told Scully in "The Erlenmeyer Flask" that the X-Files had been shut down after "word came down from the top of the executive branch"?

46. In the episode "Blood," who noted that Franklin, Pennsylvania had had "only three murders since colonial times"?
    A. Mulder
    B. Sheriff Spencer
    C. The Lone Gunmen

47. (Fill in the blank dialogue) After scanning the piece of metal from Duane Barry's stomach, Scully left a message on Mulder's answering machine that said, "What the hell is this thing? . . . It's almost like somebody was using it to _____ him."

48. Who was the doctor Mulder was referring to in "Red Museum," when he said, "Looks like the good doctor may have been delivering more than babies"?
    A. Dr. Larsen
    B. Dr. Haslett
    C. Dr. Waldie

49. What was the elderly Hal Arden's reply in "Excelsius Dei," when he was accused of raping a nurse in the convalescent home where he was a patient?
    A. "I'm seventy-four years old. I've got plumbing older than this building."
    B. "I'm seventy-three years old. My pilot light is burnt out on my furnace."
    C. "Just because there's snow on the roof doesn't mean I've got a fire inside."

50. In which episode did Mulder say in a voice-over that there was intelligent life beyond Earth, "that they're among us, and they have begun to colonize"?

X-PERT X-TRA BONUS POINTS #1

In which episode did Mulder say, "I'm betting the military never stopped the work it began fifty years ago"?

X-PERT X-TRA BONUS POINTS #2

Who told Mulder in a second season episode to "Watch your back. This is just the beginning"?

FILE NO. 2X12:

AUBREY

Declassified Case Overview: A policewoman's dreams of a murder led to the discovery of the body of an FBI agent killed nearly 50 years earlier, reopening the serial killer case he was investigating at the time. When the killer struck again, Agents Mulder and Scully questioned the connection between the police officer and the killer.

Nitpicking

At the beginning of the episode, Mulder and Scully are seen in their Washington office talking, while she casually flips through the pages of a file. Several times, Scully turns one particular page over, but when the audience sees her from Mulder's view, the page is not overturned.

This is a recurring blooper that is not indigenous to this particular episode, but we'll address it in this venue: Mulder is driving, Scully is in the front passenger's seat and they pull up to the curb where a house is on the right. He has to kill the engine, unbuckle his seatbelt, get out of the vehicle, walk around it and yet Mulder always gets to the front door before his partner.

Most victims of a heinous crime attempt to distance themselves from the scene of the trauma. Why then did Mrs. Thibodeaux remain living in the same house where all her suffering occurred, even though she admits that the spot on the stairs still haunts her?

Trivia

1. Identify Detective B.J. Morrow's superior who was also the father of her unborn child.
   A. Lt. Brian Tillman
   B. Capt. Gary Clifton
   C. Lt. Mark Wohl

2. Detective Morrow inexplicably found herself in a field, unearthing the body of an FBI agent who disappeared in 1942. What was his name?

3. In what year was Harry Cokely convicted of raping a woman and carving "sister" on her?

4. How old was the frail Cokely when Mulder and Scully questioned him?
   A. 73
   B. 74
   C. 77

5. Cokely told the two agents that he couldn't "leave the house without this damn thing" when they interrogated him about his recent whereabouts. What was he referring to?

6. (Fill in the blank dialogue) Mulder noted that "Genetic
    _____ often skip generations."

X-PERT X-TRA BONUS POINTS

(Fill in the blank dialogue) Scully quickly countered Mulder's ac-
cusation concerning her theory by saying, "I seem to recall you
having some pretty _____ hunches."

Investigative Field Report

"With that episode, I felt more confident and freer to experiment,"
said director Rob Bowman. "I learned a lot about what Chris Carter
wants, how his taste has evolved, how to do a slasher episode that
was truly scary. It was great when we shot B.J. [the policewoman] in
her bedroom when she wakes up, finds blood on her chest and goes
to the bathroom and sees that she's slashed herself. She comes out,
closes the door and there was the young Harry Cokely [her father].
The script girl couldn't watch us shoot the scene because it was so
scary."

Trivia alert: Morgan Woodward, who portrays the pathetic Cokely,
is best remembered in the sci-fi genre for the two classic *Star Trek*
episodes, "Dagger of the Mind" and "The Omega Glory."

FILE NO. 2X13:

IRRESISTIBLE

*Declassified Case Overview: Agent Scully experienced flashbacks to her abduc-
tion when the X-Files unit investigated another agent's suspicion that a
number of mutilated female bodies may have been ravaged by paranormal phenomenon.*

Nitpicking

Scully dates her autopsy 11:14 A.M., Monday, November 14th, which positions "Irresistible" in some kind of *Star Trek*-like time rift. We learn that the events in the episode "3" also took place during the month of November, which would mean that "One Breath," "Firewalker" (in which Mulder and Scully were supposed to be quarantined for a month at the conclusion), "Excelsius Dei," "Red Museum" and "Aubrey" all occurred in less than two weeks. Yeah, right.

If Pfaster was willed the car, wouldn't the DMV have it titled under his name? We would assume they would've transferred the mother's name since she was dead.

Typical location SNAFU: Donnie Pfaster is cruising the city streets looking for a prostitute, when a bus passes with a destination sign that reads UBC (University of British Columbia in Vancouver).

Trivia: The Numbers Game

(NOTE: Because of the difficulty of the following questions, all correct answers will count as a 5-point X-PERT X-TRA BONUS.)

1. At the beginning of the episode, Donnie Pfaster was discovered by his boss at the funeral home removing locks of hair off a corpse. In what year was the deceased teenage girl born?

2. How many hours did it take Mulder and Scully to get from Washington, D.C. to the crime scene in Minneapolis?

3. (True or False) Three buried bodies were desecrated within a two-day period.

4. Identify the number on the Vikings quarterback's jersey during the Minnesota-Washington NFL game on Bocks' office television.

5. Pfaster later fixated on a coed in his night school mythology class and approached her in the parking lot by inquiring about homework assignments. Which two textbook chapters did she tell him the professor had requested they read?

6. What was the time digitally displayed on Scully's alarm clock when she awoke from a nightmare?

7. (Fill in the blank dialogue with the correct number) Mulder told an obviously shaken Scully, "I've seen agents with _____ years field experience fall apart on cases like this."

8. How old was Donnie Pfaster?

9. How many late-model, white sedans fitting the description of Pfaster's car were located in the Minneapolis metropolitan area?

10. (Fill in the blank dialogue with the correct number) An angry Mulder told Agent Bocks that "people spot Elvis in _____ cities across America every day."

11. (True or False) Pfaster had three older sisters.

Investigative Field Report

This episode has often been criticized for not being an X-File, but it effectively drives home the point that not all terror comes from the paranormal, but occasionally from the mild-mannered guy next door. Interestingly, Mulder, who looks for aliens in his breakfast cereal, recognizes almost immediately that this case involves a deranged human, whereas Scully, despite her training and her usual skepticism in the face of extraterrestrials, has to presume otherwise because she just can't accept the fact that the culprit is actually a human being.

The morphing scenes where Pfaster transforms into a pointy-eared alien was an afterthought, not originally written into the script. The post-production technicians were told to add the sequences to enhance the mystery of the episode, but their inclusion makes the show less powerful.

Gillian Anderson should have been nominated for an Emmy instead of *Murder, She Wrote*'s Angela Lansbury. Her heartrending performance gives us a treasured peek beneath the ever-so-cool Dana Scully, revealing that our heroine is not imperturbable after all. When she confides in the Bureau shrink that she doesn't want Mulder to feel like he has to protect her, we realize that Scully hides certain fears from her partner and herself.

Bruce Weitz, who portrays Agent Bocks (someone even weirder than Mulder), is forever remembered as the eccentric, suspect-biting Detective Belker on *Hill Street Blues*.

The fingerprint technician was also used as an extra in the episodes "Lazarus," "Young at Heart" and "Our Town."

We remember reading an Ann Landers' letter in the newspaper not too long ago, in which a virginal young bride wrote to say that on her wedding night the groom (a mortician) had asked her to take an ice-cold bath before coming to bed. The young bride wanted to know if that was an unusual request. As Mulder points out in "Irresistible," you don't have to look to the stars to find creatures whose behavior is radically different from our own. Sometimes they're lying in bed right next to you.

FILE NO. 2X14:

DIE HAND DIE VERLETZT

Declassified Case Overview: Some male teenagers pretended that they were performing an occult ritual in an effort to score with their girlfriends, but they inadvertently piqued the interest of the town's real occult group.

Nitpicking

A thirsty Mulder turns on a water fountain in the local school and stares at the draining water in amazement. "What's wrong with it?" Scully asks. "It's going down the drain counterclockwise," Mulder answers. "The Coriolis force in the Northern Hemisphere dictates that it should go down clockwise." "That isn't possible," Scully says. "Something is here. Something is making these things happen," Mulder responds, suddenly convinced that a supernatural force permeates the town. Unfortunately, the Coriolis force has always been subject to many myths. One is that it causes water to flow down a drain clockwise. In actuality, the effect causes certain systems, low pressure ones, for example, to rotate counterclockwise. It does not, however, have a great impact on systems smaller than a hurricane.

When Shannon dies after slitting her wrists from Mrs. Paddock's demonic suggestion, the teacher states that the girl was dead when she fell off the stool. To actually die from slitting one's wrists takes a while, even after she would have passed out and fell off the stool. Also, the wounds would have started to clot over before she actually died, which is why successful suicide victims submerse their wounds in water to prevent clotting.

Trivia

1. (Fill in the Blank) The local Parents-Teachers Committee met and before adjourning lit a candle and prayed in unison to the _____ of Darkness.
    A. Masters
    B. Kings
    C. Lords

2. Identify the member of the PTC who said at a meeting, "Something is here . . . a presence."
    A. Victor Pianalto
    B. Pete Calcagni
    C. Jim Ausbury

3. (True or False) Scully scoffed at rumors of Satan worship in the town until it began raining rats.

4. What was in Mrs. Paddock's desk drawer?

5. (Fill in the Blank) In Mrs. Paddock's office, Mulder detected the smell of _____, which was used in Satanic rituals.

6. How did Jim Ausbury die after Mulder handcuffed him in the basement?

X-PERT X-TRA BONUS POINTS

The teenagers had borrowed the library book *Witch Hunt: A History of the Occult in America*. Name the book's author.

Investigative Field Report

Dedicated PTC members who are Devil worshipers? "Die Hand Die Verletzt" is almost comical (like some of Darin Morgan's third season episodes) until Shannon breaks down and confesses how she was molested. The episode suddenly becomes a very creepy, dark, disturbing installment that actually veers a little more toward the horror genre than usual.

Producer J.P. Finn remembered the scene with the python more than anything else in this episode. "John Bartley, our wonderful director of photography, was shooting at really low light levels. We had this 20-foot, 250-pound snake coming down the stairs. We had two cameras on it. The dolly grip, who was underneath the stairs, said, 'Can't see it, can't see it.' He turned around and the snake was about six inches from his face. The crew just cleared out of there."

Trivia alert: To demonstrate his appreciation for their unwavering support and dedication to the series since its debut, Chris Carter named several characters in this episode after real-life online X-Philes.

The message left on the chalkboard, "Goodbye. It's been nice working with you," also served as episode writers Glen Morgan and James Wong's farewell to the cast and crew before leaving to develop and produce the ill-fated *Space: Above and Beyond*. After missing *The X-Files'* entire third season, the two writers returned to the series at the beginning of the fourth year.

X MARKS THE SPOT: SEASON TWO

Continuing with the second season of Mulder and Scully's X-cellent adventures, match their nationwide on-site investigations with the corresponding X-Files episodes. NOTE: Locations were selected by site of main conflict; many episodes covered more than one location.

1. _____ Worcester, MA   A. "Fresh Bones"

2. _____ Marion, VA   B. "Irresistible"

3. _____ Milford Haven, NH   C. "Fearful Symmetry"

4. _____ Germantown, MD   D. "3"

5. _____ Folkstone, NC   E. "Anasazi"

6. _____ Fairfield, ID   F. "Blood"

7. _____ Minneapolis, MN   G. "Excelsius Dei"

8. _____ Los Angeles, CA   H. "Die Hand Die Verletzt"

9. _____ Arlington, VA   I. "Sleepless"

10. _____ Franklin, PA   J. "Colony"

11. _____ New York, NY   K. "Duane Barry"

12. _____ Farmington, NM   L. "The Calusari"

X-PERT X-TRA BONUS POINTS #1

Name the city in Puerto Rico in which "Little Green Men" took place.

X-PERT X-TRA BONUS POINTS #2

The southern state of Arkansas is known as the poultry capital of the world. Identify the rural town that housed the Chaco Chicken processing plant in "Our Town."

X-PERT X-TRA BONUS POINTS #3

Name the city and state populated by retired circus and sideshow performers in "Humbug."

X-PERT X-TRA BONUS POINTS #4

In the episode "Dod Kalm," Mulder and Scully journeyed to Norway. Identify the city.

X-PERT X-TRA BONUS POINTS #5

"Colony" and "One Breath" both took place in this Maryland city. Name it.

FILE NO. 2X15:

FRESH BONES

Declassified Case Overview: When a Marine stationed at a resettlement camp for Haitian refugees died after driving into a tree, Mulder and Scully investigated the widow's claim that her husband's "suicide" was the result of a voodoo curse.

Trivia

1. How fast was Private McAlpin's car traveling when it slammed into the tree?
    - A. 60 mph
    - B. 75 mph
    - C. 80 mph

2. According to McAlpin's widow, what were the only two things that her husband believed in?
    - A. God and country
    - B. The Marines and football
    - C. Good and evil

3. (True or False) Two Marines had died within two weeks from "allegedly self-inflicted injuries."

4. (Fill in the blank dialogue) Pierre Bauvais told Mulder that Haiti was "born of the blood of slaves. Freedom is our most _____ legacy."

5. Where was Private McAlpin taken after Mulder and Scully almost hit him with their car?

6. (True or False) The cemetery groundskeeper informed Mulder and Scully that bodysnatchers sold cadavers to the local medical school for $300 a head.

7. Who did Scully find dead in the bathtub of Mulder's room?

X-PERT X-TRA BONUS POINTS #1

What number was the county road on which Mulder covertly met with Mr. X?

X-PERT X-TRA BONUS POINTS #2

Identify the powerful sedative found naturally in puffer fish which was used to transform Private McAlpin into a zombie.

Investigative Field Report

"Fresh Bones" is a classic example of *The X-Files* in its best form. Seemingly flawless (we couldn't even nitpick), the writers and producers achieved their goal of keeping the voodoo storyline from becoming silly, filled with bloody chickens or all the other props that we've seen hundreds of times before in other series and movies.

In the episode, young Haitian refugee Chester Bonaparte evidently has the ability to transform into a black cat at will. The islanders trace their belief and practice of shape-shifting into animals back to their ancestors in Africa, where there are many similar accounts of humans who at times will take on the form of a hyena, wild boar, vulture or crocodile, for instance. In some tribes, the initiation of a shaman or witch doctor still generally involves the mingling of his blood with that of the animal. An intimate union between human and animal is then thought to result.

Baldheaded Daniel Benzali, who portrays base commander Colonel Wharton, starred as the high-profile L.A. lawyer on ABC's *Murder One.*

FILE NO. 2X16:

COLONY [PART 1 OF 2]

Declassified Case Overview: The search for a morphing alien bounty hunter was interrupted when Mulder was contacted by his father, who told him that his long-lost sister, Samantha, had finally returned home.

Nitpicking

Scully couldn't possibly call Mulder's cell-phone because it was destroyed when he was hit by the car. But why didn't he call Scully on her cell-phone when he reached her answering machine?

Although Mulder never returned home to tape a greeting on his answering machine, every time it's played in this episode we hear a different one ("Hi, this is Fox Mulder. Please leave me a message and I'll get back to you as soon as I can" and "Hello, this is Fox Mulder. Leave a message, please").

In the pre-credits sequence, Mulder is wearing an oxygen mask when he's in the tub. When Scully comes in and confers with the doctor, we can see Mulder in the background and he's shown not wearing one. But in the next shot, the mask is back on.

Trivia

1. (Fill in the Blank) At the beginning of the episode, Mulder was rushed into an emergency room suffering from extreme _____.

2. Name the sea in the Arctic Circle where a government research vessel rescued a Russian pilot who had crash landed.

3. The pilot then showed up at a Scranton abortion clinic, where he murdered a doctor. What color was the fluid that oozed from his body?

4. (True or False) Mulder received the obituaries of three deceased doctors who all worked at abortion clinics, looked exactly alike, and had no birth records.

5. Concluding that the killer was following a geographic pattern, in which city did Mulder locate another identical doctor?
    A. Syracuse
    B. Buffalo
    C. Boston

6. Name the FBI agent in the regional office who Mulder sent to question the other identical doctor.

7. Who called Scully on the phone after Mulder showed up at her room?

X-PERT X-TRA BONUS POINTS

How many years had Samantha been missing?

Investigative Field Report

"I thought the show was an interesting exploration of Scully and Mulder's different perspectives," remembered Chris Carter. "I wanted to reestablish what their points of view were, to reaffirm her belief in science and his belief in the paranormal. From beginning to end, I liked it. It was a different way to tell a story. I've always wanted to tell a story backward like that, an inspiration I took from the original *Frankenstein*, which is told the same way." Many fans, though, complained about the confusing pre-credits teaser, which essentially is the final scene of the *following* episode, "The End Game."

The reappearance of Samantha Mulder, who disappeared years earlier after having been abducted by aliens, is hauntingly reminiscent of the real-life case of what UFO experts call the "West Ham Disappearances" in East London. One of the initial victims was a young girl named Eliza Carter, who vanished under mysterious circumstances from her home but later appeared in the street and spoke to several of her friends. They tried earnestly to persuade her to go home to her family, but she explained that "They" would not allow her to do so. She was seen around West Ham for a couple of days before disappearing forever.

END GAME [PART 2 OF 2]

Declassified Case Overview: When the alien bounty hunter took Scully hostage in exchange for Agent Mulder's sister (who was in actuality a clone), Mulder tracked his nemesis to a submarine at the North Pole to learn the whereabouts of the real Samantha and engage the extraterrestrial in a final confrontation.

Nitpicking

After Samantha plummets off the bridge, Scully examines the body once it is retrieved from the river. In the previous installment, "Colony," a policeman was killed by the fumes emanating from one of the clones. But the noxious fumes emerging from the deteriorating Samantha clone have no effect at all on Scully.

Trivia

1. (True or False) Samantha told Mulder that the only way to kill the alien bounty hunter was to pierce the base of his skull.

2. (True or False) Samantha informed Mulder that the clones were the descendants of two extraterrestrial visitors from the 1950s who were attempting to establish an Earth colony by genetically integrating with humans.

3. Why was a bounty hunter dispatched to terminate the colonists?
    A. They had violated their planet's Prime Directive
    B. His superior had a personal vendetta to score
    C. The experiment hadn't been sanctioned

4. A trade involving Samantha for Scully was set up on a bridge in Bethesda. Whose assistance did Mulder request?

5. Samantha had left Mulder instructions that if they were separated to rendezvous at an abortion clinic, where the agent found several Samantha clones. Including the first Samantha, who Mulder

thought was his sister, and then counting the other "Samanthas" at the clinic, how many Samantha clones appeared in this episode?

6. During Mr. X and Skinner's brutal close encounter, who pulled a gun?

7. In a voice-over at the end, what did Scully say ultimately saved Agent Mulder's life?

X-PERT X-TRA BONUS POINTS

What significance did the number 4A have for Mulder?

Investigative Field Report

Even though most of *The X-Files* staff considered "End Game" the ultimate episode so far for the series, writer Frank Spotnitz's initial draft was even bigger. One scene in particular was cut because there wasn't even time to shoot it. "Mulder met his father at a bridge," Spotnitz recalled, "and as he's driving he sees his sister, wet and cold, on the side of the road. He pulls over, she gets in, and he continues driving when he suddenly realizes it's *not* her, it's the bounty hunter. She morphs right before his eyes, they struggle for the wheel of the car, they end up jumping out of the car and the car crashes, and then he rushes to the abortion clinic where the other clones are, and the bounty hunter is right after him. We ended up cutting all of that. I didn't realize it when I was writing that you can't do a show of that size in eight days."

David Duchovny performed his own stunt work during the episode's climactic Arctic scene in which Mulder drops to the ice after dangling from the top of the submarine's conning tower.

MADAM X: GILLIAN ANDERSON

"Gillian's smart, first of all. And, she's ambitious, which is what her character is. Scully is one of the few women in what is otherwise a very male-dominated institution, the FBI. So, she has to compete with these guys and still maintain a sense of her own femininity, which I think she does very well, both in life and in terms of the character."

—*Chris Carter, Creator and Executive Producer*

1. (True or False) The oldest of four children, Anderson was born in Chicago, Illinois on August 9, 1968.

2. What did she want to become when she grew up?

3. From Chicago the Anderson family moved to Puerto Rico and then spent nine years in London. Identify the prestigious English film school that Anderson's father, Edward, attended.
   A. Bristol Old Vic School of Performing Arts
   B. London School of Film and Theatre
   C. London Film School

4. How old was Anderson when her family relocated to Grand Rapids, Michigan?
   A. 9
   B. 11
   C. 12

5. Somewhat wild as a teenager, she was a genuine punker. What fashion statements did she make in her youth?

6. (True or False) While in high school, the acting bug bit Anderson and on a lark, she tried out for a community theater group.

7. In what year did she graduate from DePaul University's Goodman Theater School in Chicago with a Bachelor in Fine Arts?
   A. 1988
   B. 1989
   C. 1990

8. (Fill in the blank quote) Ric Murphy, one of her teachers at Goodman, said in a *People* magazine cover story that Anderson "had an eight-line part in a French farce but turned it into a star role just by the _____ she brought to it."

9. What New York-based talent agency offered to represent her after seeing her perform at an actors' showcase?

10. Choosing to pursue a career in theater instead of film, she loaded up her car and moved to New York. How old was Anderson at the time?
    A. 20
    B. 21
    C. 22

11. What was her day job while she struggled to support herself as an actress?

12. After replacing another more well-known actress two weeks into rehearsal, Anderson won a Theatre World Award for her performance in the off-Broadway production of *Absent Friends*. Name the actress who abandoned the play to take a role in the movie *Grand Canyon*.

13. (Fill in the blank with the correct number) Anderson continued to go out on auditions and after a discouraging dry spell she was offered _____ different roles in the same day.

14. What was the title of her first low-budget feature which starred Tess Harper and Karen Allen?

15. Identify the New Haven, Connecticut stage where she appeared in the Christopher Hampton play *The Philanthropist*.
    A. Long Wharf Theater
    B. East Coast Performing Arts Center
    C. Atlantic Theatre

16. (True or False) Anderson ultimately settled in Hollywood after she became involved with another actor in *The Philanthropist*, followed him to the West Coast, and eventually moved in with him.

17. Anderson swore she would never work in television, but after

being out of work for almost a year she began auditioning. What was her first TV role?

18.   (True or False) *The X-Files* was the only pilot for which she auditioned in 1993.

19.   How old was Anderson when she won the role of FBI Special Agent Dana Scully?
      A.   22
      B.   24
      C.   25

20.   (True or False) She learned that she had landed *The X-Files* part the day before her final unemployment check came.

21.   Who owned the condominium she leased when she relocated to Vancouver for the long, arduous months of filming *The X-Files*?

22.   Identify the date Anderson married Clyde Klotz, an art director on the series.

23.   (True or False) The Fox Network wanted Chris Carter to recast the role of Scully after learning that Anderson was pregnant.

24.   The ways *The X-Files* creative team worked around her condition ranged from the simple to the inspired. How far along was Anderson's pregnancy when the episode was filmed with Mulder imagining aliens experimenting on Scully and inflating her belly like a balloon?

25.   (True or False) Anderson's daughter, Piper, was delivered by cesarean section on September 25, 1994, two days overdue.

26.   How many days of maternity leave did she take before returning to work on the series?
      A.   10
      B.   12
      C.   14

27.   (True or False) Anderson's father, Edward, runs a movie postproduction company and her mother, Rosemary, is a computer analyst.

28. Unlike her skeptical *X-Files* character, she has "a basic belief in the paranormal." Who told Anderson and her husband that their house in Vancouver was haunted by "souls in unrest"?

X-PERT X-TRA BONUS POINTS #1

On which hole of a Hawaiian golf course were Anderson and her husband married by a Buddhist priest?

X-PERT X-TRA BONUS POINTS #2

Name the university in New York state where Anderson studied theater.

FILE NO. 2X18:

FEARFUL SYMMETRY

Declassified Case Overview: The inhabitants of a zoo located near an alleged UFO landing site—ranging from elephants to tigers to gorillas—became suspects in a string of deaths, even though witnesses stated they had not seen any animals.

Nitpicking

We admit to having a limited base of knowledge on animal reproduction, but wouldn't the zoo animals have to be abducted twice in order for the aliens to artificially inseminate them and then follow-up with a return visit to "harvest" the embryo?

Willa is armed only with a tranquilizer gun when she goes off by herself to hunt down the tiger in the office building. As a zoo keeper, she has to know that a dart does not immediately sedate an animal. Anyone who has ever watched a *National Geographic* special or the Discovery Channel knows that it takes a few minutes for the tranquilizer to take effect on the animal.

Although we are told that the elephant was African, one look at the ears will confirm that the elephant was indeed Indian.

Trivia

1. (Fill in the blank with the correct number) After an invisible force wreaked havoc and fatally injured a federal employee, a dying elephant suddenly appeared _____ miles from the zoo where it was safely locked up.
    A. 29
    B. 43
    C. 52

2. What was the name of the insurance company whose windows were imploded during the pre-credits sequence?

3. Identify the trucker who slammed on his brakes when the elephant appeared directly in front of his rig.
    A. Billy Bob Walker
    B. Winston Slade
    C. Wesley Brewer

4. (True or False) According to Willa Ambrose, the Fairfield Zoo was constructed during the 1950s.

5. Who told Mulder that the zoo was near a UFO hotspot and no animal housed there had ever brought a pregnancy to full term?

6. What strange discovery did Scully make during the elephant's autopsy?

7. How many darts did Ed Meecham tell Mulder he had in his tranquilizer gun when they went into Sophie's cage?

X-PERT X-TRA BONUS POINTS

What was the elephant's name?

Investigative Field Report

Aliens abducting animals to perhaps create their own version of Noah's Ark? Although this sometimes sentimental installment is a little quirky, it is one of *The X-Files'* most original episodes.

"A tough show schedule-wise," acknowledged producer J.P. Finn. "The hardest part was getting the elephant here. I started working on getting a permit for the elephant to come across the border to Vancouver way back at the first of December [the episode was first aired February 24, 1995]. On the day it had to leave Los Angeles to be here, we finally got the permits. Once she got here—her name was Bubbles—she was fantastic to work with, a real pro."

FILE NO. 2X19:

DOD KALM

Declassified Case Overview: While investigating the disappearance of a U.S. Navy destroyer, Agents Mulder and Scully found themselves in the Norwegian equivalent of the Bermuda Triangle and began rapidly aging while trapped on the rusting, soon-to-sink vessel.

Nitpicking

Free radicals are reactive chemicals containing extra electrons that attack DNA and proteins, causing the body to age. Eliminating them would only stop the forward process of aging, not reverse it, as shown at the end of the episode.

When Mulder tells Scully about the disappearance of several ships in an area equivalent to the Bermuda Triangle, he points to the United Kingdom on the wall map and states that one of the "vanished" boats departed from Leeds. Unfortunately, the English town is quite a way inland and does not have any ports.

If Mulder's dehydration, due to motion sickness, contributes to his hyperaging to the point where even untainted water won't help him, then why would drinking alcohol, which causes serious dehydration, extend the life of Captain Barclay?

If Harper was a lieutenant in the U.S. Navy, then why was he wearing two bars on each side of his collar? Lieutenants wear only a single bar, either gold or silver in color.

Trivia: The Numbers Game

(NOTE: Because of the difficulty of the following questions, all correct answers will count as a 5-point X-PERT X-TRA BONUS.)

1. (Fill in the blank with the correct number) The USS *Ardent*'s position in the Norwegian Sea at the beginning of the episode was 65 degrees latitude and _____ degrees east longitude.

2. How many shriveled and aged survivors of the *Ardent*'s crew were rescued by the trawler?

3. Although Scully commented that Lieutenant Harper looked ninety, how old was he in actuality?

4. According to Mulder, how many other ocean-going vessels had mysteriously vanished in the geographic area known as the 65th Parallel?

5. (True or False) The American destroyer, the USS *Eldridge*, disappeared 6 months after the Roswell incident.

6. How old was Captain Barclay?

7. In what year was the USS *Ardent* commissioned?

8. (Fill in the blank with the correct number) According to Scully's entry in the *Ardent*'s official log, Mulder lost consciousness at approximately _____ A.M. on March 12th.

9. What was the tonnage of Henry Trondheim's Norwegian trawler?

10. What was the *Ardent*'s three-digit U.S. Navy registration number?

Investigative Field Report

"I didn't want to do a Bermuda Triangle episode per se," said Chris Carter, "because I thought that was an obvious way to go with it. So what looks like a Bermuda Triangle story turns out to be something else. I thought it would be a great money saver and production value would be built in, but it ended up being very expensive, very costly time-wise. For one reason, the makeup for David and Gillian took a long time to put on, and they were miserable. The boat was cold inside, it was cramped, tight quarters. It's one of those situations where you think you're brilliant, but things don't go exactly like you planned."

In the episode, Mulder refers to the notorious "Philadelphia Experiment" in which, allegedly, the brand-new American destroyer USS *Eldridge* was the focus of a 1943 military experiment to render it invisible by manipulating wormholes on Earth. The story, which has all the ingredients of an *X-File* episode script, begins in the 1950s, with Morris Ketchum Jessup, an astronomer who wrote four books on UFOs, including the best-selling *The Case for the UFO*.

In October 1955 and again in January 1956, Jessup received several peculiar letters from a reader called "Carlos Miguel Allende," who recounted the bizarre story of a government experiment to render a ship invisible with a force field based on the principles of Nobel Prize-winning physicist Albert Einstein's Unified Field Theory. This endeavored to explain that electromagnetic, gravitational and nuclear forces were interrelated. According to Allende, the experiment had been a complete success and the USS *Eldridge* had vanished from its Philadelphia port, only to reappear in Norfolk, Virginia more than 200 miles away, all in a matter of a few minutes. Some of the crew, caught in what was later described as a "force field that surrounded the ship," became semi-transparent; others apparently walked through walls, caught fire or were paralyzed before they blurred in shape or disappeared. Some returned to speak of parallel worlds while others were never seen again.

Although Jessup did not take the story too seriously, his suicide on April 20, 1959, helped inflate the significance of the Allende letters and inevitably some people chose to believe the author was murdered because he knew too much about the Philadelphia Experiment.

FILE NO. 2X20:

HUMBUG

Declassified Case Overview: Agents Mulder and Scully's investigation into a series of horrific ritualistic killings led them to a small town built around a carnival and its collection of sideshow acts.

Nitpicking

Scully takes the cricket with her right hand, but when she shows Mulder the bug it's in her left hand. And we thought Mulder was the David Copperfield fan.

Trivia

1. What condition did Jerald Glazebrook, a reptile-skinned circus performer, suffer from?

2. Where was Glazebrook killed by an unseen attacker?

3. (Fill in the blank with the correct number) Mulder said the attack was similar to _____ other assaults over the last 28 years.
    A. 34
    B. 41
    C. 48

4. (Fill in the blank dialogue) After Dr. Blockhead emerged from under Glazebrook's casket and pounded a nail into his chest, Mulder told Scully, "I can't wait for the _____."

5. What was the name of P.T. Barnum's legendary act that was supposedly just a dead monkey with a fish's tail sewn on?

6. Name the midget proprietor of the trailer-park motel where Mulder and Scully stayed.

7. What was the tattooed man's stage name?

X-PERT X-TRA BONUS POINTS

What was Jeffrey Swaim's stage name?

Investigative Field Report

Darin Morgan writes comedic, off-beat, *very* non-traditional episodes and they are almost always a major hit with fans of the series. This is the first *X-Files* that obviously does not take itself too seriously.

"They asked me to do something about circus freaks," Morgan explained. "At first, I was a little uncomfortable joining the staff because I'm a comedy writer and this isn't a comedy show, so I was trying more or less to have an episode with a little sense of humor, without telling anybody what I was doing. I wasn't trying to be bizarre so much as I was trying to bring some humor to the show."

TORN FROM TODAY'S HEADLINES

The challenge for the writing staff of *The X-Files* is to find new phenomena to explore without getting stale, quirky, or going over-the-top. "We'll keep telling good, scary, tense, edge-of-your-seat stories," says creator and executive producer Chris Carter. "The raw material is going to be a little less obvious."

For Carter, finding that raw material is like panning for gold. "Every day of my life for the past three years has been devoted to this show, so what I've done is develop a good filter system. Everything I read, see, hear, or do, is consumed and then run through what I call my *X-Files* filter system. I trap all the little tidbits, ideas and stories that are interesting to me: anecdotes, quotes, books, magazines, it all comes through. I am constantly scavenging, selecting, and analyzing these for things I think would make good *X-Files* stories."

Much media and fan attention is given to the question of whether the stories are dramatizations of actual cases. *X-Files* episodes do not claim to be true stories—not anymore, anyway. The pilot episode, known eponymously as *The X-Files,* was prefaced by a notice that declared: "The following story is inspired by actual documented accounts." The notice was withdrawn from the second episode on.

Carter and the writing staff state categorically that the scripts are not based on true stories, but elements of the stories have been taken from true-life accounts. "Everything that's in there is an amalgam of real cases," Carter has acknowledged. "Everything you see has been written about somewhere—including the exhumation of what is believed to be an alien. Where the truth begins and ends is really up to the believer."

So, while there is no attempt to televise "true stories," Carter and the show's writers have demonstrated that they are often inspired by contemporary incidents or historical research to incorporate documented details into stories to make them appear more authentic.

For instance, the episode "Humbug" seemed to have been inspired by the real-life killing of a carnival sideshow character called Lobsterboy. "Dod Kalm" referred not only to the Philadelphia Experiment but the legendary Bermuda Triangle, an area in the Atlantic Ocean where some 200 ships and aircraft have mysteriously disappeared. "Space" connected the O-ring failure on the *Challenger* to that episode's storyline of alien beings sabotaging the shuttle program, and "Shapes" managed to work in the FBI incident at the Wounded Knee Indian reservation. Even the sewer-dwelling Flukeman in "The Host" was a quasi-vertebrate human born as Agent Scully noted, "in a primordial soup of radioactive sewage" from Chernobyl.

In reaction to "The Jersey Devil," some online X-Philes accused Carter, who wrote the episode, of getting his facts wrong about the "real" Jersey Devil. One fan on the Internet berated Carter for making "the story look farcical and amateurishly written" by describing the Jersey Devil as "some kind of wild human that was running amok in Jersey. Why would *The X-Files* execs allow a good story to be butchered by writers?"

Remember *The X-Files* is fiction, and there is no rule that Chris Carter or any of the writers are constrained to stick to what is reported in the legends. So there's something running around the East Coast woods. Who says it has to be exactly like the legends of the Jersey Devil? There are layers between the television audience and the truth, which may indeed be out there, even in the New Jersey woods.

Trivia

1. (True or False) In the episode "Humbug," the killer left tracks that appeared to be simian.

2. Mr. Nutt was pulled through his doggie door and killed. What was found in his palm?

3. Who was actually committing the murders in "Humbug"?

X-PERT X-TRA BONUS POINTS #1

What was Sheriff Hamilton's former stage name?

---

4. What was the name of the Canadian fishing trawler that rescued the crew survivors from the USS *Ardent* during the pre-credits sequence in "Dod Kalm"?
    A. *Maple Leaf*
    B. *Lizette*
    C. *Golden Maiden*

5. (Fill in the blank with the correct number) When Mulder, Scully and Trondheim rested, they awakened to find themselves _____ years older.

6. Name the pirate whaler who attacked Trondheim.

X-PERT X-TRA BONUS POINTS #2

What was Scully referring to in "Dod Kalm" when she said, "We have nothing to fear when it's over"?

---

7. Identify the supervisor of the shuttle program in "Space."

8. Who was the space shuttle commander engaged to marry?

9. Name the real-life *Mercury* astronaut who reported a glowing green object approaching his space capsule.

X-PERT X-TRA BONUS POINTS #3

What did Lt. Col. Belt urge the shuttle astronauts to do to prevent the spacecraft from burning up on re-entry?

---

10. Who was found nude and unconscious nearby after Jim Parker was ripped to pieces on his front porch in "Shapes"?

11. Name the Native American man who was killed by Jim and Lyle Parker at the beginning of the episode.

X-PERT X-TRA BONUS POINTS #4

Who was the frequent *X-Files* director at the helm of "Shapes"?

---

12. In "The Host," a Newark sanitation worker was pulled under the sewage, emerging with an odd wound on his back and grumbling about a nasty taste in his mouth. What did he erroneously believe had attacked him?

13. (Fill in the blank dialogue) After the Flukeman was caught in the sewage treatment plant, Mulder said, "It looks like I'm going to have to tell Skinner that the suspect is a giant blood-sucking _____ after all."

14. (True or False) The Flukeman had the potential to adjust at will its own sex or that of its offspring.

X-PERT X-TRA BONUS POINTS #5

A Russian seaman was suddenly dragged into the ship's sewage system during the pre-credits sequence at the beginning of "The Host." What was the translation of the Cyrillic letters tattooed on the sailor's arm?

---

15. (True or False) Mulder theorized that after the death of "The Jersey Devil," its mate had moved into the city to find food.

16.   Who scared off the female Jersey Devil when she trapped a pursuing Agent Mulder?

X-PERT X-TRA BONUS POINTS #6

What was the park ranger's full name?

FILE NO. 2X21:

THE CALUSARI

Declassified Case Overview: When a two-year-old boy was killed in a freak accident, Mulder and a group of Romanian spiritualists determined that an evil spirit had to be exorcised from the boy's older brother.

Nitpicking

During the introduction scene at the amusement park, Charlie Holvey's father has two ice cream cones in his left hand. One has two scoops and the other has only one. As he begins to hand the cone with two scoops to Charlie, the shot switches angle to the boy's perspective, and he takes the cone with only one scoop.

Trivia

1.   (True or False) Mulder analyzed a photograph of the boy's death, which with digital augmentation showed what looked like "some kind of poltergeist activity" involved in baiting the child across the amusement park's miniature railroad track.

2.   How old was Charlie Holvey?

3. What did the boy's grandmother, Golda, draw on his hand?

4. (Fill in the Blank) Scully theorized that Charlie's recurrent illnesses strongly suggested that the X-File was a case of Munchausen by _____, where a parent or caretaker induced symptoms in a child.

5. (Fill in the blank dialogue) The Calusari told Mulder that they were trying to cleanse the Holvey house of an evil that had been there through history and "doesn't care if it kills one boy or a _____ men."

X-PERT X-TRA BONUS POINTS

What was the Calusari name for the Holy Ash, which materialized out of thin air?

Investigative Field Report

Although the evil twin storyline is retread once again in this creative mix of *The Exorcist* and *The Omen,* this generally dark and rather mean-spirited episode is one the series' better installments.

Episode writer Sara B. Charno acknowledged that she developed the idea of the three Romanian exorcists after reading a quote from a 13th-century author who wrote, "Demons ride like particles of dust in the sunbeam; they are scattered everywhere . . . they come down upon us like rain; their multitude fills the whole world, the whole air, yes, the whole air is a thick mass of devils . . ." Now that's the stuff *The X-Files* are made of.

FILE NO. 2X22:

F. EMASCULATA

Declassified Case Overview: While participating in the retrieval of two escaped convicts, Agents Mulder and Scully discovered a highly contagious and deadly disease which had infected many of the inmates and, quite possibly, the escapees as well.

Nitpicking

In the episode's beginning, a scientist discovers the carcass of a wild boar covered with repulsive postules. However, there are no warthogs or wild boar in the rain forests of Costa Rica.

Didn't Scully see *Outbreak*? Here's a highly trained doctor being exposed to an obviously deadly communicable disease and what is she wearing—A surgical suit? No, only a mask and gloves.

When Scully reaches out with her tweezers to extract the bug from the postule of the dead prisoner, she is not wearing a mask. But seconds later, when she closely examines the insect, the mask is on.

Trivia

1. Identify the scientist whose sore-covered body was picked apart by vultures in the Costa Rican rain forest at the episode's beginning.
    A. Dr. Michael Bradshaw
    B. Dr. Robert Torrence
    C. Dr. Bryan Grayson

2. A convict at Cumberland Prison, Virginia, received a package and 18 hours later he, too, was covered with grotesque boils. What was in the package?

3. What were the names of the two escaped prisoners?
    A. Paul and Steve
    B. Teddy and Tom
    C. Billy and Dave

4. (Fill in the blank with the correct number) Dr. Osborne, allegedly from the Center for Disease Control, informed Scully that _____ inmates had been infected with "a flulike illness," with 10 of them dying.
    A. 14
    B. 16
    C. 18

5. Name the drug manufacturer who sent the contaminated package.
    A. Huggins Pharmaceuticals
    B. L. Mercury Jones Medical Supplies, Inc.
    C. Pinck Pharmaceuticals

6. What was the name of Paul's girlfriend, in whose house the escaped prisoners took refuge?

7. Who was Dr. Osborne's *real* employer?

8. (Fill in the Blank) Skinner told Mulder and Scully that because the scientist and the prisoner shared the same name, the controlled experiment could be dismissed as nothing more than just a simple _____ error.

X-PERT X-TRA BONUS POINTS #1

Who said that the government could "control the disease by controlling the information"?

X-PERT X-TRA BONUS POINTS #2

Who said, "Don't believe for a second that this is an isolated incident"?

Investigative Field Report

"Not a particularly emotional show," said director Rob Bowman, "but it's great because there are some things in it that are just about as disgusting as anything you could imagine. I knew I was working on *The X-Files* when I heard myself say, 'I need the pus to go from left to right.' I love that show. It was disgusting but so well done . . . It's about cover-ups, viruses; it's a chase. Basically it was a cops-and-robbers show with a twist."

Makeup effects supervisor Toby Lindala reportedly loves to do things that seem like they're impossible, especially given the tight time frame of an episodic television series. "We had actors rigged with boil pieces on their faces. The boils just keep getting larger until they blow pus. We rigged each of the pieces with two different tubes so that they could spew different distances."

And what was Lindala's response when Director Bowman told him that he was really grossing him out? The obviously grateful makeup effects genius smiled and said, "Thank you."

Trivia alert: Elizabeth's house number in this episode is 925, the birthday of Gillian Anderson's newborn daughter, Piper Maru.

The package mailed to inmate Robert Torrence is numbered DP112148, which is once again the initials and birthdate of Chris Carter's wife.

FILE NO. 2X23:

SOFT LIGHT

Declassified Case Overview: Mulder and Scully's investigation into a series of mysterious disappearances in which the only thing that remained from each victim was a burn mark on the ground, led the two agents to a scientist who had somehow become a human black hole.

Nitpicking

Whenever anyone stepped into Dr. Banton's shadow, the person and their clothes were vaporized by the dark matter. Why didn't the movable black hole swallow other matter it came into contact with—like the floor?

More location shooting problems: During the scene in the train station, one of the cars is clearly marked VIA Rail, which only runs in Canada.

Ouch! Dr. Banton unscrews two burning light bulbs with his bare hands without so much as even a slight grimace on his face.

Scully's former student at the Academy, Kelly Ryan, is vaporized into a little pile of ash, but at the funeral there is a casket.

Trivia

1. How many weeks had Dr. Banton been missing after suffering an accident while experimenting with dark matter and a particle accelerator?
    A. 4
    B. 5
    C. 6

2. (True or False) Dr. Banton's company, Polarity Magnetics, produced airline cargo movers.

3. What did Mulder shoot as Scully closed in on Banton's shadow in the train station?

4. What did Banton fear the government wanted to perform on him to learn what he knew?

5. (Fill in the blank dialogue) Dr. Banton warned the agents, "If I die, there could be nothing left to _____ this thing."

6. Who showed up at the hospital with two "paramedics" saying he was there to transfer Banton?

7. At the end of the episode Dr. Banton was seen hooked to electrodes, half-crazed and the subject of a repetitious experiment. What was it?

X-PERT X-TRA BONUS POINTS #1

What was Mr. X's weapon of choice in this episode?

X-PERT X-TRA BONUS POINTS #2

Who referred to Dr. Banton as "lightning in a bottle"?

Investigative Field Report

More of a science-fiction show than any other *X-Files* episode, the writing staff did their homework on this one and the basic scientific principles which serve as the installment's plot foundation make "Soft Light" wholly believable.

"A fair amount of work for us on that one," explained Chris Carter. "We did some work on a nuclear research facility, a particle accelerator and the necessary computers. It was a good high-tech set, and as contrast we had to build a hospital and government facility where the investigations took place. A good show for us in terms of contrast."

Trivia alert: Mulder and Scully discover that the hotel victim worked for a manufacturer of Morley's cigarettes (the smoking choice of a certain well-known and nefarious nemesis of two federal agents).

MONSTER MASH: SEASON TWO

Just like the multi-sequels to Frankenstein, Dracula, Freddy Krueger, the hockey mask-wearing Jason from the Friday the 13th film series, and a host of other cinematic monsters, we're baaaaaaaack with more M.O.T.W.s that Mulder and Scully encountered during The X-Files' second season.

1. How was Mulder able to cut the Flukeman in half?

2. What was the name of the "honey-like viscous liquid" oozing out of the walls during the exorcism in "The Calusari"?

3. Which real-life human psychopath was death fetishist Donnie Pfaster compared to in "Irresistible"?

4. (True or False) An examination appeared to validate Duane Barry's claim that aliens had previously drilled holes into his teeth.

5. (True or False) Mulder theorized that the animal abductions in "Fearful Symmetry" could have been an act of alien extermination.

6. Identify the "flesh-eating disease" that permanently terminated the teacher prior to Mrs. Paddock in "Die Hand Die Verletzt."

7. In the episode "Excelsius Dei," who saw a poltergeist hovering around Scully?

8. Who ominously declared in "Firewalker," "No one can leave"?

9. (True or False) "3"'s "vampires" Kristen and John were into what she termed "blood games."

10. What were the teenagers *actually* injected with in "Red Museum"? (Hint: Purity Control)

11. Terry O'Quinn played Lt. Tillman in "Aubrey," but he previously portrayed a killer in which movie horror series?

12. (True or False) When Scully went to examine Private McAlpin's body at the base morgue in "Fresh Bones," a jackal's corpse had taken its place.

13. (True or False) The disease-causing parasite in "F. Emasculata" attacked the hypothalamus gland in the brain.

X-PERT X-TRA BONUS

(Fill in the blank with the correct number) The federal poultry inspector's disappearance intrigued Mulder, especially in light of local tales about a _____ foot burn mark found in a nearby field.

FILE NO. 2X24:

OUR TOWN

Declassified Case Overview: Mulder and Scully's investigation of a missing poultry inspector in a small town in Arkansas held the key to the rural community's real delicacy—human beings!

Nitpicking

The autopsy scene shows Scully examining a microscopic slide of Paula's brain. How did she obtain a sample of it without cutting the woman's head open?

When townfolk contracted the extremely rare and fatal Creutzfeldt-Jacob disease, it showed up in their brain tissue within a matter of weeks. Scientists and doctors with the CDC in Atlanta claim that it takes several years for the disease to manifest itself.

Trivia

1. Name the young woman who led George Kearns, a federal poultry inspector, to his death in the woods.
    A. Paula Gray
    B. Tonya Sturtevant
    C. Robin Behan

2. Who did Paula take hostage at knife-point when she became delirious on the assembly line at the poultry processing plant?

3. Who shot and killed Paula?

4. What relation was Paula to Mr. Chaco, founder of Chaco Chicken, the processing plant?

5. (Fill in the blank with the correct number) Mulder noted that

_____ people had disappeared in the area over a span of 59 years.
   A. 76
   B. 87
   C. 93

6. What did Mulder discover in the display cases at Chaco's house?

7. At the end of the episode, what did a laborer find in the poultry feed as the chickens pecked away?

X-PERT X-TRA BONUS POINTS

According to Scully's voice-over at the end of the episode, how old was Chaco?

Investigative Field Report

After the writing staff did some research on chicken processing plants in Arkansas, they discovered that the facilities were perhaps the most despicable and vile environments ever created by human beings—essentially the perfect setting for an *X-Files* episode. Even though the network Standards department was a little concerned about the show's subject matter, Chris Carter and Company somehow pulled off a tasteful cannibalism episode.

Ironically, within a year of "Our Town" 's first TV airdate, panic spread in Europe as news reports suggested a possible link between Mad Cow Disease (formally known as bovine spongiform encephalopathy) and the deadly human brain ailment Creutzfeldt-Jacob. When several young Britons died from the tainted beef, the English government demanded the mass slaughter of English cattle herds in an effort to halt the epidemic. Even McDonald's, which serves 1.8 million customers a day at 660 restaurants in Britain, quit selling Big Macs and Quarter Pounders until supplies of Dutch beef could be imported.

Mr. Chaco and Chaco Chicken are named for Chaco Canyon, New Mexico, where the Anasazi tribe (see following episode) lived and where boiled bones as those depicted in this installment were uncovered.

ANASAZI [PART 1 OF 3]

Declassified Case Overview: Agent Mulder was given a digital audio tape that supposedly contained classified government information on UFOs, but no one could protect him from the consequences.

Nitpicking

After Mulder hauls off and slugs Assistant Director Skinner, he goes before the FBI's equivalent of a court-martial and is threatened with permanent dismissal from the Bureau. Wouldn't a federal law enforcement agency like the FBI do a physical and mental examination of a normally stable Mulder before invoking such extreme disciplinary measures? And wouldn't a physical have included blood and urine tests, which would have detected the LSD-like chemical in his body?

Mulder sure had a clean-shaven mug for a man who had been unconscious for 36 hours after Scully shot him.

Trivia

1. (True or False) The Thinker, one of the Lone Gunmen, cracked the code of the National Security Agency's ultra-secret files on UFOs and alien abductions.

2. What three foreign governments were alerted that the MJ documents had been compromised?
    A. Japanese, German, and Italian
    B. British, French, and Canadian
    C. Russian, Chinese, and British

3. What was the code-name of the multinational black ops unit that the Lone Gunmen claimed was pursuing them?

4. Mulder's neighbor shot her husband to death. How many years had the couple been married?

5. Where did Alex Krycek hide while waiting to murder William Mulder?

6. Who was Agent Mulder attempting to contact when his father called saying he had to see him urgently?

X-PERT X-TRA BONUS POINTS

Identify the World War II Navajo code talker whom Scully introduced Mulder to in New Mexico.

Investigative Field Report

Whereas the first season's finale, "The Erlenmeyer Flask," was action-oriented, season two's cliffhanger "Anasazi" was intensely character-driven. Even though Chris Carter holds fast to the "believer vs. skeptic" relationship between Mulder and Scully, in this episode she seems to have a hopeful, believing edge. Scully definitely knows now that a conspiracy is afoot and someone or some organization is trying to keep certain information from her and her partner. After all she's seen and been through, Scully is in a position to become Mulder.

Chris Carter said at the end of the second season: "I'm very proud of 'Anasazi 's' script. David Duchovny and I worked quite closely on the story and he had a lot of input, and then I sat down and wrote the script. I'm proud of the way it came together, what it did for the series and the overwhelmingly positive response it has gotten. I'm very pleased to begin season three with where this episode puts us—which is that it posed more questions than it answered."

BEHIND THE SCENES: PART II

1. Which episode did writers Glen Morgan and James Wong originally conceive as a feature film unrelated to *The X-Files*?
   A. "Blood"
   B. "Little Green Men"
   C. "Ice"

2. The producers of the show rented a decommissioned submarine from the Canadian Navy to use in three different *X-Files* episodes. Can you name all three?

3. (True or False) To simulate the deserts of New Mexico for the episodes "Anasazi" and "The Blessing Way," the *X-Files* crew sprayed 1,600 gallons of burgundy paint into a gravel pit just outside Vancouver.

4. Gordon Baines portrayed the staff physician at the Chaco Chicken plant in "Our Town." Name his character from "Young at Heart."

5. Didn't Kate Twa look familiar in "Soft Light"? What role did she play in "GenderBender"?

6. (True or False) The disgusting bugs shown on the warthog in the opening sequence of "F. Emasculata" were cockroaches, assassin beetles, and mealworms, none of which belong to the *F. Emasculata* insect group for which the episode was named.

7. (Yes or No) In "Fearful Symmetry," were real zoo animals used in all the scenes?

8. Which episode's final scene was a tribute to the Wes Craven film *The Serpent and the Rainbow*?

9. Which episode's opening credits featured James "Chargers" Wong and Glen "Bolts" Morgan, references to the name and logo of their favorite NFL team who, during the week this episode aired, were playing in the Super Bowl?

10. Name the Minnesota Vikings' player who appeared on the television in Bocks' office in "Irresistible."

11. Which *X-Files* episode was originally scripted to be a crossover storyline involving CBS' *Picket Fences*?
    A. "Fallen Angel"
    B. "Die Hand Die Verletzt"
    C. "Red Museum"

12. Why was Gillian Anderson unusually pale in "One Breath"?

13. In which episode did Darin Morgan, brother of writer Glen Morgan and an *X-Files* wordsmith himself, actually make his debut on the show in reportedly one of "the most God-awful creations ever to be deliberately wrapped around a human body"?

14. Identify the semi-regular actor on *The X-Files* who also had roles in *Return of the Living Dead*, horrormeister Wes Craven's *Shocker* and *Vampire in Brooklyn*?
    A. Mitch Pileggi
    B. Steven Williams
    C. William B. Davis

15. (True or False) The episode "Conduit" revealed Mulder's hometown to be Chilmarc, Massachusetts, though the spelling was "Chilmark" when it turned up nearly a year later in "Little Green Men."

16. In "Shadows," whose real-life name was used in the scene where the parking lot attendant painted over the name on the space that previously belonged to the dead man?
    A. Tom Braidwood
    B. Chris Carter
    C. Glen Morgan

17. Name the classic Spencer Tracy movie which inspired writer Frank Spotnitz to pen "Our Town."

18. Identify the day job of Angelo Vacco, who portrayed Angelo Garza in the "F. Emasculata" episode.
    A. *X-Files* special effects technician
    B. Production assistant in the offices of Ten Thirteen in Los Angeles
    C. A Vancouver prison guard

19. During the boy's exorcism, "The Calusari" used an herb called dragon's blood as a charm against evil. Does the plant actually exist?

20. (True or False) For those who do not speak fluent Romanian, when

Charlie stood over his grandmother before her death in "The Calusari" episode, he said, "You could not stop us, old woman."

X-PERT X-TRA BONUS POINTS #1

Name the guest star in "Darkness Falls" who was a childhood friend of David Duchovny's, was instrumental in his decision to take up acting, and worked with him for a time in New York as a bartender.

---

21. (True or False) The striking visual sequence in "Ghost in the Machine" involving Scully and a vacuum-sucking fan was a last-minute addition when the originally scripted scene with an elevator shaft was deemed too expensive.

22. Who is the famous real-life uncle of the actor who portrayed Mulder's former partner, Jerry Lamana?

23. What type of wires were used to suspend Scott Bellis in the air during the Max Fenig abduction sequence in "Fallen Angel"?

24. (True or False) In the scene in "Beyond the Sea" where Scully's father appears in his daughter's apartment, silently mouthing words, actor Don Davis was actually reciting the 23rd Psalm.

25. *X-Files* co-executive producer R.W. Goodwin's wife, Sheila Larken, has had a recurring role on the series. Name her character.

26. Rob Bowman directed several *Star Trek: The Next Generation* episodes. Which episode marked his *X-Files* directorial debut?
    A. "Ice"
    B. "GenderBender"
    C. "Sleepless"

27. Why was Chris Carter not concerned about parallels between the fictional Kindred in "GenderBender" and the real-life Amish religious group?

28. Episode titles in the series are sometimes rather obscure. What was the origin of the title "Fearful Symmetry"?

29. How many tons of snow and ice were trucked into a soundstage in order to capture the Arctic conditions for "End Game"?
     A. 85
     B. 125
     C. 140

30. Who suggested the dueling head-butts between Skinner and Mr. X for the violent elevator encounter in "End Game"?
     A. Steven Williams
     B. Mitch Pileggi
     C. David Duchovny

31. Which episode was the first one to be told in flashback?

32. Where did writers Glen Morgan and James Wong come up with the idea of the paranoid conspiracy theorists, the Lone Gunmen?

33. Which first season episode received a nomination for an Edgar Award, an honor presented by the Mystery Writers of America?

34. Who was Chris Carter's first preference to be cast in the role of Senator Richard Matheson?
     A. Author Richard Matheson
     B. Darren McGavin
     C. Raymond J. Barry

35. Name the university where "Blood" 's climactic scene in the bell tower was shot.

36. Whose bout with insomnia inspired the "Sleepless" episode?
     A. Howard Gordon
     B. Chris Carter
     C. Rob Bowman

37. As an inside joke alluding to Gillian Anderson's real-life pregnancy, what was Scully buying in the supermarket scene in "Duane Barry"?

38. Which episode was the highest-rated of the first two seasons?

39. Name the first *X-Files* episode directed by Chris Carter.

40. What was the last episode written by Glen Morgan and James Wong before they left *The X-Files* to devote their time to developing and producing the new sci-fi series, *Space: Above and Beyond?*

X-PERT X-TRA BONUS POINTS #2

Colonel Wharton performed his voodoo ritual at the end of "Fresh Bones" in French. What was the English translation?

---

41. Identify the science-fiction writer who suggested to Chris Carter that an effort be made to explain why the forces seeking to thwart Mulder's work didn't simply kill him. (Note: The conversation between Krycek and the Cigarette-Smoking Man in "Ascension" was a direct response to that prevailing question.)
     A. Richard Matheson
     B. Arthur C. Clark
     C. Harlan Ellison

42. (True or False) The song played as Captain Scully's ashes were scattered, and which inspired the title of the episode, is Bobby Darin's "Beyond the Sea."

43. (True or False) In Taipei, Taiwan, and the Republic of China, *The X-Files* airs as *X-Dang An*, while in Finland fans crowd around the tube to await *Salaiset*, which translates in English to "The Secret Files."

44. Whose decision was it to kill off Deep Throat?

45. Previously this *X-Files* actor had roles on *Star Trek: The Next Generation, Time Trax, The Twilight Zone, Quantum Leap, Starman, Lois & Clark,* and *Alfred Hitchcock Presents.* Identify the actor.

46. Name the composer whose spooky theme music for *The X-Files* was nominated for an Emmy.

47. (True or False) By the end of the second season, construction costs for a single episode ran $60,000.

48. Tasha Simms played the mother of Cindy Reardon in "Eve." What role did she have in "Excelsius Dei"?

49. (True or False) The producers considered making Scully's sister, Melissa, a romantic interest for Mulder but later nixed the idea.

50. The Club Tepes featured in the "3" episode was named after what infamous torturer?

51. Who performed David Duchovny's stunts in the aerial tram sequence in "Ascension"?

52. Steve Railsback was impressive as former FBI agent and alien abductee Duane Barry. Name the TV movie in which he originally came to prominence playing a notorious real-life mass murderer.

53. Identify the director of the third season episodes "Paper Clip," "Clyde Bruckman's Final Repose," "The Walk," and "731."
    A. R.W. Goodwin
    B. Rob Bowman
    C. David Nutter

54. (True or False) The famous "black silk boxer shorts" scene in "Fire" was originally a "Jockey underwear" scene.

55. Whose wives were Teena and Cindy named after in "Eve"?

56. (True or False) The address in Samantha Mulder's X-File, 2790 Vine Street, is the former address of *The X-Files* production office in Los Angeles.

57. Name the character whose traitorous and nefarious nature on the series has earned him the nickname "Ratboy" on the Internet.

58. (True or False) William Scully was referred to as a captain in the U.S. Navy, but in "One Breath" he appeared to Dana wearing the uniform of an admiral (one star on the shoulder).

59. What was the significance of Steveston, Massachusetts in the "GenderBender" episode?

60. Tom McBeath, who played Detective Munson in "3," made an appearance as a scientist in which first season episode?

61. In which episode did Mulder have his first and only sexual close encounter?

62. James Leard appeared in the role of Captain Lacerio in "The Erlenmeyer Flask." What was his character's name in "Colony"?

63. The episode "Red Museum" was shot in a real meat plant. Did the series film in a real poultry processing factory in "Our Town" or did the crew construct a lookalike set?

64. Who recommended Steven Williams for the recurring role of Mr. X?

65. Identify the former porn star who played a suburban housewife in "Blood."
    - A.   Lotta Hedd
    - B.   Kimberly Ashlyn Gere
    - C.   Sophie Quinlan

X-PERT X-TRA BONUS POINTS #3

Excluding David Duchovny, name the four other *Twin Peaks* alumni who appeared in various roles during the first two seasons of *The X-Files*.

X-PHILE EPISODE RANKING: SEASON TWO

Note: The following ranking of The X-Files' second season episodes (with 10.0 being the highest) have been posted by fans in various manifestations at official conventions and on the Internet.

Ranking	Episode Title	Ranking	Episode Title
1.	9.33 "Anasazi"	13.	7.69 "Soft Light"
2.	9.15 "Duane Barry"	14.	7.63 "Our Town"
3.	9.09 "Colony"	15.	7.62 "The Host"
4.	9.08 "One Breath"	16.	7.62 "Dod Kalm"
5.	8.98 "End Game"	17.	7.53 "Sleepless"
6.	8.95 "Ascension"	18.	7.44 "Aubrey"
7.	8.61 "Humbug"	19.	7.28 "The Calusari"
8.	8.40 "Die Hand Die Verletzt"	20.	7.21 "Blood"
9.	8.39 "Irresistible"	21.	6.87 "Fresh Bones"
10.	8.10 "F. Emasculata"	22.	6.73 "Firewalker"
11.	8.07 "Little Green Men"	23.	6.38 "3"
12.	7.95 "Red Museum"	24.	6.27 "Excelsius Dei"
		25.	5.25 "Fearful Symmetry"

THE BLESSING WAY
[PART 2 OF 3]

Declassified Case Overview: The Cigarette-Smoking Man continued to relentlessly pursue the missing data tape that documented the government's knowledge of alien visitors. Meanwhile, Agent Mulder hung precariously between life and death and Scully found her own life and career as an FBI agent in jeopardy.

Nitpicking

In the second season finale "Anasazi," which was the first part of "The Blessing Way" continued storyline, Scully is bloodied by a bullet graze across her forehead. Yet, in this episode there is no scar or mark of any kind.

When Scully's car is stopped for a search by camouflaged troops, the male soldier physically checks Scully for the MJ Documents while the female soldier checks out the trunk of the automobile. Rules and regulations governing the military and law enforcement agencies require that women suspects be searched by female soldiers or police officers if present.

Why do Skinner and Scully choose Mulder's apartment of all places for a covert meeting? His place has been bugged, the phone tapped and the entrance under surveillance in hopes of recovering the digital audio tape.

Trivia

1. (Fill in the blank dialogue) In a voice-over, Albert Hosteen, the Navajo tribal leader, said, "While history serves only those who seek to control it, those who would douse the flame of _____ in order to put out the dangerous fire of truth— beware these men."

2. (True or False) Back in Washington, Scully was told she was being suspended for "direct disobedience."

3. (Fill in the blank dialogue) The Cigarette-Smoking Man met with other members of the cabal in a private club in New York City, promising them that the matter of the missing MJ Documents was being handled and that the media attention would amount to "nothing more than a few scattered _____."

4. During his near-death experience, who told Mulder that if he died the truth would die?

5. Who told Scully, "You've built up walls around your true feelings"?

6. At William Mulder's funeral, who told Scully that she had been targeted for murder, perhaps by someone she knew?

X-PERT X-TRA BONUS POINTS #1

Name the New York City street address where the Cigarette-Smoking Man met with his international consortium "associates" in the private club.

X-PERT X-TRA BONUS POINTS #2

Identify the date that the Thinker's body was found at a Trenton, New Jersey landfill, the victim of an execution-style murder.

Investigative Field Report

Not only is "The Blessing Way" a bridge episode, getting us from point A in the second season cliffhanger "Anasazi" to the real action of point C in "Paper Clip," it is also the weakest link in Chris Carter's first trilogy storyline. Admittedly, it would have been difficult for any episode to have lived up to the anticipation established by the previous season finale, but "The Blessing Way" is riddled with plot oversights and inconsistencies.

When Deep Throat appears to Mulder during his near-death experience, why does he call the FBI agent "old friend"? There is nothing from the first season to suggest that their relationship was anything more than professional.

What is Bill Mulder referring to when he tells his son, "You are the memory. It lives in you"? The statement could have been simply a metaphor, but from what we've seen on the series during the past two seasons, we can only assume it must be taken literally.

Scully's reaction to Mulder's alleged death is very disappointing. In "Beyond the Sea," she almost suffered a breakdown when she believed her partner was dead, but in this episode she doesn't even tell a grief-stricken Frohike "I miss him, too," when he sobs in her kitchen about Mulder's passing.

Scully, usually the quintessential skeptic, not only becomes obsessed with government conspiracies and paranormal phenomena in this episode, she actually seems to transform into Mulder. She suffers from insomnia, walks to her mother's house in the middle of the night, is openly insubordinate to Skinner, hangs out with one of the Lone Gunmen, demands that Skinner pursue an investigation based on an obscure newspaper clipping, undergoes regression hypnosis, pulls a gun on her boss, and approaches a grieving family to give them a message based on her own obsessive beliefs and not any cold-hard facts (remember what Mulder did to the family in "Conduit"?).

"The Blessing Way" is really about losses. Scully loses her partner and her job; Mulder loses his father and nearly loses his life. But this episode is also about loss in continuity. The overall pacing of the storyline suffered enormously from the long summer intermission between "Anasazi" and this episode.

FILE NO. 3X02:

PAPER CLIP [PART 3 OF 3]

Declassified Case Overview: Reunited, Agents Mulder and Scully sought evidence of alien experimentation by Nazi war criminals pardoned through Operation Paper Clip, while Assistant Director Skinner tried to bargain with the Cigarette-Smoking Man for their lives.

Nitpicking

Real-life Nazi scientist Wernher von Braun is identified as one of the doctors allowed to escape to the United States after World War II in exchange for their research knowledge, under a secret alliance code-named Operation Paper Clip. Braun, however, defected before the end of the war.

Why would a TOP SECRET, highly secured mountain complex have a coded entrance for the front door, but have an unlocked, clap-trap wooden back door?

Why would Krycek's accomplices allow him to possess the digital audio tape when they planned on killing him with a car bomb?

The Well-Manicured Man provides Mulder and Scully with a hint to the mountain complex's access code by asking, "Do you know what Napier's constant is?" Scully, of course, knows that Napier's constant is the basis for all natural logarithms: 2.71828. Instead, the agents enter the PIN code of 27828 to access the doors.

When Mulder runs outside to see the massive hovering spacecraft, he leaves the door open. Although there is no wind (we would have seen the effects on his hair), the door is closed when Mulder ventures back inside the compound.

In "Conduit," the X-File on Mulder's sister's disappearance gives her name as Samantha T. Mulder. The medical file found at the mountain complex in this episode list her full name as Samantha Ann Mulder.

If Albert Hosteen memorized the tape's entirety, why doesn't he just relate to Mulder and Scully what it contains?

While we can speculate on secret tunnels or compartments, failing to show how Mulder escaped from the boxcar is unforgivable.

Trivia

1. In a voice-over, what animal's birth did Albert Hosteen call "a powerful omen" in Native American legend?

2. Who helped Mulder and Scully locate Victor Klemper, an ex-Nazi scientist who claimed to have known Mulder's father?

3. (True or False) Operation Paper Clip was supposed to have been scrapped in the early 1960s.

4. Who alerted the Well-Manicured Man that Mulder was still alive?

5. How did Mulder and Scully escape from the Well-Manicured Man's "small army"?

6. Skinner met with his two agents to tell them he wanted to trade the tape for their safety and reinstatement to the FBI. What was the name of the café where the covert meeting took place?

7. According to the Well-Manicured Man, what type of vaccinations were used to gather genetic data from millions of people in an effort by the government to create an alien/human hybrid?
    A. Measles
    B. Smallpox
    C. Tuberculosis

8. (True or False) Albert Hosteen had memorized the DAT's contents and related it to thirty other men under his tribe's narrative tradition.

X-PERT X-TRA BONUS POINTS #1

In the opening voice-over, what reptile did Albert Hosteen say symbolized "the healing powers of the Medicine Man"?

X-PERT X-TRA BONUS POINTS #2

In what city and state was Charlotte's Diner located?

Investigative Field Report

One of the major appeals of *The X-Files* from the very beginning was that it allowed intelligent, rational non-believers in UFOs and extraterrestrials to have fun and go along for the ride even if they didn't subscribe to these paranormal theories that defy modern science. We must now say goodbye once and for all to the notion that Mulder may have been hallucinating or was deceived by some shadowy international consortium. With "Paper Clip," Carter and Company daringly jar us out of our comfort zones to reveal that there are actually ETs cruising the skies in awesome motherships.

The *X-Files* has also now entered a new dimension with substantial character development, giving us a more coherent background against which to understand the series. Mulder learns that his sister was sacrificed for him, Scully discovers that her sister died in her place, Skinner finally decides where his loyalties are, and the Cigarette-Smoking Man loses some of his menace when it is revealed that he is merely a pawn of a darker, yet more sinister international cabal. This ambitious revamping of the series breaks the mold of the previous two seasons, appealing to new viewers as well as appeasing the appetites of the veteran X-Philes.

D.P.O.

Declassified Case Overview: Agent Mulder was skeptical over a coroner's report regarding the fifth person to be struck by lightning in a small Oklahoma town. The X-File investigation into the latest death seemed to point to a serial killer who was able to harness the power of lightning.

Nitpicking

Although the previous three episodes were pivotal in the development of Mulder and Scully's characters, this installment suffers from serious continuity problems. You would expect to see our dynamic duo attempt in some way to integrate the life-changing experiences they went through (comas, abductions, the murders of close family members), but "D.P.O." is simply back to business-as-usual. One disturbing aspect of UFO experiences are reports of alien mind manipulation as many people have claimed that large tracts of their waking and sleeping lives have been wiped from their memories. Maybe this is what happened to Mulder and Scully.

Location filming snafu: Oklahoma is our neighboring state and we've never seen it look so lush, forested and green. We understand that *The X-Files* films in Vancouver and we always try to suspend our disbelief, but the accents sounded like they had been transplanted from another Fox series: *Beverly Hills, 90210.*

Trivia

1. What was the time span between the events that concluded "Paper Clip" and the X-File investigation begun in this episode?
    A.   3 weeks
    B.   2 months
    C.   5 months

2. What did the initials D.P.O. stand for?

3. Oswald had a crush on his remedial reading teacher and wanted to run away with her. What was her name?
    A.   Sharon Kiveat
    B.   Karen Droms
    C.   Sally Dickson

4. (True or False) When Oswald finally forced his teacher to accompany him, he rambled around trying to decide whether to steal a Japanese or an American car.

5. Name the local sheriff who grilled Scully about the unorthodox medical evidence.

6. What fell to the pavement when Oswald's friend, Zero, was struck down in the parking lot?

7. What did Oswald call his unique ability to focus lightning through his body?
    A.   "Special powers"
    B.   "Gifts from heaven"
    C.   "Special talents"

8. (True or False) Mulder noted that all of Oswald's victims were males between the ages of 16 and 22.

X-PERT X-TRA BONUS POINTS #1

(Fill in the blank dialogue) The heart of one of Oswald's victims was described during post-mortem as being "_____ in the chest."

X-PERT X-TRA BONUS POINTS #2

What was *Mr.* Kiveat's first name?

Investigative Field Report

Although "D.P.O." never shows us the changes in Mulder and Scully's personalities caused by the events of the previous three-part storyline, this episode can certainly stand alone on its own merits and remind viewers that aside from the occasional government conspiracy arc, *The X-Files* is one of the creepiest and most fun shows to watch on TV.

"D.P.O." is your basic Monster-of-the-Week installment, albeit in the form of some loser redneck kid who has acquired the Zeus-like ability to focus lightning through his body. Giovanni Ribisi gives a solid performance as this classic example of wasted protoplasm and Howard Gordon, a veteran *X-Files* screenwriter who wrote "Conduit," "Fallen Angel" and "Dod Kalm," delivers an unusually straight-ahead episode. Noticeably absent is the characteristic ninety degree plot turns. With "D.P.O.," the audience knows from the beginning who the monster is and what he can do.

After three episodes of complex, multi-layered government conspiracies, it's mildly amusing to hear Mulder shout, "I'm going after Oswald!" It sounds like something the Lone Gunmen would say.

Trivia alert: The Johnson County sheriff makes reference to the town's Astadourian Lightning Observatory while lecturing Scully. Mary Astadourian is the chief researcher and office manager for Ten Thirteen Productions, as well as Chris Carter's personal assistant.

FED X

Behind the Scenes with the Supporting Cast

Although Jerry Hardin's shadowy character Deep Throat was assassinated in the first season's final episode, Mitch Pileggi (Walter Skinner), Nicholas Lea (Agent Krycek), Steven Williams (Mr. X), and William B. Davis (the really nefarious Cigarette-Smoking Man) have transformed their minor roles on The X-Files into significant supporting parts. You may know that Skinner had an out-of-body experience in Vietnam, or that the Cigarette-Smoking Man sucks endlessly on his trademark Morley's, but how well do you really know the men who portray these enigmatic Feds with mysterious pasts and equally mysterious agendas?

1. Mitch Pileggi was born in Portland, Oregon. Besides Los Angeles and Austin, Texas, in which foreign country was the actor raised?
    A. Greece
    B. Saudi Arabia
    C. Turkey

2. Which of the four actors had a recurring role as "a cop with a bad attitude" on the ABC-TV series *The Commish*?

3. Identify the cable movie in which William Davis played a gentle grandfather.
    A. *Circumstances Unknown*
    B. *Something about Grandpa*
    C. *Season of Change*

4. Which actor appeared in the feature film *Twilight Zone: The Movie*?

5. (True or False) Steven Williams has stated in interviews that people say he's cold and uncaring, not too dissimilar from the government informant he plays on the series.

6. (True or False) William Davis was once a Canadian national bob-sledding champion.

7. Nicholas Lea was the lead singer of which alternative rock band for five years?
    A. Beau Monde
    B. Crooked and Steep
    C. Before Sunrise

8. Who does Mitch Pileggi play golf with during off-hours on the set of *The X-Files*?

9. Which one of the four actors has said, "I believe in aliens, but I don't think they're among us"?

10. What was the last name of the police captain Steven Williams played for several years on *21 Jump Street*?

11. Who appeared on TV in *Stephen King's It* and *MacGyver*?

12. Which musical instrument do Pileggi and Lea both play?
    A. Trombone
    B. Saxophone
    C. Guitar

13. What was the name of Pileggi's psychotic character who returned from the grave in Wes Craven's horror movie *Shocker*?

14. Which actor appeared in guest spots on TV's nighttime soap operas *Dallas* and *Models Inc.*?

15. Which TV character has Steven Williams acknowledged as the inspiration for his Mr. X role?

16. Which one of the four men has confessed, "I don't fear ghosts and aliens, but I do fear the people who believe that there's a conspiracy"?

17. Who played a kindly doctor in *Look Who's Talking?*

18. What role did Mitch Pileggi assay in a production of *Jesus Christ Superstar*?

19. What type of books did Nicholas Lea read as background research for his role as Mulder's double-agent partner?

20. Pileggi stays in shape with in-line skates. What does Lea do for exercise?

21. Who was a boxer during a two-year stint in the Army?

22. Which actor was a model for a short time in Chicago?

23. (True or False) William Davis quit smoking in 1986.

24. Davis' character's distinctive manner of holding a cigarette between the thumb and forefinger is the way the actor used to smoke tobacco. On camera, what type of cigarette does he incessantly puff on?

25. Before becoming an actor in 1980, which one of the four was an overseas contractor, surviving coups and travels through the Middle East?

26. (True or False) Pileggi shaved his head for his first two *X-Files* auditions.

27. Where was Steven Williams raised?
    A. New Orleans
    B. Memphis
    C. Little Rock

28. Who appeared on episodes of Fox's time-travelling *Sliders* series?

X-PERT X-TRA BONUS POINTS #1

Which of the four actors received a degree in business?

X-PERT X-TRA BONUS POINTS #2

Name the Vancouver acting school that William Davis serves as a director and teacher.

CLYDE BRUCKMAN'S FINAL REPOSE

Declassified Case Overview: Agents Mulder and Scully enlisted the reluctant assistance of a truly gifted clairvoyant when fortune tellers who could not predict their own murders fell victim to a serial killer.

Nitpicking

Bruckman tells Mulder that he has the same recurring dream every night in which he is lying naked in a field of red tulips. Although we have no desire to see actor Peter Boyle even *partially* naked, the dream is dramatized by showing him in a T-shirt and underwear.

Trivia

1. Clyde Bruckman read about the Stupendous Yappi's predictions on the front page of a tabloid. Name it.

2. Identify the dead rock-and-roll star who Yappi claimed faked his own death.
    A. Elvis
    B. The Big Bopper
    C. Buddy Holly

3. What was Bruckman's favorite alcoholic beverage?

4. (True or False) Bruckman was employed as a life insurance salesman for a company called General Indemnity.

5. (Fill in the blank dialogue) Mulder informed the other crime scene investigators that "Satanists take the _____ and leave the body."

6. Bruckman had a vision of the serial killer foreseeing Mulder's

death in a kitchen immediately after the agent stepped on a pie. What flavor was it?

    A. Coconut cream

    B. Sweet potato

    C. Banana cream

7. (True or False) Bruckman, in a sly tease to Mulder, hinted that the agent would die of auto-erotic asphyxiation.

X-PERT X-TRA BONUS POINTS #1

Identify the hotel that was used as a safe house to protect Bruckman from the killer.

X-PERT X-TRA BONUS POINTS #2

How many aces was Bruckman holding in the poker game?

Investigative Field Report

As usual, episode writer Darin Morgan ("Humbug") has penned a successful mix of gripping suspense, quirky humor and genuinely moving moments. We bit our nails, we cried, and we laughed at the fast-flying one-liners and the priceless scenes between the title character and Mulder. Superbly personified by veteran character actor Peter Boyle, hapless and reluctant psychic Clyde Bruckman is certainly one of the more memorable and tragic figures to appear on *The X-Files*.

Bruckman's burdensome ability to foresee others' deaths is obviously a unique psychic gift. Abraham Lincoln foretold his assassination after a vivid dream and was proved right within a few days. The sudden death of John Lennon was also predicted when psychic Alex Tanous appeared on a radio show called "Unexplained Phenomena" in September 1980. Three months later, the former Beatle fell victim to an assassin's bullet only yards from the studio that broadcast the prediction.

Repeat Tour of Duty Award: Dwight McFee (Detective Havez) made his fourth *X-Files* appearance in this episode.

Trivia alert: Did anyone recognize the clearing in the forest as the same one from first season's "Conduit"?

Clyde Bruckman was the name of a 1920–30s Hollywood film director.

Detective Havez, the officer assigned to watch Clyde Bruckman in the hotel room, is named for Jean C. Havez, who collaborated with the real Clyde Bruckman on numerous Buster Keaton screenplays.

The dead man under the wheels of Mulder and Scully's car is named Claude Dukenfield, the real name of W.C. Fields, whom Clyde Bruckman directed in numerous short films.

FILE NO. 3X05:

THE LIST

Declassified Case Overview: An executed prisoner's enemies list and his promise to come back from the grave to wreak revenge became the focal points of Mulder's and Scully's investigation into the grisly murders at a southern prison.

Nitpicking

Considering that this episode is one of *The X-Files'* most graphic (rapidly decomposing and maggot-infested bodies, headless corpses, bloody interrogations and car wrecks), you'd think the show's staff wouldn't shy away from the actual mechanics of how prisoners die in the electric chair. In real-life, electrocution causes the eyes to bleed from the corners, but Neech Manley has his shut tight in the pre-credits sequence. Prison officials also insert a mouthguard to keep the victim from biting his tongue off. Neech, however, only grits his teeth. Unlike this episode, electrodes are not placed at the temples; one goes on top of the head and the other on the lower leg to facilitate the flow of electricity through the heart, effectively stopping it.

Trivia: The Numbers Game

(NOTE: Because of the difficulty of the following questions, all correct answers will count as a five-point X-PERT X-TRA BONUS.)

1. How long had Napoleon "Neech" Manley been on death row?

2. Not counting Neech, how many men knew the identity of his hooded executioner?

3. How many months had Vincent Parmelly been employed at Eastpoint State Penitentiary?

4. What was Neech Manley's prison number?

5. (Fill in the Blank) Danielle Manley had _____ personal visits with her husband in prison in the past eleven years.

6. How many times had Manley previously been strapped to the electric chair before the execution was finally carried out?

7. In what year was Manley convicted for double-murder?

8. How many names were on the enemy list?

9. What was the license plate number of the car Mulder and Scully were driving?

Investigative Field Report

Chris Carter himself wrote and directed this ambitious but flawed episode in which Mulder and Scully not only dismiss the paranormal aspects of this *X-File*, but they seem outright oblivious to the very human crimes being committed by the thuggish guards and sadistic warden. Considering all they've investigated in the previous two years, it almost seems as if the two agents are sleepwalking through this episode.

The word tossed around so often in "The List" is "reincarnation," which according to certain Eastern religions involves an "old" soul being reborn into a new life, usually as a child born after the death of the original person. That also was the theory behind the premise in the first season episode "Born Again." Keeping these facts in mind, why is Mulder suggesting that a full-grown adult could be the suspect in the murders that occur only days after Neech Manley's execution?

Also debated is the possibility of soul transmigration (see "Lazarus"), the theory that the soul of a dying person is transplanted into another individual's body. Once again, this is highly unlikely since the audience sees Manley in the backseat of the warden's car during the final scenes of the episode.

Perhaps, though, Neech Manley is reincarnated as a fly, since a really big one in particular keeps showing up whenever a murder is about to take place. A man reincarnated as a fly? Now *that* would make for a genuinely fresh and imaginative X-File.

FILE NO. 3X06:

2SHY

Declassified Case Overview: A series of dead bodies coated with a gelatinous fluid led Mulder and Scully in search of an Internet Cassanova who preyed on lonely and insecure overweight women.

Nitpicking

Scully dates this episode as August 29 when she performs an autopsy, but events in two previous episodes, "D.P.O." and "Clyde Bruckman's Finale Repose," occurred in September.

When Mulder interviews the first victim's roommate, she tells him about the online chat rooms. He then *immediately* calls Scully and informs his partner that he has *already* called the Internet service. We never knew that Mulder was such a fast talker.

If those Italian works of literature quoted in the letters are so rare, how does Mulder find them so easily and how can they manage to narrow a list of those who have access to them?

The building shown twice as the establishing camera shot for the Cleveland police headquarters is in actuality the First District Police Headquarters building in Washington, D.C.

Trivia

1. Identify the local detective who vehemently objected to Scully being on his investigative team.
    A. Mark Cassidy
    B. Alan Cross
    C. Rick O'Kelley

2. (Fill in the Blank) Scully's analysis revealed strange discrepancies in the victims' weight and body _____.

3. Identify the strange gelatinous substance that coated each victims' bodies.

4. (Fill in the blank dialogue) After his outrageous patronizing about women in law enforcement, the detective stated self-righteously, "I'm not being sexist here. I'm just being _____."

5. This episode's M.O.T.W. was a "fat-sucking vampire" with a truly monstrous appetite. What was its character's name?

6. Two of the women that he dated were superstitious. Identify the lucky charms that each of them had.

X-PERT X-TRA BONUS POINTS #1

(Fill in the Blank) Scully discovered that her autopsy subject had reduced itself to primordial soup and that the body seemed to have lost all its _____ tissue.

X-PERT X-TRA BONUS POINTS #2

Whose deliquescent remains were seen slopping over the morgue drawer?

Investigative Field Report

"Unlike most monster episodes on this series, this particular one was approached from a totally different angle," admitted first-time *X-Files* screenwriter Jeff Vlaming. "Incanto wasn't some weird death fetishist like "Irresistible" 's Donnie Pfaster or simply a homicidal maniac like the no-name serial killer in "Clyde Bruckman." Incanto's fat-sucking vampire was most like "Squeeze" 's Tooms in that he needed to kill simply for physical survival."

Although Timothy Carhart's solid performance as the urbane and intelligent Vincent Incanto makes "2Shy" probably the best M.O.T.W. episode since the first season, it is actually Gillian Anderson's cool, competent and self-confident portrayal of Scully that makes this *X-Files* installment such a delight to watch. When she refuses to be fazed by Detective Cross' sexist boys' club, her composure and professionalism wins his grudging respect later on and he consents to let Scully brief his men about the case. Go girl!

S & M: SEASON THREE

The rapid-fire verbal gunplay between Scully and Mulder intensified even more in the series' third season. Identify the episodes in which the following "Scullyisms" and "Mulderisms" occurred.

1. MULDER: "Scully, you are the only one I trust."
    SCULLY (holding a gun on Mulder): "You're in on it. You're one of them. You're one of the people who abducted me. You put that thing in my neck. YOU KILLED MY SISTER!"

    Episode _____

2. MULDER: "What are you watching?"
    SCULLY: "Your alien autopsy video."
    MULDER: "You mean I get my $29.95's worth after all?"

    Episode _____

3. MULDER: "Go ahead."
    SCULLY: "No, you go ahead."
    MULDER: "No, I know how much you love snapping on the latex."

    Episode _____

4. (Mulder is playing the answering machine)
    SCULLY: "Find anything?"
    MULDER: "No, but I'm really beginning to like the tune."

    Episode _____

5. (Mulder and Scully are viewing the remains of a half-eaten, waterlogged corpse)
    SCULLY: "We eat fish and fish eat us."
    MULDER: "Are fish also known for eating half and saving half for later?"

    Episode _____

6. (Mulder and Scully are in a mine in West Virginia)
    SCULLY: "What do you think your father would have been doing here?"
    MULDER: "I dunno . . . but he never came home wearing a miner's cap."

    Episode _____

7. MULDER: "Imagine if you could come back and take out five people who had caused you to suffer. Who would they be?"
    SCULLY: "I only get five?"
    MULDER: "I remembered your birthday this year, didn't I, Scully?"

    Episode _____

8. MULDER (on possible suspects): "Maybe it's just a . . . very disgruntled altar boy."
    SCULLY: "Well, that narrows down the field."

    Episode _____

9. SCULLY: ". . . because they know they could drop you in the mid-

dle of a desert and tell you the truth is out there and you'd ask them for a shovel."
MULDER: "Is that what you think of me?"
SCULLY: "Well, maybe not a shovel. (A pause) Maybe a backhoe."

Episode _____

10. SCULLY: "The dog ate the cat."
DOCTOR: "I also found what appears to be bits of rat fur. I think the rat ate the poison."
SCULLY: "The cat ate the rat."
MULDER: "And the dog ate the cat."

Episode _____

11. (Mulder and Scully are examining the body of a dead prostitute)
SCULLY: "There was some irritation, probably an allergic reaction to the latex."
MULDER: "At least they were having safe sex."

Episode _____

12. SCULLY: ". . . The very idea of intelligent alien life is not only astronomically improbable, but at its most basic level downright anti-Darwinian."
MULDER: "Scully . . . what are you wearing?"

Episode _____

X-PERT X-TRA BONUS POINTS #1

(Fill in the blank dialogue from the episode "2Shy")
MULDER: "Okay, it's not yet the finely detailed insanity that you've come to expect from me. It's just a theory, but what if he's not doing this out of a psychotic impulse but rather out of some physical hunger? Maybe he needs to replenish this _____ deficiency in order to survive.
SCULLY: "From a dry skin sample you're concluding what? That he's some kind of fat-sucking vampire?"

---

13. MULDER: "Be honest, Scully. Doesn't that propane tank bear more than a slight resemblance to a fat little white Nazi stormtrooper?"
SCULLY: "Mulder, the human mind naturally seeks the meaningful patterns and configurations in things that don't inherently have any. Given the suggestion of a particular image, you couldn't help but see that shape somewhere. If that tank weren't there, you'd see it in a . . . in a rock or in a tree."
MULDER: "Did you answer my question?"
SCULLY: "Yes, it looks like a fat little white Nazi stormtrooper, but that only proves my point."

Episode _____

14. SCULLY: ". . . I hope you're not thinking this has anything to do with government conspiracies or UFOs."
MULDER: "None of the evidence so far indicates either one of those possibilities."

Episode _____

15. SCULLY: "Chantilly Lace?"
MULDER: "You *know* what I like."

Episode _____

16. MULDER: "Will you let me drive?"
SCULLY: "I'm driving. Why do you always have to drive? Because you're the guy? Because you're the big, macho man?"
MULDER: "No, I was just never sure your little feet would reach the pedals."
SCULLY (mockingly): "I'm a macho man . . ."

Episode _____

17. SCULLY: "Mulder, this town is insane."
MULDER: "Where are you?"
SCULLY: "In a convenience store just outside . . . civilization."

Episode _____

18. SCULLY: "That's spooky."
MULDER: "That's my name."

Episode _____

19. (Mulder and Scully are reviewing a black-and-white videotape in bad condition)
     MULDER: "It looks like the fuselage of a plane."
     SCULLY: "It's an American P51 Mustang."
     US NAVAL GUY (leaning in to look at the monitor): "Yeah, it sure is."
     MULDER: "I just got very turned on."

     Episode _____

20. SCULLY: "Do you know how much the human body is worth?"
     MULDER: "Depends on the body."

     Episode _____

21. SCULLY: "What would a Japanese diplomat be doing in that house with a dead man . . . with his head stuffed in a pillow case?"
     MULDER: "Obviously not strengthening international relations."

     Episode _____

22. SCULLY (discussing the ability to reincarnate): "Being obsessed with it doesn't mean you can do it."
     MULDER: "No, unless he knew something we don't."
     SCULLY: "Like what, the magic password?"

     Episode _____

23. SCULLY: "Mr. Jarvis, my religious convictions are hardly the issue here."
     JARVIS: "But they are. How can you help Kevin if you don't believe? Even the killer, he believes."
     MULDER: "Townfolk wonder why I sleep in Sundays."

     Episode _____

24. SCULLY: "Mulder, you're not thinking about trespassing on government property again, are you? I know you've done it in the past but I don't think this case warrants . . ."
     MULDER: "Too late. I'm already inside."
     SCULLY: (Heavy sigh)

     Episode _____

25. MULDER: "If it's no bother—if it's not too big a deal—maybe you can get me a few photographs of that thing which bears absolutely no resemblance to a horned beast."
SCULLY: "Sure. Fine. (Snaps on latex glove) Whatever."

    Episode _____

26. MULDER: ". . . I believe that what we're looking for is in the X-Files. I'm more certain than ever that the truth is in there."
SCULLY: "I've heard the truth, Mulder. Now what I want are the answers."

    Episode _____

27. MULDER (referring to a female detective): "You don't suppose she's a virgin, do you?"
SCULLY: "I doubt she's even a blonde."

    Episode _____

X-PERT X-TRA BONUS POINTS #2

(Fill in the blank dialogue from the episode "War of the Coprophages")
MULDER: "Did you know that the ancient Egyptians worshipped the _____ beetle and possibly erected the pyramids to honor them, which may be giant symbolic dung heaps?"
SCULLY: "Did you know the inventor of the flush toilet was named Thomas Crapper?"

X-CEPTIONAL ONE-LINERS

(NOTE: Because of the difficulty of associating the following one-line "Scullyisms" and "Mulderisms" with their corresponding episode titles, all correct answers will count as a 5-point X-PERT X-TRA BONUS.)

28. MULDER (as he hands a pencil to Frohike): "Don't drop that. That's a finely calibrated piece of investigative equipment."

    Episode _____

29. SCULLY: "Please explain to me the scientific nature of the whammy?"

     Episode _____

30. MULDER: "You'd be surprised what's not on the map in this country and what the government will do to keep it that way."

     Episode _____

31. MULDER: "If my Miss Manners serves me right, that protrusion from his left cornea is a salad fork."

     Episode _____

32. SCULLY: "I'm not going to ask if you just said what I think you said because I know it's what you said."

     Episode _____

33. MULDER: "Personally, if someone digs me up in a thousand years, I hope there's a curse for them, too."

     Episode _____

34. SCULLY: "That was Detective Manners. He said they found your bleeping UFO."

     Episode _____

35. SCULLY: "How is it that you're able to go out on a limb whenever you see a light in the sky, but you're unwilling to accept the possibility of a miracle even when it's right in front of you?"

     Episode _____

36. SCULLY: "I think the lack of discretion is the least of his sins."

     Episode _____

37. SCULLY: "I hate to say this, Mulder, but I think you just ran out of credibility."

     Episode _____

38. SCULLY: "Yeah, scorpions predigest their food outside of their body by regurgitating onto their prey, but . . . I don't know too many scorpions who surf the Internet."

     Episode _____

39. MULDER: "Sometimes the only sane response to an insane world is insanity."

     Episode _____

40. SCULLY: "I can't take you anywhere."

     Episode _____

41. SCULLY: "So, what? Are we supposed to charge him with assaulting a cellular phone?"

     Episode _____

42. SCULLY: "If I'm right, this is one man who left his heart in San Francisco."

     Episode _____

43. MULDER: "This may not be the time to mention it, but somebody is wearing my favorite perfume."

     Episode _____

FILE NO. 3X07:

THE WALK

Declassified Case Overview: Another failed suicide attempt by a patient at a veterans hospital piqued Agent Mulder's interest with the talk of a "phantom soldier" who could walk where no man could walk, saw the Gulf War vets no matter where they hid, and seemed to know all their secrets.

Nitpicking

Captain Janet Draper is wearing infantry branch insignia on her green class "A's." Females are not permitted to either enlist or commission into the infantry branch.

Lieutenant Colonel Victor Stans is addressed during the episode as "Lieutenant Colonel." According to military regulations, the proper way to address an LTC is simply as "Colonel."

A post commander resides on almost every Army base. General Callahan, as the commanding officer of the post, should not have been living off-base.

According to standard operating military procedures, when the threat to the general is elevated, not only should he be required to have uniformed MP's guarding his quarters, he should have also been assigned plainclothes security officers.

Trivia

1. What did Mulder use to prove his theory that an "astrally projected" spirit was bent on torturing its victims?

2. Name the quadruple amputee who Mulder suspected was behind the whole scenario.

3. Who said, "I don't want to *handle it.* I want my son back"?

4. Who did Mulder tell, "You're a soldier. You knew what you were risking when you signed up"?

    A. Quinton "Roach" Freely
    B. Leonard "Rappo" Trimble
    C. Lt. Colonel Victor Stans

5. Where were General Callahan and Scully when she confronted him with a litany of tragedies erased from the records of his men?

6. Where was Captain Janet Draper, the general's aide, killed?

7. What was Trevor playing with in the sand when he was killed?

X-PERT X-TRA BONUS POINTS

Name the Sonja Henie and Glen Miller movie that was playing on the TV when Mulder and Scully questioned the amputee.

Investigative Field Report

"The Walk," written by John Shiban (another first-time *X-Files* wordsmith), gets uncomfortably up close and personal with the issue of disabled veterans, forcing the audience to look at them with both sympathy and apprehension inextricably mixed. We can actually feel Rappo's simmering hostility, the adamant integrity of General Callahan, and the anguish and pain of the disfigured Lieutenant Colonel Stans.

The highlight of this "five-star" episode (and we're not referring to the general) is Gillian Anderson's cool, competent, and self-confident Scully. Without resorting to a feminist rant that would have come across as bitchy or grating, this daughter of a Navy officer dauntlessly confronts not only the uniformed authority of the Army general but the derogatory sexual overtures of Rappo. It is a welcome relief to see Scully show a new level of strength and no-nonsense assertiveness and Mulder's slightly impressed "go girl!" expression during the scene with the general is priceless.

FILE NO. 3X08:

OUBLIETTE

Declassified Case Overview: Agent Mulder protected a suspect in a kidnapping case who seemed to have a psychic connection to the missing girl, while Scully insisted that the woman was part of the kidnap plan, a suspicion confirmed with DNA analysis.

Nitpicking

Scully, a highly trained medical doctor, stops Mulder from administering CPR on Amy after just a few seconds, which is patently wrong. Drowning victims, especially a young healthy girl suddenly drowned in cold water, have an excellent chance of revival as much as 45 minutes after CPR has commenced.

The pacing of the entire episode seems out of sync, with some scenes so hurried that we can barely discern the dialogue being rattled off at warp speed, and other scenes so needlessly stretched out we keep expecting some earth-shattering revelation that never arrives. Case in point: Mulder arrives at the halfway house, gets out of the car, climbs the stairs, walks across a porch, climbs more stairs, knocks on a door, is admitted, etc. Yet, the climactic CPR scene with Amy is only given a few seconds.

Trivia

1. What was the time digitally displayed on Amy Jacob's bedroom alarm clock when she was kidnapped and simultaneously on Lucy Householder's wristwatch?

2. What did Carl Wade say to Amy after he crawled through her open bedroom window and put his hand over her mouth?
    A. "Nobody's going to spoil our fun"
    B. "Nobody's going to spoil us"
    C. "Be a good little girl and Daddy will spoil you"

3. Identify the regional FBI Special Agent In Charge of Amy's kidnapping case.

4. Which hospital was Lucy taken to after going into a seizure at work?

5. What was the distance across town from Amy's house to the restaurant where Lucy collapsed?

6. How old was Amy?

X-PERT X-TRA BONUS POINTS #1

What was the name of the halfway house?

X-PERT X-TRA BONUS POINTS #2

How many liters of water did the state pathologist find in Lucy's lungs?

Investigative Field Report

Just as "The Walk" was Gillian Anderson's acting *tour de force*, then "Oubliette" provides David Duchovny with the opportunity to showcase an unforgettable performance. Entirely fresh dimensions of Mulder's complex character are laid bare in this episode, such as his sensitive and protective nature.

Duchovny plays his character as deadpan as ever, but the resonance in his voice, and most importantly, his body language communicate the emotion flowing past Mulder's safeguards, exposing the agent's emotions more persuasively than his more typical simple grimace would have. Mulder is compassionate without being maudlin, and his kind and indefatigable sympathy finally breaks through the anger, bitterness and self-pity that seal off Lucy Householder (Tracey Ellis) from the rest of humanity.

After several weeks of unnecessary gore such as maggot-infested bodies and morgue drawers slopping over with the remains of the killer's victims, we feel cheated when Mulder simply shoots Carl Wade in the back while he crosses the stream. Be honest, how many of you wanted to see his head explode like an overripe watermelon dropped from a six-story building? We thought so.

NISEI [PART 1 OF 2]

Declassified Case Overview: After receiving a mail order videotape of a purported alien autopsy, the agents' follow-up investigation led Scully to a group of women who claimed to have recognized her from her abduction the previous year and Mulder pursued a train car which possibly carried a living alien being.

Nitpicking

When Senator Matheson informs Mulder of the assassination of the four Japanese, he states that the murders had occurred several weeks earlier. When Mulder briefs Scully, however, he tells her that someone must have been able to identify the four doctors who were performing the alien autopsy because they were slain the day before.

The exterior camera shot of the police station in Allentown, Pennsylvania is of a building surrounded by several trees and captioned in the left corner of the TV screen as "substation B." In actuality, the police station in Allentown is located in the heart of the city and is not sectioned off alphabetically.

Trivia

1. Identify the number of the train car which was attacked by a black-clad hit squad at the beginning of the episode.
    - A. 82517
    - B. 82594
    - C. 84315

2. How much did Mulder pay for the videotape of the alien autopsy?

3. Mulder said he answered the ad for the tape from a video pirate who pulled it off a satellite dish at two in the morning. Where did this high-tech Blackbeard reside?

4. What was the name of the video pirate's production company?
    A. Secrets for Sale, Inc.
    B. They're Out There Videos, Etc.
    C. Rat Tail Productions

5. Who identified the Japanese salvage ship in the satellite photos as the *Talapus*?

6. Whose name was circled on the MUFON membership listing found in the Japanese diplomat's briefcase?
    A. Lottie Halloway
    B. Laura Christine
    C. Betsy Hagopian

7. (Fill in the blank dialogue) Senator Matheson told Mulder that "_____ are the only real currency we deal in."

8. How many Japanese nationals, all doctors and former military medical officers, were murdered on the train car in Knoxville, Tennessee?

9. In what year had Dr. Takeo Ishimaru supposedly died?

X-PERT X-TRA BONUS POINTS #1

What was Senator Matheson's three-word reply when Mulder asked him, "What am I on to here?"

X-PERT X-TRA BONUS POINTS #2

What was the number of the train car Mulder was pursuing at the end of the episode?

Investigative Field Report

As with all of the *X-Files* episodes that Chris Carter calls the "mythology" storylines—the installments dealing with aliens and government cover-ups—"Nisei" crams a great deal of complex information into a limited amount of time. Not only do the scenes rush past the audience, but the characters themselves speak at breakneck speed in an effort to elevate the tension and also convey a lot of data rapidly.

"Nisei" opens with a surreptitious autopsy aboard a train car, which is interrupted by masked commandos who machine-gun the Japanese surgeons and retrieve the patient, who appears to be an alien lifeform in the very brief glimpse we get of it. Mulder purchases a pirated videotape of the incident and Scully scoffs that the purported alien autopsy is even worse than the recent special on the Fox network which allegedly showed the medical examinations of alien bodies recovered from the legendary UFO crash at Roswell, New Mexico in 1947.

As debate continues over whether the film shown on TV is an authentic alien autopsy or a merely a deplorable hoax, potential purchasers of the videotape should be aware that hardly anything about the footage has been verified by independent research. The video is accompanied by the following caveats from the distributor: "Whilst the [film] stock has been verified as manufactured in 1947, we cannot currently warrant that the contents were filmed in 1947. Although our medical reports suggested that the creature is not human, this cannot be verified. Although we have been informed that the footage emanates from the Roswell incident, this has not yet been verified."

A THIRD HELPING OF ALPHABET SOUP

This is your last chance to fill up on your favorite soup (no, not the primordial soup from "The Host"). Continuing with where we left off before, fill in the blank with the correct answer that corresponds to the letter of the alphabet. Oh, by the way, the loser does the dishes.

L is for . . .

1. Name of the actress who portrayed Scully's mother, Margaret:
   _____.

2. He was one of the Lone Gunmen. Identify this good-natured paranoid: _____.

M is for . . .

3. In 1967, she saw a UFO with other members of a Girl Scout troop: _____.

4. He penned the third season episodes "Clyde Bruckman's Final Repose," "War of the Coprophages," and "Jose Chung's 'From Outer Space' ": _____.

5. This director helmed "Apocrypha," "D.P.O." and "Teso Dos Bichos": _____.

N is for . . .

6. It was the name of a tabloid newspaper seen in Mulder's office (Hint: It had a lizard baby on the cover): _____.

7. This actor plays the role of the shadowy and mysterious Well-Manicured Man: _____.

O is for . . .

8. The magazine Mulder wrote for in 1993: _____.

9. A lake in Iowa that Mulder described as a "UFO hotspot": _____.

P is for . . .

10. If you have this psychic ability you can influence inanimate objects by mindpower: _____.

11. This prison guard was killed by Danielle Manley in "The List" when she believed he was her reincarnated husband: _____.

12. Brenden Beiser plays this recurring federal agent: _____.

13. She played Dr. Bambi Berenbaum in "War of the Coprophages": _____.

Q is for . . .

14. Name the FBI training academy where Scully taught for two years prior to being assigned to the X-Files: _____.

R is for . . .

15. Gulf War veteran Leonard Trimble's nickname in "The Walk:" _____.

16. Vancouver twin Erika Krievins portrayed this genetic replica in "Eve": _____.

17. This rock group performs the track "Star Me Kitten" on the CD *Songs in the Key of X (Music from and inspired by* The X-Files): _____.

S is for . . .

18. Even though his body was exhumed in Oregon in the pilot episode, his tombstone was seen briefly in a Minneapolis cemetery in "Irresistible": _____.

19. This well-known actor portrayed the Norwegian captain, Henry Trondheim, in "Dod Kalm": _____.

20. He is the talented composer of *The X-Files'* theme music: _____.

21. This Florida convict tried to cut a deal with the warden in "The List" but was beaten to death instead: _____.

22. Identify the federal agent Susan Bain portrayed in "Grotesque": _____.

T is for . . .

23. Mulder lied to rescuers about this scientist's survival in "Firewalker": _____.

24. (Fill in the Blank): Scully's senior thesis at the University of Mary-

land was titled: "Einstein's _____ Paradox: A New Interpretation."

25. Dr. Ishimaru's first name in "731": _____.

U is for . . .

26. Identify the more polite and professional term for "saucer
chasers": _____.

V is for . . .

27. This *X-Files* writer penned the scripts for "2Shy" and "Hell
Money": _____.

W is for . . .

28. Name the bleached blond police detective who couldn't keep
her hands off of Mulder in "Syzygy": _____.

29. This well-known character actor played the sadistic warden in
"The List": _____.

30. Mr. Chaco's first name in the cannibalistic "Our Town":

_____.

X is for . . .

31. The title of the April 12, 1996 *TV Guide* cover story on *The X-Files:*

_____.

Y is for . . .

32. This famous psychic accused Mulder of giving off negative en-
ergy in "Clyde Bruckman's Final Repose": _____.

Z is for . . .

33. This crystal ball-reading fortune teller couldn't foresee her own
impending death: _____.

34. Jack Black portrayed this small town loser in "D.P.O.":

_____.

35. Veteran actor Robert Ito played this Japanese version of Dr. Mengele in "731": _____.

X-PERT X-TRA BONUS POINTS #1

W is for . . .

The name of the D.C. police detective who investigated Skinner in "Avatar": _____.

X-PERT X-TRA BONUS POINTS #2

T is for . . .

The actor who portrayed Dr. Bilac in "Teso Dos Bichos."

FILE NO. 3X10:

731 [PART 2 OF 2]

Declassified Case Overview: Mulder was trapped aboard a speeding, bomb-laden train with a government assassin and a mysterious quarantine subject who may or may not have been a human/alien hybrid. Meanwhile, Scully took Mr. X's advice to heart and investigated more fully the implant that was removed from her neck.

Nitpicking

Mulder runs the access card through the electronic door lock backwards. Like an ATM card, if the magnetized strip isn't in contact with the scanner, there's nothing but plastic for it to read.

The scientist's diary (although correctly written in Japanese) is in actuality simply one page of handwritten text copied over and over again to make up the remainder of the journal.

We find it hard to believe that Hansen's disease cannot be arrested even when it has progressed to disfigurement.

Trivia

1.   What was the name of the "leper colony" in Perkey, West Virginia which was raided by government death squads at the episode's beginning?

2.   Who did Scully chastise with the words, "I don't have time for your convenient ignorance"?

3.   Who saved Mulder's life when the NSA operative tried to garrote Mulder aboard the quarantined train car?

4.   (Fill in the Blank) Scully told Mulder that the *Talapus* had salvaged a piece of a _____ nuclear submarine instead of a UFO from the bottom of the Pacific Ocean.

X-PERT X-TRA BONUS POINTS #1

What was the seven-digit *entrance* code to the quarantined train car (which Dr. Zama gave to the NSA operative before his untimely death)?

---

5.   According to Mulder, what was the "most painful and slowest way to die"?

6.   (Fill in the blank dialogue) The NSA agent told Mulder "that thing" on the quarantined car was a weapon "more valuable than Star Wars, more valuable than the atomic bomb or the most advanced _____ weapons."

7.   How many seconds were left on the bomb's digital timer when Mr. X carried Mulder to safety from the train car's explosion?
     A.   32
     B.   49
     C.   58

8. According to Scully, an anonymous person called the hospital administrator where Mulder was taken after the train car explosion and alerted them to his location. From what city and state did the caller use a pay phone?
    A.   Blue Earth, Iowa
    B.   Big Sky, Montana
    C.   Greenspoint, Ohio

X-PERT X-TRA BONUS POINTS #2

Scully was able to provide Mulder with the *exit* code for the quarantined train car by stopping and slowly advancing Mulder's videotape copy of the alien autopsy. Identify the six-digit code.

Investigative Field Report

" '731' brings us full circle to where Mulder and Scully started two years ago," Chris Carter elaborated in an interview. "Mulder still believes in UFOs and aliens and Scully is still the skeptic, but in a more pragmatic way. She no longer rejects the 'evidence' that jumps right into her face, but tries to conform it into her own theory of medical experimentation and research barbarity. We don't want to turn her into a carbon copy of Mulder."

Although Scully may fall for the "medical atrocities" cover-up story told to her by one of the Well-Manicured Man's cronies, Mulder knows that the creature in the train car is indeed an alien life-form whose existence is being denied by an elusive international government coalition.

UFO researchers have alleged that major studies of alien spacecraft and their inhabitants have definitely been carried out by the governments of the U.S., Russia, France, Britain, Canada and Australia for the past thirty to forty years. Dr. Jacques Vallee, an astrophysicist who left his position with the French government in 1988 when he heard of plans to destroy vast numbers of UFO files, stated: "Something is going on . . . Something so big that international governments think we would all panic . . . We have a right to know what it is."

Perhaps, the truth *really* is out there.

FILE NO. 3X11:

REVELATIONS

Declassified Case Overview: Agents Mulder and Scully tracked a series of religiously motivated murders in which each of the victims claimed the ability to display inexplicable wounds similar to the crucified Christ.

Nitpicking

Why is Kevin removed from his mother's custody so quickly after he starts bleeding in school? Mrs. Kryder was nowhere around, so how could she have possibly caused his injury? In addition, it takes a great deal more that one questionable incident before social services will remove a child from the custody of one or both of his parents.

Scully claims that based upon her understanding of Catholic catechism, Owen Jarvis is one of the so-called "Incorruptibles" because his corpse is slow to decay and is redolent of flowers. Official Catholic doctrine, however, clearly states that incorruption following death has been ascribed under Canon Law to only one individual: Jesus Christ.

Somehow Dr. Scully fails to notice that the school nurse takes Kevin's temperature orally with a rectal thermometer.

Trivia

1. (Fill in the blank with the correct number) According to religious lore, at any given time there were _____ stigmatics in the world.

2. What was the name of the school young Kevin Kryder attended?
    A. Bridgeway Elementary
    B. Loveland Middle School
    C. Ridgeway Elementary

3. (Fill in the blank dialogue) Before he was institutionalized, Kevin's father had barricaded himself and his son in their house because the boy had been "_____ by God."

4. Mulder and Scully questioned Kevin's father at the mental hospital. Who did he allege had been after the boy since the day he was born?
    A. "The Forces of Darkness"
    B. "The Evil Ones"
    C. "The Dark One's Angels"

5. Where did Owen Jarvis tell Mulder and Scully he wanted to go just before jumping through the attic window?

6. How long had Owen been dead when Scully conducted her autopsy?

7. Simon Gates, one of the wealthiest men in the South, had been arrested three years earlier for Driving Under the Influence, which left a boy paralyzed. After he received a suspended sentence, to which country did he flee?
    A. Argentina
    B. Israel
    C. Honduras

8. What was the name of the motel where Kevin was abducted from the bathroom while Mulder and Scully were right outside the door?

X-PERT X-TRA BONUS POINTS #1

What was the math problem Kevin's teacher wanted him to work out on the chalkboard in front of the entire class as punishment for picking on a classmate?

X-PERT X-TRA BONUS POINTS #2

What was the name of the shelter for boys where Kevin stayed?

X-PERT X-TRA BONUS POINTS #3

How many years had it been since Scully's last confession to a priest?

Investigative Field Report

In a reversal of roles, Mulder and Scully both undergo tests of their faiths in "Revelations": his faith in his partner's rational, scientific nature is challenged by her acceptance of religious beliefs he finds absurd, and her faith in Mulder's devotion to the search for truth is eroded by his disdain for her Catholic convictions. Although the flip-flopping of their characters is an intriguing idea, it doesn't work out as well as might have been expected. In the end, the patented warmth, humor, and good-natured teasing that usually mark their relationship is noticeably absent.

Stigmata, as displayed by Kevin Kryder in this episode, are said to appear on those parts of the body where the crucified Christ was wounded. Since the late 19th century, however, a number of experiments have shown it is possible to bring about certain skin conditions—blistering and perhaps also wounds that resemble those of Christ—by means of hypnotic suggestion. Some researchers have also considered the possibility that the "bleeding" may be pink-colored sweat, caused by blood seeping into the sweat glands.

More importantly, it has been pointed out that many famous depictions of the crucifixion are in fact inaccurate, since the Roman method involved driving nails not through the palms but through the wrists, just below where the two small bones of the forearm meet. The hands are held together by cartilage and the weight of a body could effectively pull the nail through the hand in a relatively short amount of time, but the bones in the wrists can easily support a human for three days. In other words, stigmata victims experience the injuries where they think Christ was wounded and not where they were actually inflicted.

WAR OF THE COPROPHAGES

Declassified Case Overview: While waiting out the fumigation of his apartment complex, Mulder investigated reports of UFO activity in a small Northeastern town and discovered that three people had recently died—possibly victims of mass cockroach attacks.

Nitpicking

Dr. Ekerle's office window at ALT-FUELS, the alternative fuel research plant, reads "DR. JEFF EKERLE—PRESIDENT & CHIEF SCIENCE OFFICER." What is he the officer of? It should read something like "CHIEF RESEARCH SCIENTIST." Does this guy think he is Mr. Spock on *Star Trek*?

Toward the conclusion of the episode, Mulder tells Scully she was right about the cause of death for the victims (the exterminator, dopehead teenager, Medical Examiner and an unidentified man in the motel room). However, Mulder fails to mention what killed the first two victims, who died off-screen but were mentioned in the opening scenes.

Trivia

1. How many known cockroach species exist, according to the observations of Dr. Bugger, the exterminator in the pre-credits sequence?

2. Which 1960s science-fiction movie classic was mentioned three times in this episode?
    A. *2001: A Space Odyssey*
    B. *Planet of the Apes*
    C. *It Came from Outer Space*

3. (True or False) Mulder told Scully that the federal government was conducting secret experiments in the town under the guise of the U.S. Department of Commerce.

4. What was Dr. Berenbaum's theory for Unidentified Flying Objects?

5. What was the name of Dr. Ivanov's research lab?
    A. Massachusetts Robotics Institute
    B. Massachusetts Institute of Robotics
    C. Ivanov's Center for the Study of Artificial Life-forms

6. What fatal disease were the cockroaches rumored to be spreading?

7. What was the name of the over-the-counter insecticide spray used repeatedly (and fought over in a convenience store) by the townsfolk?

X-PERT X-TRA BONUS POINTS #1

What was ALT-FUELS' advertising slogan?

X-PERT X-TRA BONUS POINTS #2

What was the number on the bulky X-File Mulder used to kill the big bug in the final scene?

Investigative Field Report

As Mulder told Clyde Bruckman, there are hits and there are misses. For Darin Morgan, who had previously penned the black humor classics "Humbug" and "Clyde Bruckman's Final Repose," this cartoonish Bugs from Outer Space episode is definitely a miss. "War of the Coprophages" reads like some of the *really* bad fiction fans write and post on the Internet. Sadly, Morgan's desperate script displays some of the worst excesses of that genre: sophomoric humor, shallow characterization and a storyline that aims high at the beginning but achieves too little in the end.

Although Morgan's premise of a war between Earth cockroaches and their robotic counterparts from a distant galaxy is way out (out of this world, in fact), the sight of a cockroach scampering across the TV screen was a stroke of comedic genius and sent us running for the bug spray.

Trivia alert: "War of the Coprophages" pays homage to the classic sci-fi film, H.G. Wells' *War of the Worlds.* The name of the town in this episode, Miller's Grove, mirrors that of Grover's Mill in the movie.

Dr. Ivanov's name is a nod to author Isaac Asimov who wrote numerous science-fiction books dealing with the "laws of robotics."

Dr. Bambi Berenbaum is named for Dr. May R. Berenbaum, head of the Entomology Department at the University of Illinois and author of several books on insects.

Breakfast at Tiffany's, which is the book Scully is reading during one of Mulder's many telephone interruptions, is also the Final Jeopardy answer (or should we say question?) that David Duchnovy missed and cost him the game when he appeared on a celebrity version of the popular game show.

X-PERT TESTIMONY: PART III

With the grudging assistance of some influential and cryptic secret sources (whose real names and affiliations are never revealed), we have been given highly classified transcripts of wiretaps of several individuals associated in various capacities with the X-Files. Unfortunately, the surveillance equipment was not able to record all the requested information and it is now your assignment to fill in the missing gaps.

1. Identify the character from the episode "Revelations" who sermonized, "Most people today tend to vest themselves in science and cynicism. They expect proof for all they see. Miracles are wondrous by nature. They need no rationale, no justification."

2. In which episode did Skinner complain to Mulder, "Whatever you stepped in on this case is being tracked into my office and I don't like the smell of it"?
    A. "731"
    B. "Nisei"
    C. "Paper Clip"

3. Who said in "The Blessing Way," "We predict the future, and the best way to predict the future is to invent it"?

4. Identify the character who issued the warning, "Anyone who thinks that alien visitation will come not in the form of robots but living beings with big eyes and gray skin, has been brainwashed by too much science-fiction"?

5. In which episode did Mulder tell a police detective, "If, uh, you detect a hint of skepticism or incredulity in Agent Scully's voice, it's because of the overwhelming evidence gathered by the FBI debunking virtually all claims of ritual abuse by Satanic cults"?

6. Who said, "Oh, sometimes it just seems that everyone's having sex but me"?

7. (Fill in the blank dialogue) The Well-Manicured Man asked in "Paper Clip," "My God, you presume to make us believe and simply fix it with enough _____?"

8. Who chastised Skinner in "The Blessing Way," "With all due respect, sir, I think you overestimate your position in the chain of command"?

9. (Fill in the blank dialogue) When it was obvious that Danielle Manley was seeing another man, Scully commented, "Woman gets lonely. Sometimes she can't wait around for her man to be _____."

10. In "Piper Maru," who sarcastically responded with "Remind me not to move there" when told by a MIB that he worked for "the intelligence community"?

11. Who told Mulder to "muster whatever resources you have to make sure you find Scully first" when she became psychotic and disappeared in "Wetwired"?

12. In which episode did Scully utter the conspicuously un-Scully-like phrase, "Mulder, you're nuts!"?

13. Who said, "Although we may not be alone in the universe, in our own separate ways, on *this* planet we are all alone"?
    A. Mulder
    B. Melissa Scully
    C. Jose Chung

14. Identify the human monster who Scully said wanted "to go out in a blaze of glory" after a failed life.

15. Who warned Mulder through a mouthful of blood, "It will find you. Maybe it already has"?

16. In "Grotesque," who did Mulder tell to "Look at your hands. Now tell me what you're doing here"?

17. (Fill in the blank dialogue) In the episode "Syzygy," Mulder apologized for Scully's rather inflexible behavior by saying, "She tends to be rather rigid, but rigid in a _____ way—not like she was today."

18. Who said in "Revelations," "Moses hadn't really parted the Red Sea. He said that high winds and ocean currents had been responsible"?

19. (Fill in the blank dialogue) Mulder, while aiming his revolver at the relentless, arrogant assassin aboard the bomb-laden train car in "731," warned, "As an employee of the National Security Agency, you should know that a gunshot wound to the _____ is probably the most painful and slowest way to die. But I'm not a very good shot. And when I miss . . . I tend to miss low."

20. In which episode did Mulder compare Skinner to "a beacon in the night"?

21. Which alleged psychic in "Clyde Bruckman's Final Repose" confessed, "I guess I can't see the forest for the trees"?

22. Which two characters said in unison in "Syzygy," "Hate him, wouldn't want to date him"?

23. In which episode did the leader of a gun-toting mob declare at

the conclusion, "It *was* Satan" (and the enlightened townfolk respond with a chorus of "Ohhhhh!")?

24. Who told Mr. X, "I don't have time for your convenient ignorance"?

25. (Fill in the blank dialogue) Albert Hosteen said in a voice-over at the beginning of "The Blessing Way," "Memory, like fire, is _____ and immutable."

26. In "Talitha Cumi," whose diatribe consisted of "Men can never be free because they're weak, corrupt, worthless and restless. The people believe in authority. They've grown tired of waiting for miracle and mystery. Science is their religion. No greater explanation exist for them"?

X-PERT X-TRA BONUS POINTS #1

In which episode did Mulder hand a gun to an innocent bystander and say, "I just want you to point it at him. Don't pull the trigger (clicks empty gun). Kinda gives away the game"?

X-PERT X-TRA BONUS POINTS #2

(Fill in the blank dialogue) Mulder lectured Scully in "Revelations": "These people are simply fanatics behaving fanatically, using religion as a justification. They give bona fide _____ like myself a bad name."

FILE NO. 3X13:

SYZYGY

Declassified Case Overview: Mulder and Scully are called to a small community by a semi-hysterical police detective to investigate the murder of several high school students as rumors of a Satanic cult whipped the normally placid towns-folk into a panic.

Nitpicking

Stellar objects do not adhere to the same time schedules as humans, especially not down to the second. If an astrological alignment was causing the rise in fear and anger, then the tension should build up in increments and gradually decrease the same way, not escalate over a period of days then disappear abruptly when the clock strikes midnight.

Mulder tells Detective White that he never drinks alcoholic beverages. Yet, in the previous episode he shared a bottle of Johnny Walker Red with Dr. Ivanov.

Scully comments that she and Mulder have been working together for two years, but the date indicated in the pilot episode is March 1992. The events in "Syzygy" occur in January 1996, making it almost four years that Mulder and Scully have been assigned together in the X-Files division.

Trivia

1. Identify the name of the teenage boy killed in the pre-credits sequence.
    A.   Jake "Bam" Bambler
    B.   Jay "Boom" DeBoom
    C.   Jimmy "Boomer" Elliot

2. Which three planets were re-aligning into some sort of cosmic G-spot?

3. What was the name of the astrologist Mulder interviewed?
    A. Madame Wylene
    B. Zirinka
    C. Zelma

4. Whom did the Ouija board foresee Brenda Summerfield marrying?

5. What was the name of the 14-year-old dog whose skeletal remains were found buried in Dr. Richard Godfrey's medical bag?

6. Identify the names of the two telekinetic blond cheerleaders who were born on the same day.
    A. Sherri and Mary
    B. Nancy and Tracy
    C. Terri and Margi

7. (True or False) Comity was known as "The City of Sunshine and Smiles."

X-PERT X-TRA BONUS POINTS #1

(Fill in the correct number) In a voice-over at the end of the episode, Mulder commented, "We are but visitors on this rock, hurtling through time and space at _____ miles an hour."

X-PERT X-TRA BONUS POINTS #2

According to its city limits sign, what was the population of Comity?

Investigative Field Report

"Syzygy" (which means "imminent astrological alignment") was the turning point for a season that many critics and X-Philes were referring to as a "mid-life crisis" for the series. Rumors were circulating on the Internet that Duchovny was possibly leaving the show, and some fans were grumbling that the season at the halfway point (already littered with re-runs) felt "off"—perhaps Chris Carter, the creative juice behind the phenomenally successful series, was cooling down or burning out.

Carter, who started out in the business writing comedy, tries to re-turn to his roots with "Syzygy" and fails miserably. The erosion (even if it is temporary) of the bond between Mulder and Scully is no laughing matter. Carter had said that this episode would "change the dynamics" of our heroes' relationship, and in the process he transformed the usually suave and urbane Mulder into a boozing, insensitive clod and Scully into a chain-smoking, jealous and whiny bitch. This entire sick joke of an episode is nothing more than a Keystone Kops escapade with the two agents being seesawed frantically from one ridiculously contrived scene to another under the pretense of a cosmic realignment.

The consensus among X-Philes on the Internet was loud and clear: Return the show to its base or risk losing its fans.

FILE NO. 3X14:

GROTESQUE

Declassified Case Overview: When a three-year-old serial murder case continued even after the killer was apprehended, Mulder and Scully were assigned to aid Mulder's former mentor at the FBI's Behavioral Sciences Unit in tracking down the perpetrator's accomplice or copycat.

Nitpicking

If Mostow is in a straightjacket, how could he possibly draw the face of a gargoyle on the floor of his jail cell? Even if he wasn't physically restrained, it is highly unlikely that an alleged serial killer (who mutilated his victims' faces) would be given art supplies.

Trivia

1. How many young men between the ages of 17 and 25 had Mostow killed during a three year period?

2. How many days had Mostow been incarcerated when another murder matching his M.O. occurred?

3. Who said, "If you want to know an artist you have to look at his art"?

4. What reason did Mostow give for his artistic obsession with gargoyles?

5. (True or False) The bodies of seven young men were discovered inside life-size clay gargoyles in Mostow's secret gallery.

6. At which university's library did Mulder conduct his gargoyle research?
    A. Georgetown
    B. George Washington
    C. Howard

X-PERT X-TRA BONUS POINTS #1

Identify the room number at FBI Headquarters in which evidence was maintained in Mostow's murder case.

X-PERT X-TRA BONUS POINTS #2

What time was it when FBI agents burst into Mostow's apartment and arrested him?

Investigative Field Report

With "Grotesque" the series gets back on track with not only a top-notch M.O.T.W. episode, but with an Emmy-deserving showcase of David Duchovny's acting talents as well.

Mulder's old boss and guru, Agent Bill Patterson, reminds his former star pupil that "If you want to catch a monster, you must become one yourself." In one of his finest performances to date, Duchovny takes Mulder on a foray into the core of madness and realistically demonstrates the terrible price some law enforcement agents must pay in tracking the real monsters among us.

Descending into the bowels of hell, Mulder covers the walls of his apartment with the killer's drawings of gargoyles, sleeps where the killer slept, and steals the killer's murder weapon from the FBI's evidence room. Although more experienced agents have lost their souls in such a nightmarish heart of darkness, Mulder somehow maintains the fundamental ability to stay sane. Duchovny's Mulder not only rises above this episode's monster mash, he towers over it.

Trivia alert: This episode's Agent Nemhauser is named in honor of Post Production Supervisor Lori Jo Nemhauser.

FILE NO. 3X15:

PIPER MARU [PART 1 OF 2]

Declassified Case Overview: When the crew of the French salvage ship Piper Maru began to die from severe radiation burns after discovering a life-form trapped in a sunken World War II aircraft, Mulder and Scully became entangled in a deadly conspiracy dating back to Hiroshima.

Nitpicking

The miniature submarine used in the black-and-white Commander Johansen flashback scene looks very much like the toy that it is. As it moves away from the underwater camera, it slowly goes out of focus, which is something a large ship wouldn't do but a small-scale model would.

This episode accurately points out that it is highly illegal to possess a gun in Hong Kong. If Mulder's revolver was taken from him by authorities when he entered the country, then how is Krycek able to get past the metal-detectors at the airport with a handgun concealed under his clothing?

Trivia

1. How many months had the *Piper Maru* been at sea searching for the sunken remains of the aircraft squadron?

2. Identify the three words scrawled in large letters on the fuselage of the P51 Mustang.
    A.   DROP DEAD RED
    B.   REMEMBER PEARL HARBOR
    C.   DAY OF INFAMY

3. Whose satellite system did Mulder utilize to track the *Piper Maru*'s course from the Pacific Ocean to San Diego?

4. What was the name of the submarine on which Commander Johansen served as the Executive Officer?

5. The French diver Bernard Gauthier lived with his wife, Joan, in the Pacific Heights section of San Francisco. What was their house number?
    A.   1310
    B.   64
    C.   42

6. (True or False) Scully located Commander Johansen at the Grand Prairie Naval Air Station.

X-PERT X-TRA BONUS POINTS #1

(Fill in the blanks with the correct numbers) The *Piper Maru* located the remains of the World War II squadron at a latitude of _____ degrees north and at a longitude _____ degrees east.

X-PERT X-TRA BONUS POINTS #2

The *Zeus Faber* had a crew complement of 144. How many survived the TOP SECRET mission to find the P51 Mustang?

Investigative Field Report

When Mulder and Scully aren't busy tracking down fat-sucking vampires, astral-projecting war veterans, alien robotic cockroaches, or reincarnated death-row convicts, *The X-Files* returns to its base: Mulder's quest for the Truth. Indeed, his quest forms the series' principal story arc, linking episodes from the pilot to the most recent conspiracy revelations in "Nisei," "731" and now with "Piper Maru," undeniably one of *The X-Files'* finest, most intense hours.

Like the conspiracy itself, episode writers Chris Carter and Frank Spotnitz play a cat-and-Mulder game with this first installment in a two-part storyline: Who shot Skinner? Who now possesses Krycek? And what do the aliens want with the digital audio tape? "Piper Maru" is the reason that *The X-Files* is truly Must-See TV.

X MARKS THE SPOT: SEASON THREE

1. Identify the Washington State county in which the alien abductions profiled in "Jose Chung's 'From Outer Space' " took place.
    A.   Washington
    B.   Klass
    C.   Benton

2. In which ocean did the French salvage ship *Piper Maru* discover alien-inhabiting sunken World War II aircraft?

3. Name the Virginia city in which the climactic mind-control scene between the "Pusher" and Mulder occurred.

4. (True or False) Mulder's and Krycek's car was run off County Road 512 in Maryland during the conspiratorial events of "Apocrypha."

5. Identify the small Maryland town in which several people committed murder while under the paranoid psychotic effects of a covert government experiment involving subliminal TV signals.

6. Name the city and state in which Mulder and Scully tracked a series of religiously motivated murders.

7. Victims of Hansen's Disease watched as other patients were rounded up by a death squad and murdered in this state's remote leper colony.

8. In which city and state did Mulder apprehend a Japanese diplomat carrying secret spy satellite photographs?
   A. Boston, Massachusetts
   B. Allentown, Pennsylvania
   C. Rockville, Maryland

9. A young girl was kidnapped from her own bedroom in which Pacific Northwest city?

10. (Fill in the Blank) While strapped to the electric chair, convict Napoleon "Neech" Manley vowed to come back and wreak vengeance on his enemies at the state prison in _____ County, Florida.

11. The cockroaches of "War of the Coprophages" were attacking and killing the populace of what small Massachusetts community?

12. In which New Hampshire town did the astrological events of "Syzygy" take place?
   A. Callahan
   B. Franklin
   C. Comity

13. Members of an archaeological expedition were killed after bringing the skeletal remains of a South American shamaness to a museum in the northeast corridor of the United States. Name the city.

14. In which state did the emotionally charged "D.P.O." murder several townfolk with lightning?
   A. Arkansas
   B. Oklahoma
   C. Kansas

15. "Grotesque"'s John Mostow killed a male model from his art class at one of this city's universities during the episode's pre-credits sequence.

16. (True or False) Mulder returned from Hong Kong with an alien-possessed Alex Krycek at the beginning of "Apocrypha."

17. (True or False) In the episode "Paper Clip," Mulder and Scully located an ex-Nazi scientist who directed them to an abandoned West Virginia mine housing a vast filing system containing detailed medical records on millions of people.

18. Reluctant clairvoyant Clyde Bruckman helped Mulder and Scully identify and apprehend a serial killer in what Minnesota city?

19. (Fill in the Blank) The "Pusher" was captured by FBI agents while standing in line at the check-out counter at the Mt. Foodmore Supermarket in _____ County, Virginia.

20. (True or False) William Mulder's funeral took place at the Garden of Reflection Cemetery in Boston, Massachusetts.

21. (True or False) Scully's car was stopped and searched by armed soldiers northwest of Los Alamos, New Mexico during the events in "The Blessing Way."

22. In which southern mountain range did pre-historic Big Blue have a lake home?

23. FBI Agent Bonnecase was reassigned from this Virginia city to Washington, D.C. to investigate ADA Skinner's involvement in the murder of prostitute Carina Sayles. (Hint: The name of the bay this city overlooks is also the name of the bar where Skinner met Sayles.)

X-PERT X-TRA BONUS POINTS #1

In the third season finale, "Talitha Cumi," Agent Mulder's mother suffered a debilitating stroke after a confrontation with the Cigarette-Smoking Man at her former summer home. Name the small Rhode Island coastal town.

X-PERT X-TRA BONUS POINTS #2

In which Virginia city did a crazed gunman go on a shooting rampage in a fast food restaurant during the pre-credits sequence of "Talitha Cumi"?

THE LONE GUNMEN

Behind the Scenes with the Paranoid Conspiracy Trinity

You know them as Frohike, Langly and Byers—the trio of nerdy characters who publish a newsletter on government conspiracies called The Lone Gunman (so-called after a Kennedy assassination theory). Stripped of their aliases and cover roles on the series, how familiar are you with the dossiers of Tom Braidwood, Dean Haglund and Bruce Harwood—the three actors who portray the intensely paranoid and eccentric operatives?

1. Which actor was a first assistant director on *The X-Files* before being drafted for the role of one of the Lone Gunmen?

2. Who was beaten and hanged before the first commercial aired during an episode of *Lonesome Dove: The Series*?

3. Which two of the three actors previously worked with Steven Williams (Mr. X) on the former Fox series *21 Jump Street*?

4. (True or False) Harwood has said in interviews that his inspiration for the role of Byers was linguist/activist Noam Chomsky.

5. Which actor trained as a figure skater when he was younger?

6. Who performs regularly as a stand-up comic with the Vancouver TheaterSports improv group?

7. Which of the three men is the oldest?

8. (True or False) Braidwood's two favorite *X-Files* episodes are "Dod Kalm" and "The Host."

9. Who played a computer technician in *The Fly II*?

10. Which actor has asked fans at *X-Files* conventions, "If Mulder has all these people helping him, why is he nowhere near the Truth?"

11. Who won the part of one of the Lone Gunmen by beating out more than thirty other aspiring actors?

12. Which of the three men has appeared on stage in the parodies *Star Trick: The Next Improvisation* and *Free Willy Shakespeare*?

13. (True or False) Braidwood laughingly considers himself "the only romantic interest on a major TV hit."

14. What is the nickname that the series' crew has given to the bicycle Braidwood rides around the set of *The X-Files*?

15. Which actor has appeared on *The Commish, Sliders,* and *Street Justice*?

16. Whose hobby is gardening when he is not busy working on *The X-Files*?

17. Identify the actor who made an appearance in the TV movie remake of *Bye Bye Birdie*.

18. Who has said at fan conventions, "I believe there's life on other planets, but I don't believe that UFOs are saucers from another world"?

19. Which of the three actors practices yoga in his off-duty hours?

20. Who had a recurring role as environmentalist expert Willis on *MacGyver*?

21. Which actor was basically unfamiliar with *The X-Files* until he was awarded the role of one of the Lone Gunmen?

22. Who has said during interviews that all conspiracy theories are true—"but only to certain people"?

X-PERT X-TRA BONUS POINTS #1

Name Haglund's two favorite *X-Files* episodes.

X-PERT X-TRA BONUS POINTS #2

Which of the three actors writes scripts during his time off from the series?

FILE NO. 3X16:

APOCRYPHA [PART 2 OF 2]

Declassified Case Overview: Mulder returned from Hong Kong with Krycek while Scully coordinated the investigation into Skinner's attempted assassination in hopes that it would bring her sister's murderer to justice.

Nitpicking

Skinner has post-operative cardiac telemetry leads attached to his chest, but there isn't a cardiac monitor in sight. He is also receiving a blood transfusion, but the blood is not on an intravenous delivery pump. The naso-gastric tube is neither positioned nor taped correctly and is not attached to a drainage canister.

Scully tells the two D.C. cops that based upon the waitress' description in the coffee shop, they know Skinner's "shooter" is male with a blood type of B+. How can a waitress determine a man's blood type just by looking at him?

Skinner is left alone and unattended in the back of the ambulance with an IV infusing. Patients with IVs are always accompanied by a nurse or paramedic during transfer in the event that life support has to be initiated.

Trivia

1. During the pre-credits sequence, a young Bill Mulder and Cigarette-Smoking Man interrogated a hospitalized sailor from the *Zeus Faber* at Pearl Harbor. What was the date?
    A.   April 15, 1951
    B.   May 23, 1952
    C.   August 19, 1953

2. Identify the hospital where Skinner was taken after he was shot.

3. What was the assumed name of the Hispanic Man, Skinner's would-be assassin?

4. Where did Mulder covertly meet with the Well-Manicured Man in New York?
    A.   In Central Park off 79th Street
    B.   In an underground parking garage adjacent to the New York Public Library
    C.   In the alleyway behind a Chinatown restaurant

5. What was the medium that the alien used to jump from one human host to another?

6. Where did the Cigarette-Smoking Man have the salvaged UFO relocated to in Black Crow, North Dakota?

X-PERT X-TRA BONUS POINTS #1

What was the number on the locker the Lone Gunmen opened at the ice skating rink in Rockville, Maryland?

X-PERT X-TRA BONUS POINTS #2

Identify the door number of the radiation containment room which housed the UFO and Krycek at the end of the episode.

Investigative Field Report

Although this second part of the "Piper Maru" storyline is well-paced and maintains a taut narrative throughout, too many threads are left unexplained. The involvement of the French government was introduced in "Piper Maru," then barely mentioned in "Apocrypha." What happened to all the human hosts who were occupied by the alien (Gauthier and his wife, Jeraldine Kallenchuk, etc.)? Did they just purge the ET from their bodies and go back to work? What happened to the officers guarding Skinner's hospital room door? Were they in actuality working for the Cigarette-Smoking Man or were they killed?

As with anything teased and stretched too often, the evil-cabal-with-the-secret-alien-agenda conspiracy storyline may be in danger of wearing thin. How many times will Mulder come within a hair's breadth of a critical piece of evidence, only to have it pulled out from under him at the last minute?

FILE NO. 3X17:

PUSHER

Declassified Case Overview: Mulder and Scully became involved in a case whose suspect had apparently murdered 14 people by controlling their minds. Deeply sunk in his fantasy of being a masterless Japanese samurai, the killer escaped and left clues for Mulder, whom he considered a "worthy opponent."

Nitpicking

During the pre-credits sequence, Modell is captured in a Virginia supermarket by federal agents. If his security is such an important issue, why is he placed in the last car of a multi-vehicle motorcade and why is that car separated from all the others simply by stopping at a stop sign?

If Modell is arrested by federal law enforcement officers, why does his pre-trial hearing take place in a Loudoun County courtroom with a state judge presiding?

Toward the end of the episode, Mulder radios back to the SWAT team that he heard two gunshots and then discovers a hospital technician and a security guard dead from wounds to the head. Mulder surmises that Modell induced the guard to shoot the technician and then to kill himself. However, there are more than two casings on the floor near the bodies.

Trivia

1. Which former *X-Files* M.O.T.W. was on the front cover of the tabloid *World Weekly Informer* in the Mt. Foodmore Supermarket at the beginning of the episode?

2. (Fill in the Blank) Modell induced the officer to pull the police car into the path of an oncoming 18-wheeler semi truck by calmly telling him that his uniform was a _____ blue, like a gentle breeze.

3. What is the Japanese word for a samurai without a master?

4. In which Virginia city did Modell reside?
    A. Roanoke
    B. Alexandria
    C. Fairfax

5. Modell initially tried to become a Navy SEAL and then a Special Forces Green Beret, but promptly failed at both attempts. Identify the military installation where he served as a supply clerk for two years.

6. Under Modell's control, Holly in the FBI's Computer Records Office sprayed Skinner with mace and kicked him repeatedly while he lay on the floor. What was Holly's shoe size?

X-PERT X-TRA BONUS POINTS #1

What is the Japanese word for "push"?

X-PERT X-TRA BONUS POINTS #2

Where is the Computers Records Section located at FBI Headquarters in Washington, D.C.?

Investigative Field Report

"While not of the tragic or terrifying dimensions of 'Grotesque' or 'Oubliette,' episode writer Vince Gilligan penned a good, solid story about a true sociopath whose only motive is, as Scully says, 'to go out in a blaze of glory' after a failed, miserable life," said director Rob Bowman. "Finally, in a self-destructive last act he sets out to take Mulder, his 'worthy opponent,' with him into oblivion."

During the episode's climactic game of Russian Roulette between Mulder and Modell (reminiscent of Michael Cimino's 70s classic *The Deer Hunter*), we were sitting on the edge of our seats. Mulder's utter desperation as he realizes he cannot overcome Modell's manipulative mind control, his despairing "Scully, run!", his humiliation afterwards as he hands the revolver to his partner without looking at her and buries his face in his hands, are all deeply affecting scenes.

FILE NO. 3X18:

TESO DOS BICHOS

Declassified Case Overview: Members of an archaeological expedition began dying mysteriously after they forcibly removed the remains of a South American shamaness. Agents Mulder and Scully investigated whether the string of murders were part of a curse from beyond the grave or the result of political terrorism.

Nitpicking

The entire basis of Mulder and Scully's federal investigation of Dr. Bilac doesn't seem very credible. Since when does writing a letter of protest to the State Department place you on the short list for political terrorism?

Why does the shaman murder Mona and Dr. Bilac, both of whom were sympathetic to the idea of returning the remains of the female shamaness to the government of Equador?

Can anyone explain why Mulder, an experienced FBI agent, is stupid enough to walk around the museum with the lights off? Scully pulled the same stunt at the exact same time at Dr. Bilac's house. When people enter a room that is dark, they usually reach for the light switch.

What happened to Mulder and Scully's famous $4,000, 6-million-candlepower flashlights, which they have used quite often during the course of their investigations over the past two-and-a-half years? In this episode, they venture into a maze of underground tunnels with a couple of your basic bargain basement flashlights.

Why are the rats trying to escape from the sewer if the cats are in the heating tunnels?

Mulder and Scully discover their prime suspect, Dr. Bilac, covered in blood at the scene of two previous murders, but they don't handcuff him or take him into custody. Instead, they violate police procedure and simply leave him alone in one of the museum's rooms with a solitary policeman standing guard outside the door.

We've seen Scully work wonders in the lab many times in the past, but being able to identify a victim solely from the gnawed remains of a single small intestine does not make us suspend our disbelief.

Trivia

1. Name the archaeologist killed in the Equadorian Highlands during the episode's pre-credits sequence.

2. Identify the museum in Boston which became cursed after it received the shamaness' remains.

3. What type of vehicle did Dr. Lewton drive?

4. (Fill in the blank dialogue) Dr. Bilac warned Mulder and Scully, "This is more powerful than any man. This is a spirit you are dealing with—the spirit of the Amaru. This is not something you can put in _____."

5. (True or False) Dr. Lewton had been snacking on corn chips and bean dip on the afternoon of his untimely death.

6. What did Mulder and Scully discover floating in the toilets of the museum's restrooms?

X-PERT X-TRA BONUS POINTS #1

Identify Dr. Bilac's house number.

X-PERT X-TRA BONUS POINTS #2

What was the English translation for the greenish hallucinogenic Yaje?

Investigative Field Report

Just when we thought the series had returned to its roots, Carter and Company threw in this outright rip-off of the horror movie classic *Cat People* and the best-selling book *Relic* by D. Preston, a thriller in which a monster is brought back by a South American expedition and set loose in the bowels of a natural history museum. According to episode writer John Shiban ("The List"), "Teso Dos Bichos" is ancient Brazilian Portuguese meaning "burial mound of small animals." Most X-

Philes surmised, however, that its English translation was a more suitable "excrement of small animals."

It is painfully obvious that this episode is going downhill fast when most fans find themselves actually laughing out loud at supposedly horrific monster attacks. These have to be the worst special effects *The X-Files* staff has ever attempted. In the predictable opening sequence we see the shadow of the jaguar attacking what is obviously a dummy with its hands sticking out in an effort to ward off the big cat. Even worse is the climax in which Scully is attacked by what appears to be Morris the Cat on LSD. Both scenes confirm the B-movie feel of the whole episode. This is supposed to be a M.O.T.W. show, but the monster stays hidden until the final seven minutes. Be grateful. When the resolution of an X-File is to call the city animal control department, that episode fails to deliver what it promised.

Writer John Shiban acknowledged that Dr. Lewton's name is an homage to producer Val Lewton who headed up a B-movie unit at RKO Studios in the 1940s, with the mission of turning out a string of psychological horror classics, including the unforgettable *Cat People*, *Curse of the Cat People*, and *The Leopard Man*.

A recent newspaper article (and not a tabloid) related the story of a man in the Netherlands who died and was not missed for several weeks. He had lived with almost two dozen cats and by the time his disappearance was investigated there wasn't much left of him to identify. Din-din time, Morris!

THE WRITE STUFF

It was a dark and stormy night . . . Match the X-Files wordsmiths below with the episodes they wrote during the series' first three seasons.

1. ____ Charles Grant Craig

A. "Revelations"

2. ____ Frank Spotnitz

B. "Fallen Angel"

3. ____ John Shiban   C. "End Game"

4. ____ Kenneth Biller & Chris Brancato   D. "2Shy"

5. ____ Vince Gilligan   E. "Roland"

6. ____ Sara Charno   F. "Eve"

7. ____ Scott Kaufer & Chris Carter   G. "Teso Dos Bichos"

8. ____ Howard Gordon & Chris Carter   H. "Fearful Symmetry"

9. ____ Jeffrey Vlaming   I. "Ascension"

10. ____ Darin Morgan   J. "Oubliette"

11. ____ Glen Morgan & James Wong   K. "Miracle Man"

12. ____ Kim Newton   L. "Shapes"

13. ____ Paul Brown   M. "Jose Chung's 'From Outer Space' "

14. ____ Larry & Paul Barber   N. "Soft Light"

15. ____ Marilyn Osborn   O. "Aubrey"

16. ____ Steven DeJarnatt   P. "Young at Heart"

17. ____ Chris Ruppenthal   Q. "Beyond the Sea"

18. ____ Alex Gansa & Howard Gordon   R. "GenderBender"

X-PERT X-TRA BONUS POINTS #1

David Duchovny was the co-author (with Kim Newton and Chris Carter respectively) on two original stories during the third season. Name the episodes.

X-PERT X-TRA BONUS POINTS #2

The writing team of Glen Morgan & James Wong wrote eleven *X-Files* episodes before leaving the series to devote their time producing and developing *Space: Above and Beyond*. Which second season episode was the last one they penned before departing?

X-PERT X-TRA BONUS POINTS #3

How many episodes has Chris Carter written or co-written during *The X-Files* three seasons?

FILE NO. 3X19:

HELL MONEY

Declassified Case Overview: When a young Chinese immigrant was found burned to death, Mulder and Scully investigated a series of murders in Chinatown where a lottery ticket could cost participants an arm and a leg.

Nitpicking

One major drawback of this entire episode is the extensive foreign dialogue. And if subtitles are to be used, then it's only fair to translate *all* of the dialogue. There are several scenes in which vital information is withheld from the audience by simply not subtitling (such as Detective Chao's conversation with Mr. Hsin).

Couldn't Mulder and Scully foresee the danger Detective Chao faced because of his involvement with the gambling ring/black market organ thieves?

Trivia: The Numbers Game

(NOTE: Because of the difficulty of the following questions, all correct answers will count as a 5-point X-PERT X-TRA BONUS.)

1. How many phantom-like figures in masks did the guard see in the crematorium room at the beginning of the episode?

2. (Fill in the blank with the correct number) Mulder informed Scully and the investigating detective that _____ Chinese men had been cremated alive recently in Seattle, Los Angeles, Boston and San Francisco.

3. (Fill in the blank dialogue) Detective Chao, commenting on the "Festival of the Hungry Ghosts," said, "On the _____ day of the seventh moon in the Chinese calendar, it is believed that the gates of hell are opened and the ghosts of unwanted souls roam the earth."

4. How many mask-clad, ghostly figures did the patrolling guard catch a glimpse of at Highland Park Cemetery?

5. What was Mr. Hsin's apartment number?

6. (Fill in the blank with the correct number) When Mr. Hsin begged to quit the lottery, the pot was allegedly at almost _____ million dollars.

7. (Fill in the blank with the correct number) Mr. Hsin's daughter had been diagnosed with a treatable form of leukemia _____ months earlier.

8. Combined, how many Chinese immigrants (from the ages of 20 to 40) had been cremated alive in Seattle and Los Angeles?

Investigative Field Report

"Writer Jeffrey Vlaming ["2Shy"] delved into a very realistic and unpretentious topic with the appropriate amount of flair and drama,"

Chris Carter said during an interview to defend the episode's lack of supernatural elements. "As happens so often in history, unfortunately, the immigrant community finds that it must guard against its own people rather than 'outsiders.' Like the Mafia, which originally terrorized only Italian immigrant ghettos, the greedy organ robbers in 'Hell Money' were less than human monsters that preyed upon their own people."

Nice try, Chris, but you still haven't satisfactorily explained why this episode is even an X-File. Although there are the faint apparitions (which are nothing more than drug-induced hallucinations), there isn't even the barest whiff of a paranormal bouquet about "Hell Money." At best, this disappointing installment of the series is nothing more than a run-of-the-mill cop story.

The jar of eyes that Mulder and Scully find is Vlaming's in-joke homage to veteran character actor James Wong (who portrays this episode's Hard-Faced Man) and his performance in the contemporary sci-fi classic *Blade Runner*, in which he proclaims, "I only do eyes!"

FILE NO. 3X20:

JOSE CHUNG'S "FROM OUTER SPACE"

Declassified Case Overview: Flattered by the attention of one of her favorite authors, Scully discussed a recent case in which two teenagers mysteriously vanished, only to reappear later with conflicting stories of alien abduction.

Nitpicking

Amazingly, this intricately structured episode (which unfolds into deeper and deeper complexity via conflicting flashbacks from its characters) is the first episode of the third season to be totally free of plot oversights, production problems, equipment oddities and scientific impossibilities.

Trivia

1. Who suggested to author Jose Chung that he write a book about alien abduction?

2. Identify the literary genre that Chung wanted to create with his new book (which would guarantee its landing on the best-seller list).

3. (True or False) Chung had spent six months in Klass County researching the alien abduction of two teenagers.

4. Identify the syndrome from which Mulder believed Chrissy was suffering.

5. (Fill in the blank dialogue) Chung commented to Scully about hypnosis: "As a storyteller, I'm fascinated how a person's sense of consciousness can be so transformed by nothing more _____ than listening to words."

6. Which planet did one of the MIBs tell Roky Erikenson was most often misidentified as a flying saucer?
    A. Saturn
    B. Venus
    C. Mars

7. What was the title of the Stupendous Yappi's videotape in which Scully supposedly conducted an "alien" autopsy?

X-PERT X-TRA BONUS POINTS #1

Identify the title of Roky's handwritten UFO "manifesto."

X-PERT X-TRA BONUS POINTS #2

According to Roky and Lt. Schaeffer, what was the name of the third alien from inner space?

Investigative Field Report

Writer Darin Morgan ("Humbug" and "Clyde Bruckman's Final Repose") came dangerously close to degenerating his needle-like wit into mere sophomoric shtick with "War of the Coprophages," but redeems not only himself with this episode, but the declining imagination, originality and boldness of *The X-Files'* latest scripts.

Full of in-jokes and self-parody, "Jose Chung's 'From Outer Space' " challenges our assumptions of what we know about UFOs, addresses the effects of the commercialization of ufology (to which *The X-Files* has greatly contributed of late) and even makes us question the principal government conspiracy story arc of the series. We may never be able to watch another UFO-related episode of *The X-Files* with straight faces.

Mulder points out in "Jose Chung's 'From Outer Space' " that not only do many alien contactees develop mysterious ailments, but some are later visited by nefarious Men in Black (MIB), who persuade them to remain silent about their close encounters.

Although no two stories are identical, many follow a similar pattern. The UFO contactee is visited by a man—or several men—dressed in 1950s-style black suits and hats, crisp white shirts and black ties. Occasionally, they wear thick, black sunglasses that completely conceal their eyes. Most fantastic, however, is the fact that MIB often arrive so quickly after a sighting that it seems unlikely they learned of it through normal means. Sometimes the witness has not related the story to anyone—yet the MIB still arrive.

The MIB usually turn up in a large black car (a celebrated model such as a Cadillac or a Rolls Royce). The vehicles look brand-new, but later license plate checks reveal that the numbers are bogus.

Physically, the men often look slightly Oriental, and sometimes speak with accents to match. Their speech is over-precise and their vocabulary comes straight out of a Humphrey Bogart gangster movie. The fact that MIBs speak and move in an artificial manner has given credence to the theory that they are not the government officials they claim to be, but the extraterrestrials themselves.

The MIB in "Jose Chung's 'From Outer Space' " comments that former American President Jimmy Carter was quite convinced that he saw what he described as a "flying saucer." The sighting took place in the company of several other witnesses on January 6, 1969, when he was the governor of Georgia. It is widely rumored that once he became president in 1977, he issued an Executive Order to NASA to launch a public inquiry into reported accounts that a crashed UFO and remains of dead aliens were being sequestered somewhere in America. The story goes that he repealed the presidential order at the behest of his advisors, who thought that the matter should remain classified.

Trivia alert: Roky Erikenson, the character who witnesses the teenagers' abduction in this episode, is named in honor of the psychedelic lead singer for the "13th Floor Elevators" who later formed a band called "Roky Erickson and the Aliens."

Klass County is also a nod to famous UFO debunker Philip J. Klass, who wrote in his book *UFOs Explained*, the familiar line, "No single object has been misinterpreted as a 'flying object' more often than the planet Venus."

FILE NO. 3X21:

AVATAR

Declassified Case Overview: When Assistant Director Skinner woke up in a hotel bed next to a murdered prostitute, Mulder and Scully joined the investigation to prove their boss' innocence. As they unraveled the threads of a conspiracy, Mulder also became convinced that Skinner had been visited by a medieval apparition known as a succubus.

Nitpicking

After hearing about Skinner's lurid nightmares of an old woman visiting him, Mulder concludes that his boss is encountering a succubus. Unfortunately, Mulder must have misplaced his mythology reference books, because the creature who keeps appearing to Skinner is more like the Night-Riding Hag of European legend. The traditional conception of a succubus is that of a sexually alluring demon which rises from the underworld to introduce infernal sexual pleasures to humanity. The most common physical appearance of a succubus is tall and voluptuous, not old and wrinkled as in "Avatar."

If Skinner has such a caring and devoted wife, then where was she a few weeks earlier when he was shot and hospitalized?

Trivia

1. On which date did the events in this episode begin?
    A. March 7, 1996
    B. April 26, 1996
    C. May 3, 1996

2. How many years had Skinner been married?

3. (True or False) Skinner picked up a prostitute in the Chesapeake Lounge of the Ambassador Hotel in Washington, D.C.

4. Identify the naturally occurring substance that Scully detected surrounding the dead woman's mouth and nose during her autopsy.

5. What color was the raincoat that the succubus/Skinner's wife was wearing while standing in front of the Second District Police Station?

6. What was Skinner's wife's name?

7. (Fill in the blank dialogue) Scully told investigators during Skinner's OPR hearing: "Whatever extreme cases I have encountered, I have always viewed through the _____ of science."

8. Which three words were engraved on the inside of Skinner's wedding band?
    A. LOVE ALWAYS SHARON
    B. SHARON AND WALTER
    C. LOVE FOREVER SHARON

X-PERT X-TRA BONUS POINTS #1

Skinner had been treated for the previous three months at the Bethesda Sleep Disorder Center. Identify the illness for which he was receiving psychiatric treatment.

X-PERT X-TRA BONUS POINTS #2

How long had Skinner and his wife been separated?

Investigative Field Report

"It's been a rough third season for Walter Skinner," acknowledged David Duchovny, who co-wrote this storyline with co-executive producer Howard Gordon. "He began the year with an armed confrontation with Mulder and Scully, got shot in the gut for pursuing the murder investigation of Scully's sister, was sprayed with mace and repeatedly kicked by a mind-controlled FBI clerk, and finally was framed for the murder of a prostitute."

Although "Avatar" is disappointing because the enigmatic Skinner still remains a mystery man (thanks to Mitch Pileggi's over-controlled performance), the conspiracy subplot hangs together better than the succubus theory proposed by Mulder. Bringing in the same Gray-Haired Man who warned Skinner to back away from the Melissa Scully murder investigation in "Piper Maru" was a successful attempt at storyline continuity.

Gillian Anderson's young daughter, Piper Maru (Gee, we wonder where the staff comes up with episode titles?), can be seen sitting in a window seat on a bus when Skinner runs back across the street to catch the woman in the raincoat.

ON CLOSER X-AMINATION: PART III

During The X-Files' third season, Agents Mulder and Scully continued to come into contact with a diversified range of highly competent and trained specialists. Typically, some of these skilled professionals were committed to eradicating disease and crime, but several others were only concerned with their own selfish, covert agendas. Correctly match the X-Perts below with the third year episodes in which they appeared.

1. _____ Warden Leo Brodeur

A. "The Walk"

2. _____ Dr. Seizer

B. "Clyde Bruckman's Final Repose"

3. _____ Agent Greg Nemhauser

C. "Teso Dos Bichos"

4. _____ Dr. Richard Godfrey

D. "The List"

5. _____ Mona Wustner

E. "2Shy"

6. _____ Dr. Mark Pomerantz

F. "War of the Coprophages"

7. _____ Agent Kazanjian

G. "Syzygy"

8. _____ Captain Janet Draper

H. "Piper Maru"

9. _____ Detective Cline

I. "The Blessing Way"

10. _____ Dr. Berenbaum

J. "Grotesque"

X-PERT X-TRA BONUS POINTS

Who was the bleeping detective named after in "Jose Chung's 'From Outer Space' "?

ON CLOSER X-AMINATION: THE FINAL X-AM

1. _____ Dr. Bugger

A. "Oubliette"

2. _____ Dr. Ishimaru

B. "Nisei"

3. _____ Agent Caleca

C. "Wetwired"

4. _____ Agent Burst

D. "Pusher"

5. _____ Dr. Fingers

E. "D.P.O."

6. _____ Lorraine Kelleher

F. "Teso Dos Bichos"

7. _____ Dr. Stroman

G. "Jose Chung's 'From Outer Space' "

8. _____ Dr. Winters

H. "Apocrypha"

9. _____ Agent Eubanks

I. "Avatar"

10. _____ Sheriff Teller

J. "War of the Coprophages"

X-PERT X-TRA BONUS POINTS

He played Ray, the foreman of the sewer treatment plant, in season two's "The Host" and more recently, Mr. Decker, the security guard at the museum in "Teso Dos Bichos." Identify this bearded character actor.

FILE NO. 3X22:

QUAGMIRE

Declassified Case Overview: When a series of mysterious deaths and disappearances occurred near a small town lake, Agents Mulder and Scully investigated reports of a killer aquatic serpent.

Nitpicking

Although the attack and consumption of children and small animals by alligators occurs, unfortunately, quite often in the Everglades, animal behavior experts in Florida are in agreement that it is highly unlikely that one alligator could eat three large adults within a few hours. In addition, these experienced handlers state that they have never seen a gator attack a boat the size of the one Mulder and Scully are in—especially from the bottom—nor have they seen one move as quickly as the one chasing Mulder through the woods during the episode's climax. The alligator's short, stubby legs make rapid movement on the ground a physical impossibility.

The scene of Big Blue surfacing on the lake during the episode's final moments, supposedly confirms to the audience that despite what Mulder and Scully are led to believe about the alligator, the Loch Ness-like prehistoric creature was indeed the culprit behind all the deaths and disappearances. If Big Blue was *really* the insatiable, man-eating beast in this episode (at a rate of three bodies within a few hours), wouldn't he still be devouring the townfolk at a steady rate?

"Quagmire"'s special effects left much to be desired: The mangled bodies were far from realistic-looking and the shot of Big Blue at the episode's conclusion was B-movie cheesy.

Trivia

1. Identify the lake in which Big Blue lived.
    - A.   Harroway
    - B.   Heuvelmans
    - C.   Hawkins

2. Under what conditions did this case become an FBI matter?

3. (Fill in the Blank) Big Blue was also known as "the _____ Serpent."

X-PERT X-TRA BONUS POINTS #1

What was the date on Big Blue's scale on display in the bait and tackle shop?

---

4. What was the name of Scully's dog (heavy emphasis on *was*)?

5. To what classic literary character did Scully compare Mulder?

6. Name the boat Mulder and Scully rented and lost when it was sunk.

X-PERT X-TRA BONUS POINTS #2

According to the sheriff, how many miles of shoreline encompassed the lake?

Investigative Field Report

The "rock" conversation between Mulder and Scully is the most intelligent aspect of an otherwise average *X-Files* installment. The electricity between these two characters in this memorable scene demonstrates their intimate knowledge of each other and the complexity of their relationship. Unfortunately, the rest of the episode is disappointing, especially the unnecessary ending which wraps up everything just a little too neatly.

Mulder states in "Quagmire" that a prehistoric animal living in a lake is not without precedent. Lake creatures have been reported for centuries in dozens of countries. A classic example, of course, is the Loch Ness monster. Seen by thousands of people and allegedly photographed, its existence continues to be a point of lively debate. The Siberian equivalent, the monster of Labinkir, is said to lurk in the freezing waters of Lake Labinkir. The Swedish authorities take the existence of their famous lake monster, Storjooduret, reputed to be a huge serpentine creature measuring up to 65 feet long living in Lake Storsjon, much more seriously. It was recently declared that anyone trying to capture or kill the creature could face prosecution.

Trivia alert: Big Blue's home turf, Heuvelmans Lake, is named after Van Heuvels, a Dutch cryptozoologist who wrote *In the Wake of the Sea Serpents*.

Ansel, the town photographer in pursuit of Big Blue, is named in honor of famed photographer Ansel Adams.

WETWIRED

Declassified Case Overview: Agents Mulder and Scully's partnership was tested to the extreme when they uncovered a dark conspiracy behind a bizarre series of seemingly unrelated murders in a small town.

Nitpicking

In the past, Mulder has been able to tell the difference between green alien blood and red human blood. Making Mulder red/green color-blind in this episode is nothing more than a convenient plot device to explain why he's rendered immune to the mind-controlling subliminal TV signals. A more suitable and believable explanation would have had the motel manager apologizing for a temporary black-and-white TV model in one of the two rooms available when Mulder and Scully checked in and then having Mulder graciously insist that Scully stay in the room with the color set. Besides, as any X-Phile can attest, Mulder prefers to watch old black-and-white movies.

When Mulder sees the cable guy (was that Jim Carrey?) examining a high-line pole on the street, he chases after the fleeing service van. Unable to catch up with the vehicle, Mulder climbs the pole to examine the signal box. However, when he comes back down he steps on the hood of his car, which wasn't parked there before he climbed up the pole.

If Skinner and his men are conducting a manhunt for Scully "as if searching for an escaped convict," then why isn't her mother's home under surveillance?

Law enforcement officers are taught to *always* lock their vehicle when exiting. Yet, every time Mulder gets out of his car in this episode, he leaves the driver's side window rolled all the way down (even in Washington, D.C.).

It is a rather big assumption on Mulder's part to accuse Mr. X of being a coward and never putting his life on the line. Mulder knows absolutely nothing about his shadowy informant and, from what we've seen in the past two years, Mr. X gets into his share of scrapes (the head-butt scene with Skinner in "End Game," saving Mulder from the exploding train in "731," and the near-miss with the scientist in "Soft Light").

Skinner tells Mulder that "Scully fired four rounds at you and a civilian last night," but there are five shots on the soundtrack and it sure looks like she pulls the trigger six times.

There are several photos of Dana (including pictures of her and/or possibly her sister Melissa as young girls) on Mrs. Scully's nightstand and none of Dana's two brothers. We know it's difficult to supply still photos of characters who haven't been cast yet, but couldn't Mrs. Scully at least have had some boyhood photos of her sons?

Trivia

1. On which date did the events in the episode initiate?
   - A.   April 19, 1996
   - B.   April 27, 1996
   - C.   May 10, 1996

2. How many people did Joseph Patnick kill, believing that each of them was the Bosnia equivalent of a "modern-day Hitler"?

3. What was the name of the motel where Mulder and Scully stayed?

4. Why did Mrs. Riddick kill her next-door neighbor while he lay resting in a backyard hammock?

5. What was the first thing Mulder did when he visited a recovering Scully in her hospital room?

6. Name the doctor who was killed by Mr. X during the episode's climactic scene.

X-PERT X-TRA BONUS POINTS

What was the telephone number of the motel where Mulder and Scully stayed?

Investigative Field Report

The phenomenon of previously peaceful people suddenly cracking up and going on killing sprees is certainly frightening . . . hey, wait a minute, that was our **Investigative Field Report** for second season's "Blood." Now that we think about it, "Wetwired" does resemble that episode a little too much. Although the government-conspiracy-of-setting-up-innocent-civilians-with-subliminal-messages is not very original, the brisk execution of this episode certainly is.

"Wetwired," which at first glance looks like a center-stage opportunity for Duchovny to strut his stuff, is, in fact, Gillian Anderson's big chance to impress the Emmy voters. She absolutely shines as the psychotic Scully, from her frantic search for the listening device in her motel room to her complete breakdown in her mother's arms when confronting Mulder.

Duchovny, too, is outstanding as Mulder, alternating between his quest for the Truth and his deep concern for his partner. His brief moment of grief, when he pulls into a parking space at the coroner's office and leans against the steering wheel before he has to identify the body of a woman who may or may not be Scully, says more than a ream of script paper.

Steven Williams' portrayal of the mysterious and paradoxical Mr. X is, as always, superlative. His fierce insistence that the outcome of this case is Mulder's failure, followed by his cool reaction as Mulder threatens to shoot him, appear effortless. The man can speak volumes simply with those cold, piercing eyes.

Skinner's critique of Mulder's field report, which segues into the parallel between Mr. X and the Cigarette-Smoking Man, shows that there *are* similarities between the opposing forces of the government and the international consortium, even though we'd like to think otherwise.

Episode writer Mat Beck is also the Visual Effects Producer and has worked on *The X-Files* since the pilot episode.

FILE NO. 3X24:

TALITHA CUMI [PART 1 OF 2]

Declassified Case Overview: Agent Mulder's mother's life hung in the balance as the X-Files team raced against time to save an extraterrestrial life-form with healing powers from the Cigarette-Smoking Man and the alien bounty hunter from "Colony" and "End Game."

Nitpicking

The Cigarette-Smoking Man reminisces to Mrs. Mulder about "so many good times at the Mulders' summer place" when Fox and Samantha were "so young and energetic." Mulder has extensive memories about his childhood with his sister, but he can't remember CSM visiting his parents' vacation home so many times over the years?

Why would Mulder's murder turn his quest for the Truth into a crusade, when just a few weeks earlier the same shadowy government elements attempted an even more high-profile murder—Walter Skinner, the assistant director of the FBI?

In "Colony/End Game" the clones who worked as doctors at abortion clinics all had different names, but in this episode the Jeremiah Smith clones all work at the Social Security Administration and share the same name. At least those Gregor clones had the common sense to use different aliases.

The first time the viewing audience hears the phrase "the date is set," it is spoken by the Cigarette-Smoking Man to a restrained Jeremiah Smith. The next person to utter the words is Mulder during his confrontation with Mr. X. How does Mulder get the information about the project's date being set, especially when he has not yet met the "real" Jeremiah Smith?

The Samantha clone told Mulder in "Colony/End Game" that a bullet to the base of the neck would kill the alien bounty hunter, but in this episode Mr. X tells Mulder that a simple gunshot wound to the same area will not work. Also, wouldn't your basic kitchen drawer ice pick produce the same result as the special alien-terminating weapon?

The alien bounty hunter apparently does not have a tracking device to find the clones (as evidenced in "Colony/End Game" and in this episode). So how does he know that Jeremiah Smith is in the Cigarette-Smoking Man's private jail and how does he know where to find Mulder, Scully, and Smith at the episode's cliffhanger conclusion?

A frantic Mulder tells Scully that the Cigarette-Smoking Man and his minions are after Jeremiah Smith, yet he gives her directions to a covert meeting place over the airwaves of an unsecured cellular phone. The Lone Gunmen would be *very* disappointed by Mulder's unnecessary and flagrant breach of security.

Mrs. Mulder has just suffered a serious cerebral vascular incident, but she gains consciousness just long enough to write PALM as an anagram for the word LAMP. With time so precious and her health rapidly deteriorating, wouldn't you think she'd impart such invaluable information without resorting to word games? If, on the other hand, it's supposed to be because the debilitating stroke has as Scully points out, damaged her language skills, how is she able to get that close to the word she meant (and have such neat handwriting)?

Mulder asks Scully if she thinks it is a "leap" for him to make a correlation between the shootings at the fast food restaurant and his mother writing the word PALM. Yes, Mulder, it is one *hell of* a leap and so is the scene where you find the special alien-killing device so easily in the second lamp you break. We're surprised the Cigarette-Smoking Man and/or Mr. X didn't trash the summer house before Mulder did.

Why would an alien-terminating weapon still be hidden in a lamp at the Mulder's abandoned summer house after all these years?

If Mulder's mother had to be transferred to a larger, more metropolitan hospital for better care, then why didn't her son move her to a hospital closer to Washington, D.C., where he could visit her more often and oversee her medical care?

Trivia

1. How many hostages did the gunman shoot in the fast food restaurant during the opening scenes of the episode?

2. What was the cell number of Jeremiah Smith's "cage within a cage"?
    A. 1013
    B. 128
    C. B18

3. (True or False) The Cigarette-Smoking Man told Mulder that he had known the agent's mother since before he was born.

4. What was Mrs. Mulder's room number at the hospital in Providence?
    A. 1123
    B. 128
    C. 118

5. What two words were printed in bright red on the concrete support column next to Mr. X in the hospital's underground parking garage?

6. (True or False) The Cigarette-Smoking Man was visibly shaken when the restrained Jeremiah Smith transformed into Deep Throat and Bill Mulder.

X-PERT X-TRA BONUS POINTS #1

Identify the six cities where the Jeremiah Smith clones lived according to the Social Security Administration Employee computer records that Scully accessed.

X-PERT X-TRA BONUS POINTS #2

What was the name of the fast food restaurant shown during the pre-credits sequence?

Investigative Field Report

Although not as fast-paced as first year's "The Erlenmeyer Flask" (Deep Throat murdered and the X-Files division shut down) and year two's "Anasazi" (with Mulder trapped in a burning boxcar), *The X-Files'* third season ends with a cliffhanger that offers "all kinds of possible outcomes," according to Chris Carter, who wrote the original story with David Duchovny. But he also leaves us hanging for four months (as he does every spring) with at least 200 more questions than we had before "Talitha Cumi" aired. It's frustrating and maddening, but also wonderfully intriguing, and one of the prime reasons we stay addicted to the series. What a letdown it would be if we knew all the answers. Speculation, like anticipation, is sometimes *much* more fun than satisfaction.

As did most fans, we concluded from "Talitha Cumi" that the Cigarette-Smoking Man and Mrs. Mulder had been lovers (CSM: "I was a better waterskier than he [Bill] was, but that could be said about many things."). Is Mulder the Cigarette-Smoking Man's son? Although Carter announced that the episode would reveal more about CSM and "how he may have impacted Mulder's life in ways we never expected," a plot thread of this nature is just too predictable and obvious, too much like the Darth Vader/Luke Skywalker father/son revelation of *Star Wars*, and just too soap operaish.

In part two, will Mulder try to kill the alien bounty hunter in hopes of using Jeremiah Smith to save his mother's life and discover his sister's whereabouts? Has the brutal confrontation over the alien-terminating device exposed an insurmountable schism between Mulder and Mr. X? What is the Cigarette-Smoking Man's and the international consortium's role in the alien colonization project? How will Scully scientifically explain away the morphing aliens? Will Samantha finally be returned to her brother ("Talitha Cumi" is Aramaic for "arise, girl")? Remember, though, that Chris Carter has always admitted that he has a multi-year overview of the series, which means that most of the "basics" from the conspiracy/alien arc (which is the central core of the show) won't be revealed until the final episodes air in the last year. Sure, he'll drop a few bread crumbs along the way to keep us intrigued, but he can't disclose everything about Samantha or the Cigarette-Smoking Man or Mulder's parents at this point in the series or he'd lose his audience.

"I'm the only one who knows where the show is going," Carter admitted during an interview with *Entertainment Weekly*. "I keep it in my head. That way they can't fire me."

Trivia alert: Roy Thinnes (benevolent alien Jeremiah Smith) was the star of the short-lived 1967–68 science-fiction series *The Invaders* (which Carter has acknowledged as inspiration for *The X-Files*); the Cigarette-Smoking Man makes a reference to waterskiing with the Mulders and, ironically, William B. Davis (who portrays CSM) was once a Canadian national waterskiing champion; the young man who gets shot in the fast food restaurant at the beginning of the episode is *X-Files* Production Assistant Angelo Vacco, who also played the gas station attendant in "F. Emasculata"; Mrs. Mulder's hospital physician is played by actor John MacLaren, who portrayed federal inspector George Kearns in "Our Town"; and sorry ladies, Mitch Pileggi's character ADA Skinner, is definitely back to wearing his wedding band in this episode.

MONSTER MASH: SEASON THREE

Match the third year M.O.T.W.s with the correct description.

1. _____ Fat-sucking vampire

2. _____ Homicidal maniac

3. _____ Alien robotic cockroaches

4. _____ Lightning producing redneck

5. _____ Curse from beyond the grave

6. _____ Shape-shifting alien

7. _____ Prehistoric lake serpent

8. _____ Astral-projecting spirit

9. _____ Transmigrated soul

10. _____ Grotesque-shaped gargoyle

11. _____ Mind-controlling hit man

A. Regular or premium, Agent Collins?

B. Oklahoma boy scored a Zero

C. What's bugging you, Dr. Bugger?

D. Did he eat the Budweiser frogs, too?

E. It had the soul of an FBI agent

F. They *really* were on Death Row

G. He put overweight women on a liquid diet

H. They couldn't see the forest for the trees

I. He was a veteran attacker

J. Krycek couldn't keep *it* down

K. Members of an archaeological expedition were casualties of feline-ious assault

---

X-PERT X-TRA BONUS POINTS

Where was Skinner when he first encountered the female succubus in "Avatar"?

BEHIND THE SCENES:
THE NAME GAME

1. *Star Trek* fans never warmed to the seemingly derogatory sobri-
    quet "Trekkie," so *Next Generation* followers changed the name
    to "Trekkers." What did Chris Carter originally call members of
    X-Files fandom before they, too, changed their nickname to "X-
    Philes"?

2. When Mulder went "B-ba-ba-booey" in "Tooms," it was an in-
    side joke by Duchovny showing that he listens to a certain con-
    troversial New York radio DJ. Name him.

3. Who was the professional photographer/filmmaker who took
    many "UFO" photos which later proved to be hoaxes, including
    the one on the I WANT TO BELIEVE poster hanging above Mul-
    der's desk?

4. Identify the actor who played the Satie piece heard in "Irre-
    sistible" and went on to play the unnamed "homicidal maniac"
    in "Clyde Bruckman's Final Repose." (Hint: He is also married
    to the former *X-Files* writer who penned the episodes "Aubrey"
    and "The Calusari.")

5. Who narrates the R.E.M. song "Star Me Kitten" on the *Songs in
    the Key of X* CD?

6. Name the leader singer/guitarist for the Foo Fighters who had a walk-on part for the episode "Pusher."

7. Which two members of *The X-Files* production staff appeared on Los Angeles' KCRW's radio show "Morning Becomes Eclectic" for three hours on April 2, 1996?

8. Name the irreverent comedy show that David Duchovny hosted on May 20, 1995.

9. Who has said of *The X-Files*, "People are hungry for transcendence, they're looking for that feeling of mystery, that tingle you get when you feel God. I'm not making those kinds of claims for *X-Files*, but we're dealing with the same kinds of issues. We're dealing with the unexplainable"?

10. Identify the actor whose recurring role on *The X-Files* led to a Showtime *Outer Limits* portrayal of an evil prep school principal who controlled his students by inserting neural implants.

11. Who wrote the lyrics to PM Dawn's "If You Never Say Goodbye" on *The Songs in the Key of X* CD?

12. Which *X-Files* actor doesn't wear his pants when filming head shots on the series (yes, he does have on boxer shorts)?

13. Name the magazine in which Gillian Anderson discussed her loss of privacy and fear of *X-Files* fans.

14. Which *X-Files* performer was in Washington, D.C. in 1996, petitioning Congress to provide funds to support research for Neurofibromatosis?

15. Who narrated the third season TV special *More Secrets of the X-Files*?

16. How does David Duchovny's father, Amram, spell his last name?

17. What is the name of Duchovny's character on the Showtime original anthology series, *Red Shoe Diaries*?

18. Identify the classic black-and-white movie which made a brief cameo on Modell's television set in "Pusher."

19. Duchovny made a surprise guest appearance as a pool-shark on *Space: Above and Beyond*. What was his character's name?

20. Identify the waste removal company whose three-letter name is often seen on the blue dumpsters in episodes of *The X-Files*. (Hint: It was also a demon-god of the Old Testament.)

21. He is known as "Mr. FiX-it," a producer of the series and the guy who oversees all aspects of physical production. Who is he?

22. Who does Duchovny credit as the creator of the "extended stories," those alien-conspiracy arcs that span two-to-three episodes?

X-PERT X-TRA BONUS POINTS #1

Name the episode in which the visual effects technicians used condoms to impersonate asparagus-shaped monsters?

---

23. Who recalled Gillian Anderson's audition for Agent Scully by stating, "What it came down to was that the network wasn't sure how Gillian would look in a bathing suit"?

24. Identify the *X-Files* performer who has flatly said that he doesn't want to see anybody he works with on the series off the set?

25. Who was the French deep-sea diver in the opening scenes of "Piper Maru" named after?

26. Who has said that "Mulder thinks about UFOs the way other men think about sex"?

27. What magazine's Australian edition had its biggest best-seller ever when David Duchovny and Gillian Anderson appeared on the cover?

28. Identify the hip performers whose two hidden CD tracks are tucked away at the beginning of *Song in the Key of X*?

29.   Name the playwright/actor Duchovny admires the most.

30.   Comedian Charles Nelson Reilly portrayed an author researching an alien abduction in the episode "Jose Chung's 'From Outer
Space.' " What was the name of the TV celebrity game show he
regularly appeared on for several years?

31.   Identify the *X-Files* writer whose distinctive idiosyncratic touch,
which works the funny bone while chilling the spine, has earned
him a huge fan following. (Hint: He was once a starving actor
who put on a grotesque rubber suit for money.)

32.   Name the composer whose first five attempts at a theme song
were rejected by Chris Carter.

33.   What is the name of the L.A. pub where David Duchovny used
to perform poetry readings?

34.   Which *X-Files* performer is allergic to cats (which made for a lot
of fun while filming the cat-infested climax to "Teso Dos Bichos")?

35.   Name the best-selling horrormeister who has asked Chris Carter
for the opportunity to write an *X-Files* script.

36.   He's a legendary crooner from way back and an unabashed X-
Phile. Who is he?

37.   Identify the star trekking, Oscar-winning actress who wants to
make a guest-appearance on *The X-Files.*

38.   Which performer on the series was spotted in the audience at the
last date on the Rolling Stones' "Voodoo Lounge" 1995 tour?

39.   Name the country which was first to get *The X-Files* episodes on
videotape.

40.   Which *X-Files* regular narrated the Discovery Channel's *Spies
Above,* an absorbing and undeniably rare look inside the classified world of spy surveillance and information-gathering from
space?

41. Identify the entertainment magazine which said in its "The Best (and the Worst) of '95" special issue, "But just as we know that Mulder will never prove to the world that there are aliens among us, we know he will never cross over the line from platonic love."

42. Who is the actor whom many fans consider to be the most popular guest star *The X-Files* has ever had?

43. After playing the fresh-faced faith healer Samuel Hartley in the episode "Miracle Man," he went on to star as Newt Call in *Lonesome Dove: The Series*. Name the actor.

44. Identify the character actor whose memorable and unique features have been a frequent and well-loved sight in movies and television from the Subway Spirit of *Ghost* to the freakish Lanny in *The X-Files* classic "Humbug."

45. Which *X-Files* performer described the series' shooting schedule to the *Los Angeles Times* as "a death sentence"?

46. Who often called Duchovny "ugly" when he was growing up?

47. This veteran *X-Files* director/producer helmed the *Star Trek: The Next Generation* episode "When the Bough Breaks." What's his name?

48. *Kolchak: The Night Stalker* is probably more famous as being the stimulus for *The X-Files* than for being a show in its own right. But whose talk show provided Chris Carter with the inspiration for his characters being FBI agents?

49. Who did Duchovny lose to on *Celebrity Jeopardy*?

50. Which *X-Files* performer was chosen among *People* magazine's "50 Most Beautiful People in the World 1996"?

51. Name the two famous faces who played the infamous MIB in "Jose Chung's 'From Outer Space.' "

52. Who has stated publicly that *The X-Files* is "all about religion, really. Not necessarily Christian religion, but it's about beliefs—and meaning and truth and why are we here and why are they here and who's lying to us. It's religion with a lower case 'r' "?

X-PERT X-TRA BONUS POINTS #2

David Duchovny's senior thesis at Princeton, where he earned a Bachelor's degree, was entitled *The Schizophrenic Critique of Pure Reason in Beckett's Early Novels.* What was the title of his unfinished doctoral dissertation?

X-PHILE EPISODE RANKING: SEASON THREE

Note: The following ranking of The X-Files' third season episodes (with 10.0 being the highest) have been posted by fans in various manifestations at official conventions and on the Internet.

Ranking	Episode Title	Ranking	Episode Title
1. 9.24	"Clyde Bruckman's Final Repose"	13. 8.49	"Wetwired"
2. 9.06	"731"	14. 8.08	"Quagmire"
3. 9.02	"Apocrypha"	15. 8.01	"Avatar"
4. 9.01	"Nisei"	16. 8.00	"Oubliette"
5. 9.00	"Talitha Cumi"	17. 7.72	"Grotesque"
6. 8.97	"Paper Clip"	18. 7.60	"Syzygy"
7. 8.96	"War of the Coprophages"	19. 7.38	"The Walk"
8. 8.95	"Jose Chung's 'From Outer Space' "	20. 7.30	"Hell Money"
9. 8.79	"Piper Maru"	21. 7.26	"2Shy"
10. 8.71	"Pusher"	22. 7.09	"D.P.O."
11. 8.69	"Revelations"	23. 6.89	"The List"
12. 8.57	"The Blessing Way"	24. 6.77	"Teso Dos Bichos"

ANSWER KEY

(Note: Each correct answer is worth one point. For every X-PERT X-TRA
BONUS POINTS *answered correctly, add an additional 5 points.)*

The Realm of X-treme Possibility: The Beginning of The X-Files

1. C   2. True   3. No   4. Yes   5. True   6. Darren McGavin, who played the title character on *Kolchak: The Night Stalker*   7. *Silence of the Lambs*
8. True   9. mother   10. Vin Scully   11. The Watergate scandal
12. False (Fox was Carter's first and only network)   13. B   14. A
15. TV screens   16. Carter's   17. True   18. True   19. It's his birthday
20. 1) There are a great many forests; 2) Offers monetary savings compared to Los Angeles; and 3) Able to visually approximate almost any city in North America   21. March   22. C   23. *The Adventures of Brisco County, Jr.*   24. False (It was tacked on to the first episode to mollify Fox's desire to provide resolution to the story)   25. True   26. B   27. *Lois and Clark: The New Adventures of Superman* and *seaQuest DSV*

X-PERT X-TRA BONUS POINTS #1: Nathan Couturier, son of supervising sound editor Thierry Couturier
X-PERT X-TRA BONUS POINTS #2: *Star Trek*
X-PERT X-TRA BONUS POINTS #3: 7.4 million

MAXIMUM SCORE POTENTIAL: 42

YOUR SCORE: _____

The X-Files: Pilot

1. 2   2. 2   3. physics   4. A   5. True   6. Congress

X-PERT X-TRA BONUS POINTS: Dr. Heitz Werber

MAXIMUM SCORE POTENTIAL: 11

YOUR SCORE: _____

Deep Throat

1. B   2. A   3. B   4. six   5. He was strapped to a gurney and injected with drugs   6. Deep Throat

X-PERT X-TRA BONUS POINTS: fish food

MAXIMUM SCORE POTENTIAL: 11

YOUR SCORE: _____

Squeeze

1. False (through an air vent)   2. an elongated fingerprint   3. B   4. He passed a polygraph   5. B   6. newspapers

X-PERT X-TRA BONUS POINTS: They're chronically anemic

MAXIMUM SCORE POTENTIAL: 11

YOUR SCORE: _____

FBI Service Record: Special Agent Fox Mulder

1. William   2. B   3. A   4. False (Chilmark, Massachusetts)   5. C
6. Right field   7. B   8. C   9. False ("T")   10. A   11. False (1986)   12. B
13. True   14. True   15. Reggie Purdue   16. John Barnett   17. 1989

X-PERT X-TRA BONUS POINTS #1: 650

18. Section Chief Scott Blevins   19. False (Sec. Chief Joseph McGrath)
20. Eugene Victor Tooms   21. Smith & Wesson 1076   22. C   23. FBI Agent Alex Krycek   24. Yes   25. B   26. C   27. Washington Redskins tickets   28. Sunflower seeds   29. "Spooky"   30. True   31. TRUSTNO1
32. C   33. False (classic science-fiction)   34. B   35. A   36. *Video*   37. C
38. False (Marty)   39. True

X-PERT X-TRA BONUS POINTS #2: M.F. Luder
40. B   41. B   42. Heinrich   43. True

X-PERT X-TRA BONUS POINTS #3: X-42053

MAXIMUM SCORE POTENTIAL: 52

YOUR SCORE: _____

Conduit

1. She reported a UFO sighting   2. satellite   3. C   4. pages of his number-pictures   5. motorcycles   6. In church   7. A

X-PERT X-TRA BONUS POINTS: They formed the binary code

MAXIMUM SCORE POTENTIAL: 12

YOUR SCORE: _____

The Jersey Devil

1. C   2. leg   3. human bite marks were found   4. True   5. A park ranger
6. A human bone

X-PERT X-TRA BONUS POINTS: 756

MAXIMUM SCORE POTENTIAL: 11

YOUR SCORE: _____

Shadows

1. 2   2. True   3. A   4. False (bathtub drain)   5. B   6. A   7. C

X-PERT X-TRA BONUS POINTS #1: Ben Franklin's

MAXIMUM SCORE POTENTIAL: 12

YOUR SCORE: _____

S & M: Season One

1. "Miracle Man"   2. "The X-Files: Pilot"   3. "Ghost in the Machine"
4. "The Erlenmeyer Flask"   5. "Roland"   6. "The X-Files: Pilot"
7. "Fallen Angel"   8. "Fire"   9. "GenderBender"   10. "GenderBender"
11. "Young at Heart"   12. "Darkness Falls"   13. "E.B.E."   14. "Deep

Throat" 15. "Squeeze" 16. "The Jersey Devil" 17. "Conduit" 18. "The Erlenmeyer Flask" 19. "Darkness Falls" 20. "GenderBender" 21. "Space" 22. "The X-Files: Pilot" 23. "Squeeze" 24. "The Jersey Devil" 25. "Beyond the Sea" 26. "E.B.E." 27. "Young at Heart" 28. "Miracle Man"

X-PERT X-TRA BONUS POINTS: anti-gravity

MAXIMUM SCORE POTENTIAL: 33

YOUR SCORE: _____

Ghost in the Machine

1. A   2. Jerry Lamana   3. False (voice analysis)   4. C   5. Deep Throat 6. B

X-PERT X-TRA BONUS POINTS: "Brad, why?"

MAXIMUM SCORE POTENTIAL: 11

YOUR SCORE: _____

Ice

1. False (they shot themselves)   2. ammonia   3. C   4. days   5. hypothalamus   6. False (Mulder did)   7. She inserted a full-grown worm into the dog, curing him   8. Da Silva

X-PERT X-TRA BONUS POINTS #1: The military
X-PERT X-TRA BONUS POINTS #2: 200,000 years

MAXIMUM SCORE POTENTIAL: 28

YOUR SCORE: _____

Space

1. False (*Gemini* 8)   2. True   3. ghost   4. True   5. Albuquerque, New Mexico   6. Mulder

X-PERT X-TRA BONUS POINTS: Mission Control Communications Commander

MAXIMUM SCORE POTENTIAL: 11

YOUR SCORE: _____

Alphabet Soup
(Note: Every correct answer will count as a 5-point X-pert X-tra Bonus)

1. The Central Operating System   2. Arctic Ice Core Project   3. Auxiliary Power Unit   4. National Investigative Committee of Aerial Phenomena   5. Deoxyribonucleic acid   6. International Extraterrestrial Biological Entity Directive   7. Federal Forest Service   8. Search for Extraterrestrial Intelligence   9. American Sign Language   10. Army Criminal Investigative Command   11. The Air Force Office of Special Investigations   12. Special Agent in Charge   13. Violent Crimes Unit   14. Office of Professional Responsibility   15. Department of Justice   16. Naval Intelligence Service   17. Assistant Special Agent in Charge   18. Immigration and Naturalization Service   19. International Criminal Police Organization   20. National Crime Information Computer   21. The Center for Disease Control and Prevention   22. Bureau of Alcohol, Tobacco and Firearms   23. Drug Enforcement Administration   24. Wild Again Organization   25. Extraterrestrial Biological Entities

MAXIMUM SCORE POTENTIAL: 125

YOUR SCORE: _____

Fallen Angel

1. meteor   2. B   3. FALCON   4. Roswell   5. False (Scully came to his aid)   6. B   7. C   8. lies

X-PERT X-TRA BONUS POINTS: jurisdiction

MAXIMUM SCORE POTENTIAL: 13

YOUR SCORE: _____

Eve

1. C   2. True   3. exsanguinate   4. B   5. False (They overdosed her with digitalis)   6. Yes

X-PERT X-TRA BONUS POINTS: 265

MAXIMUM SCORE POTENTIAL: 11

YOUR SCORE: _____

X-pert Testimony: Part I

1. C 2. B 3. True 4. C 5. sins 6. "Ice" 7. A 8. False (The state was Wisconsin) 9. B 10. A 11. C 12. A 13. C 14. False (Agent Mulder) 15. False (Bill Mulder) 16. B 17. Mr. X 18. B 19. False (Dr. Osborne) 20. "Fearful Symmetry" 21. C 22. A 23. Bocks 24. Mulder 25. C 26. arm 27. C 28. True 29. Ten 30. Luther Lee Boggs 31. B 32. A 33. C 34. forest 35. False (Mulder) 36. C 37. B 38. C 39. spontaneously 40. A 41. we 42. B 43. "Red Museum" 44. C

X-PERT X-TRA BONUS POINTS: Melissa Scully in "One Breath"

MAXIMUM SCORE POTENTIAL: 49

YOUR SCORE: _____

Fire

1. caretaker 2. A bar 3. A 4. women 5. A 6. Phoebe Green 7. False (5th and 6th degree burns)

X-PERT X-TRA BONUS POINTS: Bob

MAXIMUM SCORE POTENTIAL: 12

YOUR SCORE: _____

Beyond The Sea
(Note: Every correct answer will count as a 5-point X-pert X-tra Bonus)

1. 1:47 2. $39.92 3. 1935766 4. noon 5. X-167512 6. 8 7. five 8. 6 9. 6509137 10. 5 11. 14 12. 2 sisters, 1 brother

MAXIMUM SCORE POTENTIAL: 60

YOUR SCORE: _____

GenderBender

1. False (in a bar)   2. A   3. B   4. animal   5. False (Andrew told Scully of Brother Martin)   6. B   7. pleasures   8. earthly

X-PERT X-TRA BONUS POINTS: Marty

MAXIMUM SCORE POTENTIAL: 13

YOUR SCORE: _____

X Marks the Spot: Season One

1. D   2. G   3. J   4. C   5. L   6. B   7. H   8. E   9. F   10. A   11. K   12. I

X-PERT X-TRA BONUS POINTS #1: Idaho
X-PERT X-TRA BONUS POINTS #2: Olympia
X-PERT X-TRA BONUS POINTS #3: Philadelphia, Pennsylvania
X-PERT X-TRA BONUS POINTS #4: Icy
X-PERT X-TRA BONUS POINTS #5: Baltimore, Maryland

MAXIMUM SCORE POTENTIAL: 37

YOUR SCORE: _____

Lazarus

1. C   2. A   3. Lula   4. True   5. "Happy 35th"   6. Philips

X-PERT X-TRA BONUS POINTS: Dupre's tattoo on his forearm

MAXIMUM SCORE POTENTIAL: 11

YOUR SCORE: _____

Young at Heart

1. A   2. Irvin   3. 95   4. False (A hunted fox eventually dies)   5. Strangled while on the phone   6. research   7. salamander   8. A

X-PERT X-TRA BONUS POINTS: Delaware

MAXIMUM SCORE POTENTIAL: 13

YOUR SCORE: _____

E.B.E.

1. False (Iraq/Turkey border)   2. Reagan   3. C   4. $20 bill   5. C   6. Washington   7. Roswell

X-PERT X-TRA BONUS POINTS: three

MAXIMUM SCORE POTENTIAL: 12

YOUR SCORE: _____

FBI Service Record: Special Agent Dana Scully, M.D.

1. B   2. False (2/23/64)   3. False (P.O.B. unknown)   4. A   5. Yes   6. C   7. Captain   8. "Ahab"   9. False (January 1994)   10. B   11. False (when she turned 15)   12. Yes   13. True   14. C   15. C   16. True   17. B

X-PERT X-TRA BONUS POINTS #1: "Einstein's Twin Paradox: A New Interpretation"
18. Forensic pathology   19. A   20. Jack Willis   21. False (Section Chief Blevins)   22. Duane Barry   23. A   24. True   25. Alex Krycek

X-PERT X-TRA BONUS POINTS #2: 202-555-3564
26. A   27. C   28. B   29. Instructor, Quantico Academy   30. A   31. B   32. False (Trent)   33. Mac Powerbook 540C

X-PERT X-TRA BONUS POINTS #3: D_Scully@FBI.gov

MAXIMUM SCORE POTENTIAL: 48

YOUR SCORE: _____

Miracle Man

1. B   2. False (two)   3. His sister   4. True   5. C   6. B   7. Leonard Vance

X-PERT X-TRA BONUS POINTS #1: Mississippi
X-PERT X-TRA BONUS POINTS #2: ten

MAXIMUM SCORE POTENTIAL: 27

YOUR SCORE: _____

Shapes

1. C   2. False (His cattle had been slaughtered)   3. A   4. False ('54, '59, '64, '78 and then '94)   5. Lewis and Clark   6. Scully   7. Manitou 8. eight

X-PERT X-TRA BONUS POINTS: Charley

MAXIMUM SCORE POTENTIAL: 13

YOUR SCORE: _____

Darkness Falls

1. A   2. sixty   3. C   4. cocoon   5. enemy   6. B

X-PERT X-TRA BONUS POINTS: Steve Humphreys

MAXIMUM SCORE POTENTIAL: 11

YOUR SCORE: _____

On Closer X-amination: Part I

1. H   2. A   3. L   4. D   5. B   6. K   7. C   8. J   9. E   10. F   11. I 12. G

MAXIMUM SCORE POTENTIAL: 12

YOUR SCORE: _____

On Closer X-amination: Part II

1. G   2. I   3. A   4. C   5. K   6. B   7. D   8. E   9. F   10. H   11. J

X-PERT X-TRA BONUS POINTS #1: Frohike, Langly, Byers, and the Thinker
X-PERT X-TRA BONUS POINTS #2: Progeria

MAXIMUM SCORE POTENTIAL: 21

YOUR SCORE: _____

Tooms

1. False (Druid Hill Sanitarium)   2. False (Contingent on the results of a psychiatric hearing)   3. 100   4. No   5. B   6. B   7. A   8. fifth

X-PERT X-TRA BONUS POINTS: A caterpillar cocoon

MAXIMUM SCORE POTENTIAL: 13

YOUR SCORE: _____

Born Again

1. C   2. B   3. Psychokinetic   4. Her mother   5. His scarf got caught in a bus that dragged him to death   6. pre-existence   7. False (Michelle's mother refused to allow her daughter to be studied any further)

X-PERT X-TRA BONUS POINTS: Judy

MAXIMUM SCORE POTENTIAL: 12

YOUR SCORE: _____

Roland
(Note: Every correct answer will count as 5-point X-pert X-tra Bonus)

1. 315   2. four   3. six   4. 12:31   5. 15626   6. 15th 7. Three   8. 70   9. 18   10. 320 degrees Fahrenheit   11. 15   12. 150 degrees Fahrenheit

MAXIMUM SCORE POTENTIAL: 60

YOUR SCORE: _____

The Erlenmeyer Flask

1. Green   2. B   3. Crew-Cut Man   4. False (Dr. Carpenter)   5. "Purity Control"   6. nucleotide   7. B

X-PERT X-TRA BONUS POINTS #1: Zeus Storage, 1616 Pandora Street
X-PERT X-TRA BONUS POINTS #2: Five

MAXIMUM SCORE POTENTIAL: 27

YOUR SCORE: _____

Monster Mash: Season One

1. teeth   2. B   3. "Because he likes it."   4. C   5. Litchfield   6. The off-spring of the male and female Jersey Devil   7. Deep Throat   8. Mulder   9. eradication   10. False (an elongated claw)   11. Locusts   12. True   13. False (It escaped his body, heading skyward)   14. two

X-PERT X-TRA BONUS POINTS: Through a vent

MAXIMUM SCORE POTENTIAL: 19

YOUR SCORE: _____

Behind the Scenes: Part I

1. A frozen calf's liver   2. C   3. "Squeeze"   4. C   5. True   6. True   7. False (She confided in her co-star first, then Carter)   8. A sewer worker literally coughs up a large worm in his shower   9. A   10. Industry achievement in graphic design and title sequences   11. "The Erlenmeyer Flask" changed the opening tag line of the credits from "The Truth is Out There" to "Trust No One." In "Ascension," it was changed to "Deny Everything." In "Anasazi," the tag line displayed the Navajo translation of "The Truth is Out There."   12. False ($1.1 million per episode in season one, $1.2 million the second year and a bit more for the third season)   13. True   14. A   15. It's Carter's wife's birthday   16. True   17. B   18. "Conduit"   19. "Ghost in the Machine"   20. True   21. C   22. Rob, in "The Jersey Devil"   23. A   24. True   25. Yes   26. Jack the Ripper   27. "3"   28. A nightclub Romeo   29. "The Host"   30. Colonel Budahas' wife, Anita   31. True   32. "Young at Heart"   33. B

X-PERT X-TRA BONUS POINTS #1: "Fearful Symmetry"
X-PERT X-TRA BONUS POINTS #2: Phoebe Green ("Fire"), Kristen Kilar ("3") and his mother ("Colony")

34. It's the name of Gillian Anderson's daughter   35. False (They were made up by the makeup department)   36. B   37. C   38. Mario Mark Kennedy   39. They have an intimate relationship   40. A   41. "Our Town"   42. A cricket   43. B   44. A   45. C   46. False (They were plastic)   47. "Excelsius Dei"   48. B   49. "Sleepless"   50. Charles Grant   51. *I am Legend*   52. "Born Again"   53. "Tooms"   54. True   55. "Darkness Falls"   56. "Fire"   57. Yes, from Vancouver   58. B   59. "Space"

60. A   61. Agent Barry Weiss   62. False (Only one table-dancing girl named Peaches)   63. "Ice"

X-PERT X-TRA BONUS POINTS #3: "He who eats my flesh and drinks of my blood shall have eternal life and I shall raise them up on the last day."
X-PERT X-TRA BONUS POINTS #4: The hand that wounds
X-PERT X-TRA BONUS POINTS #5: An influential founding father of modern Wicca

MAXIMUM SCORE POTENTIAL: 88

YOUR SCORE: _____

Little Green Men

1. *Voyager*   2. B   3. "Contact"   4. The Cigarette-Smoking Man   5. The physiognomy of an alien   6. time

X-PERT X-TRA BONUS POINTS: Brandenburg Concerto Number Two by Bach

MAXIMUM SCORE POTENTIAL: 11

YOUR SCORE: _____

The Host
(Note: Every correct answer will count as a 5-point X-pert X-tra Bonus)

1. 2   2. 5A221147   3. DP112148   4. 165 pounds   5. 40   6. 560,000
7. 277-1628   8. 5:27 A.M.   9. 4   10. three

MAXIMUM SCORE POTENTIAL: 50

YOUR SCORE: _____

X-Man: David Duchovny

1. False (August 7)   2. B   3. B   4. B   5. False (He went to Princeton and then pursued grad lit studies at Yale)   6. False (Gargoyles)   7. William
8. spiritual   9. A   10. B   11. A   12. B   13. False (cinematographer)
14. 1992's *Ruby*   15. True   16. *Kalifornia*   17. *Don't Tell Mom the Babysit-*

ter's Dead   18. C   19. C   20. *Beethoven*   21. *Red Shoe Diaries*   22. The transvestite detective in *Twin Peaks*   23. False (AT&T and NYNEX) 24. B   25. C   26. C   27. True   28. C   29. C   30. B   31. True   32. Creator Chris Carter   33. Himself   34. B   35. A   36. A   37. A teeny-weeny red Speedo bikini   38. 5   39. Poetry   40. True   41. vampire   42. True 43. B   44. Writing   45. C   46. A   47. Blue   48. C   49. No   50. No 51. B   52. *Playing God*

X-PERT X-TRA BONUS POINTS #1: *The Schizophrenic Critique of Pure Reason in Beckett's Early Novels*
X-PERT X-TRA BONUS POINTS #2: September 29, 1995

MAXIMUM SCORE POTENTIAL: 62

YOUR SCORE: _____

Blood

1. B   2. C   3. False (The display read: HE'LL RAPE YOU. HE'LL KILL YOU. KILL HIM FIRST.   4. Sheriff Spencer   5. True   6. Flies   7. C

X-PERT X-TRA BONUS POINTS: Fiber-Optics Lens Micro Video Camera #CCDTH21-38

MAXIMUM SCORE POTENTIAL: 12

YOUR SCORE: _____

Sleepless

1. A   2. Sleep-disorder   3. True   4. B   5. B   6. Mr. X   7. False (24 years) 8. False (Train station)

X-PERT X-TRA BONUS POINTS: 606

MAXIMUM SCORE POTENTIAL: 13

YOUR SCORE: _____

Duane Barry (Part 1 of 2)

1. B   2. A   3. False (Only one hostage)   4. It destroyed its moral center, making him both delusional and violent   5. Scully   6. B

X-PERT X-TRA BONUS POINTS: Lucy

MAXIMUM SCORE POTENTIAL: 11

YOUR SCORE: _____

S & M: Season Two

1. "F. Emasculata" 2. "End Game" 3. "Aubrey" 4. "Blood"
5. "Blood" 6. "The Host" 7. "Anasazi" 8. "Our Town" 9. "Colony"
10. "Fearful Symmetry" 11. "One Breath" 12. "Blood" 13. "The Host"
14. "Sleepless" 15. "The Host" 16. "Die Hand Die Verletzt"
17. "Colony" 18. "Dod Kalm" 19. "Die Hand Die Verletzt" 20. "The
Calusari" 21. "Fresh Bones" 22. "Colony" 23. "The Calusari"

X-PERT X-TRA BONUS POINTS #1: hairiness
X-PERT X-TRA BONUS POINTS #2: The Lone Gunmen

MAXIMUM SCORE POTENTIAL: 33

YOUR SCORE: _____

Ascension (Part 2 of 2)

1. He played his answering machine and heard Scully being kidnapped
2. Her mother   3. With the help of computer enhancement   4. Krycek
5. Krycek killed the operator, stranding Mulder   6. Krycek   7. crusade
8. A

X-PERT X-TRA BONUS POINTS: Route 229

MAXIMUM SCORE POTENTIAL: 13

YOUR SCORE: _____

3

1. B   2. Her small gold cross   3. six   4. drawstring   5. Taste her blood
6. Four

X-PERT X-TRA BONUS POINTS: John 52:54 (which doesn't really exist)

MAXIMUM SCORE POTENTIAL: 11

YOUR SCORE: _____

One Breath

1. Scully's patient chart   2. DNA   3. player   4. Skinner   5. Mr. X   6. It was ransacked   7. beliefs

X-PERT X-TRA BONUS POINTS: 900 W. Georgia Street

MAXIMUM SCORE POTENTIAL: 12

YOUR SCORE: _____

Another Helping of Alphabet Soup

1. ALL DONE. BYE BYE.   2. *Adult Video News*   3. "All Along the Watchtower"   4. "Beyond the Sea"   5. Briggs, Detective Frank   6. Bear   7. Crew-Cut Man   8. Colton, Agent Tom   9. Club Tepes   10. Deadhorse   11. Eurisko   12. Folkstone   13. Fuller   14. Gordon, Howard   15. Gerdes, George   16. Hodge, Dr.   17. Harris, Harriet   18. "Irresistible"   19. Jarvis, Owen Lee   20. Kyte, Lauren   21. KILL 'EM ALL

X-PERT X-TRA BONUS: Ermy, R. Lee

MAXIMUM SCORE POTENTIAL: 26

YOUR SCORE: _____

Firewalker

1. Mt. Avalon   2. Trepkos   3. False (Trepkos' notes)   4. Silicon   5. Erikson   6. True

X-PERT X-TRA BONUS POINTS: Ludwig

MAXIMUM SCORE POTENTIAL: 11

YOUR SCORE: _____

Red Museum

1. twelve   2. Church of the Red Museum   3. B   4. He was a doctor   5. growth   6. A   7. Sheriff Mazeroski

X-PERT X-TRA BONUS POINTS: Richard Odin

MAXIMUM SCORE POTENTIAL: 12

YOUR SCORE: _____

Excelsius Dei

1. Hal Arden   2. B   3. An invisible force   4. Upshaw   5. suffer
6. Nurse Charters

X-PERT X-TRA BONUS POINTS: Bituen

MAXIMUM SCORE POTENTIAL: 11

YOUR SCORE: _____

X-pert Testimony: Part II

1. "Fire"   2. B   3. False (Scully)   4. C   5. Scully   6. Deep Throat   7. A
8. B   9. Donnie Pfaster   10. John Barnett   11. B   12. B   13. False (John)
14. friend   15. C   16. L'ively   17. Deep Throat   18. A   19. Krycek
20. "Aubrey"   21. Mr. X   22. science   23. tape   24. A   25. an elongated
fingerprint   26. C   27. Lt. Col. Marcus Aurelius Belt   28. A   29. Duane
Barry   30. "Die Hand Die Verletzt"   31. C   32. Charlie's grandmother
33. False (Mr. X)   34. Mr. X   35. A   36. C   37. True   38. True   39. Elvis
40. B   41. C   42. False (Doug Spinney)   43. True   44. C   45. Mulder
46. B   47. catalogue   48. A   49. A   50. "Colony"

X-PERT X-TRA BONUS POINTS #1: "Dod Kalm"
X-PERT X-TRA BONUS POINTS #2: Skinner

MAXIMUM SCORE POTENTIAL: 60

YOUR SCORE: _____

Aubrey

1. A   2. Sam Chaney   3. 1945   4. C   5. An oxygen machine   6. traits

X-PERT X-TRA BONUS POINTS: extreme

MAXIMUM SCORE POTENTIAL: 11

YOUR SCORE: _____

Irresistible
(Note: Every correct answer will count as a 5-point X-pert X-tra Bonus)

1. 1973   2. 3   3. True   4. 12   5. 11 and 12   6. 11:21   7. twenty   8. 28
9. 60,000   10. three   11. False (4)

MAXIMUM SCORE POTENTIAL: 55

YOUR SCORE: _____

Die Hand Die Verletzt

1. C   2. B   3. False (toads)   4. The dead boy's heart and eyes   5. incense
6. He was devoured by a python

X-PERT X-TRA BONUS POINTS: M.R. Krashewski

MAXIMUM SCORE POTENTIAL: 11

YOUR SCORE: _____

X Marks the Spot: Season Two

1. G   2. K   3. H   4. J   5. A   6. C   7. B   8. D   9. L   10. F   11. I   12. E

X-PERT X-TRA BONUS POINTS #1: Arecibo
X-PERT X-TRA BONUS POINTS #2: Dudley
X-PERT X-TRA BONUS POINTS #3: Gibsonton, Florida
X-PERT X-TRA BONUS POINTS #4: Tildeskan
X-PERT X-TRA BONUS POINTS #5: Georgetown

MAXIMUM SCORE POTENTIAL: 37

YOUR SCORE: _____

Fresh Bones

1. A   2. B   3. True   4. sacred   5. The base's Psychiatric Infirmary
6. False ($200)   7. Private Dunham

X-PERT X-TRA BONUS POINTS #1: 10
X-PERT X-TRA BONUS POINTS #2: Tetrodotoxin

MAXIMUM SCORE POTENTIAL: 17

YOUR SCORE: _____

Colony (Part 1 of 2)

1. hypothermia   2. Beaufort   3. Green   4. True   5. A   6. Agent Weiss
7. Mulder

X-PERT X-TRA BONUS POINTS: 22

MAXIMUM SCORE POTENTIAL: 12

YOUR SCORE: _____

End Game (Part 2 of 2)

1. True   2. False (1940s)   3. C   4. Skinner's   5. Five   6. Mr. X   7. Science

X-PERT X-TRA BONUS POINTS: It was the number on the keycard
Samantha left for Mulder

MAXIMUM SCORE POTENTIAL: 12

YOUR SCORE: _____

Madam X: Gillian Anderson

1. False (She's the oldest of the three)   2. A marine biologist   3. C   4. B
5. She wore a ring in her nose and dyed her hair blue, purple and black
6. True   7. C   8. attitude   9. William Morris   10. C   11. Waitress
12. Mary-Louise Parker   13. three   14. *The Turning*   15. A   16. True
17. Fox's *Class of '96*   18. True   19. B   20. False (The same day)
21. Steven Williams (aka Mr. X)   22. New Year's Day, 1994   23. False
(Chris Carter *emphatically* denies)   24. 8 months   25. True   26. A
27. True   28. A Native American who eventually cleanses the house with
an Indian purification ritual

X-PERT X-TRA BONUS POINTS #1: 17TH
X-PERT X-TRA BONUS POINTS #2: National Theatre of Great Britain
at Cornell University in Ithaca, New York

MAXIMUM SCORE POTENTIAL: 38

YOUR SCORE: _____

Fearful Symmetry

1. B   2. Idaho Mutual Insurance Trust   3. C   4. False (1940s)   5. The Lone Gunmen   6. She was pregnant despite having never mated   7. One

X-PERT X-TRA BONUS POINTS: Genesia

MAXIMUM SCORE POTENTIAL: 12

YOUR SCORE: _____

Dod Kalm
(Note: Every correct answer will count as a 5-point X-pert X-tra Bonus)

1. 8   2. 18   3. 28   4. 9   5. False (9 months)   6. 35   7. 1991   8. 4:30   9. 50   10. 925

MAXIMUM SCORE POTENTIAL: 50

YOUR SCORE: _____

Humbug

1. Ichthyosis   2. In his swimming pool   3. C   4. wake   5. Fiji Mermaid   6. Mr. Nutt   7. The Conundrum

X-PERT X-TRA BONUS POINTS: Dr. Blockhead

MAXIMUM SCORE POTENTIAL: 12

YOUR SCORE: _____

Torn from Today's Headlines

1. True   2. One of Dr. Blockhead's pins   3. Lanny's congenital twin, Leonard

X-PERT X-TRA BONUS POINTS #1: Jim-Jim, the Dog-Faced Boy
4. B   5. 30   6. Olaffson

X-PERT X-TRA BONUS POINTS #2: Life

7. Lt. Col. Belt   8. NASA Mission Control Communications Commander Michelle Generoo   9. Major Gordon Cooper

X-PERT X-TRA BONUS POINTS #3: Alter the shuttle's angle of trajectory
10. Lyle Parker   11. Joe Goodensnake

X-PERT X-TRA BONUS POINTS #4: David Nutter
12. A big snake (Python or boa constrictor)   13. worm   14. False (It had no sex organs)

X-PERT X-TRA BONUS POINTS #5: Dimitri
15. True   16. Scully

X-PERT X-TRA BONUS POINTS #6: Peter Boulle

MAXIMUM SCORE POTENTIAL: 46

YOUR SCORE: _____

The Calusari

1. True   2. 8 years old   3. A swastika   4. Proxy   5. million
X-PERT X-TRA BONUS POINTS: Vibuti

MAXIMUM SCORE POTENTIAL: 10

YOUR SCORE: _____

F. Emasculata

1. B   2. A bloody pig's leg   3. A   4. A   5. C   6. Elizabeth   7. Pinck Pharmaceuticals   8. postal

X-PERT X-TRA BONUS POINTS #1: The Cigarette-Smoking Man
X-PERT X-TRA BONUS POINTS #2: Dr. Osborne

MAXIMUM SCORE POTENTIAL: 18

YOUR SCORE: _____

Soft Light

1. B   2. False (Electric people movers)   3. The lights   4. A "brain suck"
5. tether   6. Mr. X   7. A flashing white light

X-PERT X-TRA BONUS POINTS #1: Sig Sauer P228
X-PERT X-TRA BONUS POINTS #2: Dr. Davey

MAXIMUM SCORE POTENTIAL: 17

YOUR SCORE: _____

Monster Mash: Season Two

1. By dropping the sewer drain gate   2. Amrith   3. Jeffrey Dahmer
4. True   5. False (Alien conservation)   6. Necrotizing facilitis
7. Dorothy   8. Trepkos   9. False ("blood sports")   10. Alien DNA
11. *The Stepfather*   12. False (A dog's corpse)   13. False (The immune system)

X-PERT X-TRA BONUS POINTS: twelve

MAXIMUM SCORE POTENTIAL: 18

YOUR SCORE: _____

Our Town

1. A   2. The plant manager   3. Sheriff Arens   4. She was his granddaughter   5. B   6. Human heads   7. A human hair

X-PERT X-TRA BONUS POINTS: 93 years old

MAXIMUM SCORE POTENTIAL: 12

YOUR SCORE: _____

Anasazi (Part 1 of 3)

1. False (The Defense Department)   2. A   3. Garnet   4. 30   5. In the shower   6. Mr. X

X-PERT X-TRA BONUS POINTS: Albert Hosteen

MAXIMUM SCORE POTENTIAL: 11

YOUR SCORE: _____

Behind the Scenes: Part II

1. B   2. "Colony," "End Game," and "Dod Kalm"   3. True   4. Dr. Ridley   5. The female Marty   6. True   7. No, Sophie was an actor in a gorilla suit   8. "Fresh Bones"   9. "Die Hand Die Verletzt"   10. Chris Carter   11. C   12. Less than a week earlier she had undergone a cesarean section   13. "The Host"   14. A   15. True   16. A   17. *Bad Day at Black Rock*   18. B   19. Yes   20. False ("You're too late to stop us")

X-PERT X-TRA BONUS POINTS #1: Jason Beghe, who portrayed Ranger Larry Moore
21. True   22. Wayne Duvall's father is Robert Duvall   23. Piano   24. False (The Lord's Prayer)   25. Margaret Scully   26. B   27. Carter said, "They don't watch TV," so he wasn't worried   28. William Blake's poem "The Tyger"   29. C   30. A   31. "Colony"   32. They saw a trio of similar-looking guys at a UFO convention in Los Angeles in June 1993   33. "The Erlenmeyer Flask"   34. B   35. University of British Columbia   36. Episode writer Howard Gordon   37. Pickles and ice cream   38. "Fresh Bones"   39. "Duane Barry"   40. "Die Hand Die Verletzt"

X-PERT X-TRA BONUS POINTS #2: "To the spirit of the stars. To the spirit of the moon."
41. C   42. True   43. True   44. Chris Carter's   45. Jerry Hardin (aka Deep Throat)   46. Mark Snow   47. False ($70,000)   48. The daughter of Stan Phillips   49. True   50. Prince Vlad Tepes (aka Vlad the Impaler, the inspiration for Bram Stoker's *Dracula*)   51. David Duchovny, hoping to provide a greater sense of authenticity in the scene   52. *Helter Skelter*   53. B   54. True   55. Glen Morgan's and James Wong's   56. False (Vancouver)   57. Agent Alex Krycek   58. True   59. In real life, Steveston is a community near Vancouver beloved by *The X-Files* production manager for its diversity of settings   60. "Space"   61. "3"   62. Sgt. Al Dixon   63. They constructed a set   64. Glen Morgan   65. B

X-PERT X-TRA BONUS POINTS #3: Don Davis, Jan D'Arcy, Michael Horse, and Michael Anderson

MAXIMUM SCORE POTENTIAL: 80

YOUR SCORE: _____

The Blessing Way (Part 2 of 3)

1. memory   2. True   3. obituaries   4. His father   5. Her sister, Melissa   6. The Well-Manicured Man

X-PERT X-TRA BONUS POINTS #1: 46th Street
X-PERT X-TRA BONUS POINTS #2: April 16

MAXIMUM SCORE POTENTIAL: 16

YOUR SCORE: _____

Paper Clip (Part 3 of 3)

1. A white buffalo   2. The Lone Gunmen   3. False (In the 50s)   4. Victor Klemper   5. They followed the small aliens through a secret exit
6. Charlotte's Diner   7. B   8. False (20)

X-PERT X-TRA BONUS POINTS #1: The Gila Monster
X-PERT X-TRA BONUS POINTS #2: Craiger, Maryland

MAXIMUM SCORE POTENTIAL: 18

YOUR SCORE: _____

D.P.O.

1. C   2. Darren Peter Oswald   3. A   4. True   5. Teller   6. A shower of small change   7. A   8. False (17 and 21)

X-PERT X-TRA BONUS POINTS #1: cooked
X-PERT X-TRA BONUS POINTS #2: Frank

MAXIMUM SCORE POTENTIAL: 18

YOUR SCORE: _____

Fed X: Behind the Scenes with the Supporting Cast

1. C   2. Lea   3. A   4. Williams   5. True   6. False (Waterskiing champion)   7. A   8. Lea   9. Pileggi   10. Fuller   11. Davis   12. C   13. Horace Pinker   14. Pileggi   15. Avery Brooks' Hawk on *Spenser: For Hire*
16. Davis   17. Davis   18. Pontius Pilate   19. Books on the FBI and double agents   20. Runs   21. Williams   22. Williams   23. False (1979)
24. Clove   25. Pileggi   26. True   27. B   28. Lea

X-PERT X-TRA BONUS POINTS #1: Pileggi

X-PERT X-TRA BONUS POINTS #2: William Davis Centre for Actors' Study

MAXIMUM SCORE POTENTIAL: 38

YOUR SCORE: _____

Clyde Bruckman's Final Repose

1. *Midnight Inquisitor*   2. C   3. Malt scotch whiskey   4. False (General Mutual)   5. eyeballs   6. C   7. True

X-PERT X-TRA BONUS POINTS #1: Le Damfino
X-PERT X-TRA BONUS POINTS #2: 3

MAXIMUM SCORE POTENTIAL: 17

YOUR SCORE: _____

The List
(Note: Every correct answer will count as a 5-point X-pert X-tra Bonus)

1. 11 years and 56 days   2. 3   3. 6   4. 50416   5. Three   6. Two   7. 1984
8. 5   9. DKE-46J

MAXIMUM SCORE POTENTIAL: 45

YOUR SCORE: _____

2Shy

1. B   2. composition   3. Digestive mucous   4. honest   5. Vincent In-canto   6. A four-leaf pendant and a rabbit's foot keychain

X-PERT X-TRA BONUS POINTS #1: adipose
X-PERT X-TRA BONUS POINTS #2: Lauren MacKalvey's

MAXIMUM SCORE POTENTIAL: 16

YOUR SCORE: _____

S & M: Season Three

1. "Wetwired"   2. "731"   3. "Syzygy"   4. "The Walk"   5. "Quagmire"
6. "Paper Clip"   7. "The List"   8. "Revelations"   9. "Piper Maru"
10. "Teso Dos Bichos"   11. "Avatar"   12. "War of the Coprophages"

X-PERT X-TRA BONUS POINTS #1: chemical
13. "Clyde Bruckman's Final Repose"   14. "D.P.O."   15. "Clyde Bruckman's Final Repose"   16. "Syzygy"   17. "War of the Coprophages"
18. "Oubliette"   19. "Piper Maru"   20. "Hell Money"   21. "Nisei"
22. "The List"   23. "Revelations"   24. "War of the Coprophages"
25. "Syzygy"   26. "Paper Clip"   27. "Syzygy"

X-PERT   X-TRA   BONUS   POINTS   #2:   scarab
(NOTE: Each of the following X-ceptional one-liners count as a 5-point X-PERT X-TRA BONUS if answered correctly)
28. "Apocrypha"   29. "Pusher"   30. "Paper Clip"   31. "Clyde Bruckman's Final Repose   32. "War of the Coprophages"   33. "Teso Dos Bichos"   34. "Jose Chung's 'From Outer Space' "   35. "Revelations"
36. "Avatar"   37. "Oubliette"   38. "2Shy"   39. "The Walk"   40. "Clyde Bruckman's   Final   Repose"   41.   "D.P.O."   42.   "Hell   Money"
43. "Syzygy"

MAXIMUM SCORE POTENTIAL: 117

YOUR SCORE: _____

The Walk

1. Dental x-rays   2. Sgt. Leonard "Rappo" Trimble   3. General Callahan's wife, Frances   4. B   5. In the den of his own house   6. She was drowned in the swimming pool   7. Toy soldiers

X-PERT X-TRA BONUS POINTS: *Sun Valley Serenade*

MAXIMUM SCORE POTENTIAL: 12

YOUR SCORE: _____

Oubliette

1. 10:05 P.M.   2. B   3. Walt Eubanks   4. University Medical Center
5. 20 miles   6. 15

X-PERT X-TRA BONUS POINTS #1: Bright Angel
X-PERT X-TRA BONUS POINTS #2: Five

MAXIMUM SCORE POTENTIAL: 16

YOUR SCORE: _____

Nisei (Part 1 of 2)

1. B   2. $29.95, plus shipping and handling   3. Allentown, Pennsylvania
4. C   5. The Lone Gunmen   6. C   7. secrets   8. Four   9. 1965

X-PERT X-TRA BONUS POINTS #1: "Monsters begatting monsters."
X-PERT X-TRA BONUS POINTS #2: 82517

MAXIMUM SCORE POTENTIAL: 19

YOUR SCORE: _____

A Third Helping of Alphabet Soup

1. Larken, Sheila   2. Langly   3. Morris, Darlene   4. Morgan, Darin
5. Manners, Kim   6. *National Comet*   7. Neville, John   8. *Omni*
9. Okobogee   10. Psychokinesis   11. Parmelly, Vincent   12. Pendrell
13. Phillips, Bobbie   14. Quantico   15. "Rappo"   16. Reardon, Cindy
17. R.E.M.   18. Soames, Ray   19. Savage, John   20. Snow, Mark
21. Speranza, John   22. Sheherlis   23. Trepkos, Dr. Daniel   24. Twin
25. Takeo   26. Ufologists   27. Vlaming, Jeffrey   28. White, Angela
29. Walsh, J.T.   30. Walter   31. "X Exposed: 20 Things You Need to
Know About *The X-Files*"   32. Yappi, The Stupendous   33. Zelma,
Madame   34. Zero   35. Zama, Dr. Shiro

X-PERT X-TRA BONUS POINTS #1: Waltos, Detective
X-PERT X-TRA BONUS POINTS #2: Trevino, Vic

MAXIMUM SCORE POTENTIAL: 45

YOUR SCORE: _____

731 (Part 2 of 2)

1. Hansen's Disease Research Facility   2. Mr. X   3. The conductor
4. Russian

X-PERT X-TRA BONUS POINTS #1: 1111471
5. A gunshot wound to the stomach   6. biological   7. C   8. A

X-PERT X-TRA BONUS POINTS #2: 101331

MAXIMUM SCORE POTENTIAL: 18

YOUR SCORE: _____

Revelations

1. twelve   2. C   3. chosen   4. A   5. "To Heaven"   6. 14 hours   7. B
8. Westward Inn

X-PERT X-TRA BONUS POINTS #1: 11 divided into 170
X-PERT X-TRA BONUS POINTS #2: Linley Home for Children
X-PERT X-TRA BONUS POINTS #3: Six

MAXIMUM SCORE POTENTIAL: 23

YOUR SCORE: _____

War of the Coprophages

1. 4000   2. B   3. False (Department of Agriculture)   4. Nocturnal insect swarms passing through electrical airfields   5. B   6. Ebola Virus   7. *Die! Bug Die!*

X-PERT X-TRA BONUS POINTS #1: "Waste is a Terrible Thing to Waste"
X-PERT X-TRA BONUS POINTS #2: 667386

MAXIMUM SCORE POTENTIAL: 17

YOUR SCORE: _____

X-pert Testimony: Part III

1. Reverend Finley   2. B   3. The Well-Manicured Man   4. Dr. Ivanov
5. "Syzygy"   6. Clyde Bruckman   7. bullets   8. Scully   9. reincarnated
10. Skinner   11. Skinner   12. "Jose Chung's 'From Outer Space' "
13. C   14. Robert Modell (aka the Pusher)   15. John Mostow   16. Agent

Bill Patterson   17. wonderful   18. Reverend Finley   19. stomach
20. "Nisei"   21. Clyde Bruckman   22. Margi and Terri   23. "Syzygy"
24. Scully   25. radiant   26. The Cigarette-Smoking Man

X-PERT X-TRA BONUS POINTS #1: "731"
X-PERT X-TRA BONUS POINTS #2: paranoids

MAXIMUM SCORE POTENTIAL: 36

YOUR SCORE: _____

Syzygy

1. B   2. Mercury, Mars and Uranus   3. B   4. S-A-T-A-N   5. Mr. Tippy
6. C   7. False ("The Perfect Harmony City")

X-PERT X-TRA BONUS POINTS #1: 66,000
X-PERT X-TRA BONUS POINTS #2: 38,825

MAXIMUM SCORE POTENTIAL: 17

YOUR SCORE: _____

Grotesque

1. Seven   2. Five   3. Agent Patterson   4. They kept his "demons away"
5. False (Five)   6. A

X-PERT X-TRA BONUS POINTS #1: L-7
X-PERT X-TRA BONUS POINTS #2: 6:30

MAXIMUM SCORE POTENTIAL: 16

YOUR SCORE: _____

Piper Maru (Part 1 of 2)

1. Three   2. A   3. The National Weather Service's   4. *Zeus Faber*   5. B
6. False (Miramar Naval Air Station)

X-PERT X-TRA BONUS POINTS #1: 42, 171
X-PERT X-TRA BONUS POINTS #2: Seven

MAXIMUM SCORE POTENTIAL: 16

YOUR SCORE: _____

X Marks the Spot: Season Three

1. B   2. Pacific   3. Fairfax   4. True   5. Braddock Heights   6. Loveland, Ohio   7. West Virginia   8. B   9. Seattle   10. Leon   11. Miller's Grove   12. C   13. Boston   14. B   15. Washington, D.C.   16. True   17. True   18. St. Paul   19. Loudoun   20. False (Parkway Cemetery)   21. True   22. The Blue Ridge Mountains   23. Norfolk

X-PERT X-TRA BONUS POINTS #1: Quonochontaug
X-PERT X-TRA BONUS POINTS #2: Arlington

MAXIMUM SCORE POTENTIAL: 33

YOUR SCORE: _____

The Lone Gunmen: Behind the Scenes with the Paranoid Conspiracy Trinity

1. Braidwood   2. Haglund   3. Braidwood and Harwood   4. True   5. Harwood   6. Haglund   7. Braidwood   8. False ("Dod Kalm" and "Duane Barry")   9. Harwood   10. Harwood   11. Haglund   12. Haglund   13. True   14. The Frohike Mobile   15. Haglund   16. Braidwood   17. Harwood   18. Harwood   19. Haglund   20. Harwood   21. Haglund   22. Haglund

X-PERT X-TRA BONUS POINTS #1: "E.B.E." and "War of the Coprophages"
X-PERT X-TRA BONUS POINTS #2: Braidwood

MAXIMUM SCORE POTENTIAL: 32

YOUR SCORE: _____

Apocrypha (Part 2 of 2)

1. C   2. Northeast Georgetown Medical Center   3. Luis Cardinal   4. A   5. 50 weight diesel oil   6. An abandoned missile site

X-PERT X-TRA BONUS POINTS #1: 517
X-PERT X-TRA BONUS POINTS #2: 1013

MAXIMUM SCORE POTENTIAL: 16

YOUR SCORE: _____

Pusher

1. The Flukeman   2. cerulean   3. Ronin   4. B   5. Fort Bragg   6. Seven

X-PERT X-TRA BONUS POINTS #1: Osu
X-PERT X-TRA BONUS POINTS #2: 4th floor, west wing

MAXIMUM SCORE POTENTIAL: 16

YOUR SCORE: _____

Teso Dos Bichos

1. Dr. Carl Roosevelt   2. Museum of Natural History   3. Jaguar
4. handcuffs   5. False (Sunflower seeds)   6. Dead rats

X-PERT X-TRA BONUS POINTS #1: 356
X-PERT X-TRA BONUS POINTS #2: "The vine of the soul"

MAXIMUM SCORE POTENTIAL: 16

YOUR SCORE: _____

The Write Stuff

1. J   2. C   3. G   4. F   5. N   6. O   7. P   8. K   9. D   10. M   11. Q
12. A   13. I   14. R   15. L   16. H   17. E   18. B

X-PERT X-TRA BONUS POINTS #1: "Avatar" and "Talitha Cumi"
X-PERT X-TRA BONUS POINTS #2: "Die Hand Die Verletzt"
X-PERT X-TRA BONUS POINTS #3: 24

MAXIMUM SCORE POTENTIAL: 33

YOUR SCORE: _____

Hell Money
(Note: Every correct answer will count as a 5-point X-pert X-tra Bonus)

1. Three 2. Eleven 3. fifteenth 4. Two 5. 29 6. two 7. six 8. Six

MAXIMUM SCORE POTENTIAL: 40

YOUR SCORE: _____

Jose Chung's "From Outer Space"

1. His publisher 2. The non-fiction science-fiction 3. False (Three months) 4. Post-abduction 5. magical 6. B 7. *Dead Alien! Truth or Humbug?*

X-PERT X-TRA BONUS POINTS #1: *The Truth About Aliens*
X-PERT X-TRA BONUS POINTS #2: Lord Kinbote

MAXIMUM SCORE POTENTIAL: 17

YOUR SCORE: _____

Avatar

1. A 2. Seventeen 3. True 4. A residual phosphorus 5. Red 6. Sharon 7. lens 8. C

X-PERT X-TRA BONUS POINTS #1: REM Sleep Disorder
X-PERT X-TRA BONUS POINTS #2: Eight months

MAXIMUM SCORE POTENTIAL: 28

YOUR SCORE: _____

On Closer X-amination: Part III

1. D 2. H 3. J 4. G 5. C 6. I 7. E 8. A 9. B 10. F

X-PERT X-TRA BONUS POINTS: *X-Files* producer/director Kim Manners

MAXIMUM SCORE POTENTIAL: 15

YOUR SCORE: _____

On Closer X-amination: The Final X-am

1. J   2. B   3. H   4. D   5. G   6. I   7. C   8. F   9. A   10. E

X-PERT X-TRA BONUS POINTS: Ron Sauve

MAXIMUM SCORE POTENTIAL: 15

YOUR SCORE: _____

Quagmire

1. B   2. When a U.S. Forestry Service employee disappeared, the missing-person case became an FBI matter   3. Southern

X-PERT X-TRA BONUS POINTS #1: February 20, 1965
4. Queequeg   5. Captain Ahab   6. Patricia Rae

X-PERT X-TRA BONUS POINTS #2: Forty-eight

MAXIMUM SCORE POTENTIAL: 16

YOUR SCORE: _____

Wetwired

1. B   2. Five   3. 2400 Court   4. She believed he was her husband and his dog was a blond woman   5. Turned off her TV   6. Dr. Henry Stroman

X-PERT X-TRA BONUS POINTS: 555-0135

MAXIMUM SCORE POTENTIAL: 11

YOUR SCORE: _____

Talitha Cumi (Part 1 of 2)

1. Two   2. C   3. True   4. B   5. NO SMOKING   6. True

X-PERT X-TRA BONUS POINTS #1: Seattle, Washington; Chicago, Illinois; Cupertino, California; Miami, Florida; New York, New York; and Washington, D.C.

X-PERT X-TRA BONUS POINTS #2: Brothers K

MAXIMUM SCORE POTENTIAL: 16

YOUR SCORE: _____

Monster Mash: Season Three

1. G   2. H   3. C   4. B   5. K   6. J   7. D   8. I   9. F   10. E   11. A

X-PERT X-TRA BONUS POINTS: In Vietnam

MAXIMUM SCORE POTENTIAL: 16

YOUR SCORE: _____

Behind the Scenes: The Name Game

1. "File-o-philes"   2. Howard Stern   3. Billy Wylde   4. Stu Charno
5. William S. Burroughs   6. Dave Grohl   7. Chris Carter and Mark Snow
8. *Saturday Night Live*   9. David Duchovny   10. Peter Donat (aka Bill Mulder)   11. Chris Carter   12. David Duchovny   13. *McCalls*
14. Gillian Anderson   15. Mitch Pileggi   16. Duchovny   17. Jake
18. *Svengali*   19. Handsome Alvin   20. BEL   21. Robert Goodwin
22. Gillian Anderson, whose real-life pregnancy forced the writers to develop a three-episode story arc in which Scully was abducted

X-PERT X-TRA BONUS POINTS #1: "Firewalker"
23. Chris Carter   24. David Duchovny   25. *The X-Files* physical effects supervisor, David Gauthier   26. David Duchovny   27. *Rolling Stone*
28. Nick Cave and Dirty Three   29. Sam Shepard   30. *The Match Game*
31. Darin Morgan   32. Mark Snow   33. Largo's   34. Gillian Anderson
35. Stephen King   36. Tony Bennett   37. Whoopi Goldberg
38. David Duchovny   39. Japan   40. Gillian Anderson   41. *TV Guide*
42. Doug Hutchinson (aka Eugene Tooms)   43. Scott Bairstow   44. Vincent Schiavelli   45. Gillian Anderson   46. His brother   47. Kim Manners
48. CNN's *Larry King Live*, on which an FBI agent who investigated Satanic cults was a guest   49. Stephen King   50. David Duchovny
51. Alex *Jeopardy!* Trebek and Jesse *The Body* Ventura   52. Chris Carter

X-PERT X-TRA BONUS POINTS #2: *Magic and Technology in Contemporary American Fiction and Poetry*

MAXIMUM SCORE POTENTIAL: 62

YOUR SCORE: _____

X.Q. SCORESHEET

After you have totaled the points from each section to calculate your overall X.Q., determine your standing as an X-Phile:

2681–2234

Congratulations! You have been transferred from the Bureau's Violent Crimes Unit (great work on the Roman Ripper case, by the way) to the X-Files division at FBI Headquarters in Washington. You'll be replacing recently retired Special Agent Fox Mulder, whose latest book *The Great Alien Cover-Up: Fact or Fiction?* stayed atop the *New York Times* best-seller list for over a year.

2233–1767

When you graduate from Quantico Academy next week, do we have a surprise for you! FBI Assistant Director Walter Skinner has personally requested your posting to the new X-Files field office in Los Angeles. Because of the past successes of the Washington-based branch of this Bureau section, certain influential members of Congress sought and obtained funding for this division expansion without going through "normal budgetary channels." Watch your back, though. You may be a pawn in a bigger game.

1766–1277

Your reassignment from wiretap duty to the X-Files division has been approved. Beginning at 0800 hours on Monday morning, you are to report to Special Agent Dana Scully's office in the basement of the J. Edgar Hoover Building. You may wish you were back to eavesdropping on mobsters and hit men after Scully attempts to deter you from becoming actively involved in the world of paranormal nightmares and extraterrestrial activities—a place where you can truly trust no one. Not even your partner—since she just might shoot you one day.

1276–903

Your X.Q. scores at Quantico are too low to justify an assignment to the X-Files' field operations. However, ADA Skinner has approved a divisional clerical posting. You will be barred from directly assisting the agents in the field, but you will be permitted to type their investigative reports/case summaries and conduct deep background research. We know it's not exactly what you wanted, but at least you're in the basement office.

902–401

Better luck next time you take the test. You've got the basics of the cases committed to memory, but the **X-PERT X-TRAS** left you scratching your head. Obviously, you need to spend more time studying the videotaped exploits and paranormal investigations of the X-Files' two legendary agents instead of watching endless reruns of *Star Trek*.

400–0

If you scored less than four hundred, you probably think Deep Throat is just a porno movie, the Lone Gunmen assassinated Kennedy, and the Cigarette-Smoking Man is TV's latest version of the Marlboro Man. You must be one of those people who turns on the TV thirty minutes after the show starts and then wonders why absolutely nothing about the episode makes any sense. Get a life!

ALL DONE.
BYE BYE.

BIBLIOGRAPHY

Abbott, Jon. "The X-Files Guide." *The Dark Side*, September 1995: 23–33.

Auerbach, Lloyd. "Paranormal Programming Invades Primetime." *Fate*, November 1994: 30–34.

Bonario, Steve. "Opening the X-Files." *Sci-Fi TV Fall Preview*, October 1995: 42–49.

Bonario, Steve. "X-Files: A Mid-Life Crisis?" *Sci-Fi Channel Entertainment*, April 1996: 44–47.

Bush, Alan. "More Paranormal Programming Sighted in Prime Time." *USA Today*, 4 October 1994: Sec. 3:D.

Carlson, H.G. *Mysteries of the Unexplained*. Contemporary Books, Chicago: 1994.

Cinescape's 1995 Science Fiction Television Yearbook, Fall 1995.

Coleman, Loren. "The Truth Behind the X-Files." *Fortean Times*, August 1995: 22–28.

Emery, Gene. "X-Files' Coriolis Error Leaves Viewers Wondering." *Skeptical Inquirer*, May/June 1995: 5.

Fretts, Bruce. "A Genuine X-centric." *Entertainment Weekly*, December 2, 1994: 32.

Gliatto, Tom, and Tomashoff, Craig. "X-ellence." *People*, October 9, 1995: 72–78.

Gross, Edward. "X-Files: The Truth Is Here." *Cinescape*, November 1994: 34–45.

Gross, Edward. "Homeward Bound." *Cinescape*, June 1996: 74–75.

Gross, Edward. "Mister FiX-it." *Cinescape*, May 1996: 74–75.

Gundersen, Edna. " 'X'tra Something Out There on CD." *USA Today*, 1 April 1996: Sec. 1:D.

Jacobs, A.J. "Parting Shots." *Entertainment Weekly*, May 10, 1996: 39

Kahn, Sheryl. "Sci-Fi Mama: *The X-Files'* Gillian Anderson." *McCalls*, June 1996: 52–55.

Kennedy, Dana. "The X-Files Exposed." *Entertainment Weekly*, March 10, 1995: 18–24.

Killick, Jane. "The X-Files: Report #1." *Starburst*, March 1996: 25–40.

Lee, Julianne. "Mutants, Psychics & Freaks." *Starlog*, May 1996: 52–54.

Lowry, Brian. *The Truth is Out There: The Official Guide to The X-Files.* Harper-Prism, New York: 1995.

Maccarillo, Lisa. "Trust No One." *Sci-Fi Entertainment,* December 1994: 74–77.

Miller, Leslie. " 'X-Files' Flirts with its Fans." *USA Today,* 26 April 1996: Sec 2:D.

Mitchard, Jacquelyn. "Mom was an X-Phile." *TV Guide,* 23–29 May 1996: 60.

Nazzaro, Joe. "The X-Men." *Starburst,* January 1996: 27–30.

Nazzaro, Joe. "Fantasies in Dark & Light." *Starlog,* June 1996: 70–73.

Nollinger, Mark. "X Exposed: 20 Things You Need to Know about The X-Files." *TV Guide,* 6–12 April 1996: 18–24.

Oberg, James E. *UFOs & Outer Space Mysteries: A Sympathetic Skeptic's Report.* Donning Press, Norfolk, VA: 1982.

Rickard, Bob. "A Fortean Guide to the X-Files." *Fortean Times,* February/March 1996: 33–34.

Roush, Matt. "An Out-There 'X-Files' Writer." *USA Today,* 12 April 1996: Sec.3:D.

Roush, Matt. " 'Murder' and Mayhem Reign as Season Draws to a Close." *USA Today,* 17 May 1996: Sec. 3:D.

Russo, Tom. "Gillian Anderson: X-Files." *Us,* March 1996: 52–54.

Scully, Frank. *Behind the Flying Saucers.* Henry Holt and Company, New York: 1950.

Starlog Presents The X-Files & Other Eerie TV #1, December 1995.

Svetkey, Benjamin. "No Wonder He's Called Fox." *Entertainment Weekly,* September 29, 1995: 20–26.

Swallow, James. "X-aminations." *Starlog,* December 1995: 30–33; 64.

Thomas, Mike. "The X-Files: The Story So Far . . . " *Starburst,* October 1995: 12–15.

Watson, Bret. "A Gillian to One." *Entertainment Weekly,* February 9, 1996: 18–21.

Watson, Bret. "X-tra Credits: A Guide to the X-Files Supporting Players." *Entertainment Weekly,* February 9, 1996: 22–25.

Wild, David. "The X-Files Undercover." *Rolling Stone,* May 16, 1996: 38–41; 74.

Wilson, Ian. *All in the Mind: Reincarnation, Hypnotic Regression, Stigmata, Multiple Personality, and Other Little-Understood Powers of the Mind.* Doubleday, Garden City, NY: 1982.

X-Files Official Magazine, Premiere Issue #1, Winter 1996.

ABOUT THE AUTHORS

James Hatfield is the former film critic for *The Texas Women's News* and a frequent contributor to other Lone Star State regional publications. Having returned to his native Arkansas from Dallas in 1994, where he was for many years the vice-president of a large real estate management company, he now lives in a small town at the foothills of the Ozarks. He divides his time between writing books, computer troubleshooting, reviewing movies, hunting for antiques, and fishing on Beaver Lake for "that trophy Bass."

George Burt, Ph.D. (affectionately known as "Doc") is a computer consultant to major businesses and industries in Texas, specializing in software application development. Doc met his co-author while working on a major computer project for one of America's largest retail companies and, after discovering they were both die-hard X-Philes and Trekkers, have been writing partners ever since. Doc makes his home in Dallas, Texas, where he spends his leisure time reading law books (he's also a paralegal) or indulging in his real passion—cheering for the Super Bowl champion Dallas Cowboys!

Other Books by the Authors

The Ultimate Trek Trivia Challenge for the Next Generation
Patrick Stewart: The Unauthorized Biography